Not held?

RAG

KED?

BIG BROTHER
In Britain Today

To my parents

BIG BROTHER
In Britain Today

ANTONY A. THOMPSON

LONDON
MICHAEL JOSEPH

First published in Great Britain by
MICHAEL JOSEPH LTD.
52 Bedford Square
London W.C.1.
1970

7181 0511 7

Printed in Great Britain by
Northumberland Press Limited, Gateshead
in Ten on Twelve Point Times Roman
and bound by Dorstel Press Ltd.,
on paper supplied by P. F. Bingham Ltd.

Contents

Acknowledgements

My especial thanks are due to Mr. Brian Edwards of the *Daily Express* Legal Department, for his generosity in providing me with both research facilities and invaluable introductions; to Mr. Chapman Pincher for his kind advice; to Mr. David Williams of Emanuel College, Cambridge, whose own excellent books and articles I found immensely useful in my research, for commenting so helpfully on several chapters in the draft; and to Brian Neill Q.C. for directing me to material that I would otherwise have missed, and for his expert guidance on numerous points that would otherwise have defeated me.

My thanks are also due to the following for permission to quote extracts from works in which they hold the copyright: *George Allen & Unwin Ltd.*, British Government Observed by Brian Chapman, An Expenditure Tax by Nicholas Kaldor, The Power of the Prime Minister by Humphry Berkeley, Patronage in British Government by P. G. Richards, and The Inland Revenue by Sir Alexander Johnston; *Anthony Blond Ltd.*, Crisis in the Civil Service by Professor Hugh Thomas; *The Bodley Head*, Will Parliament Survive? by Christopher Hollis; *Butterworth & Co. (Publishers) Ltd.*, Moriarty's Police Law; *Jonathan Cape Ltd.*, The Technological Society by Jacques Ellul; *The Clarendon Press*, Studies in the Public Records by Professor V. Galbraith; *Collins Publishers*, Bagehot's English Constitution; *Conservative Political Centre*, Government by Deceit by Brian Reading, and 'Auntie' by H. Sewell; *Conservative Research Department*, Old Queen Street Paper 8, Computers and Freedom, published 2nd December, 1968; *The Daily Telegraph & Morning Post*, articles contained in their issue of 20th June, 1968; *André Deutsch Ltd.*, Scotland Yard by ex-Commissioner Scott; *Gerald Duckworth Ltd.*, Private Enquiries —a Handbook for Detectives by V. Meek; *The Electoral Reform Society of Great Britain and Ireland*, Memorandum from 1965 Speakers' Conference; *I. W. Fotheringham, Esq., T.D., M.A., A.C.A.*, extract from his lecture, 'Computers and Politics', delivered to The World Liberal Union in 1967; *Leslie Frewin Ltd.*,

The Gnomes of Zurich by T. R. Fehrenbach; *The Guardian*, extract from the supplement on the G.P.O. of 28th October, 1968, and an extract from an issue of July, 1968; *Hampstead & Highgate Express*, an article by Nicholas Walter in the issue of 6th September, 1963; *George Harrap & Co. Ltd.*, They Didn't Declare It by H. J. Browning; *H.M.S.O.*, extracts from The Denning Report (Cmnd. 2152), The Report of the Committee on Security Procedures in the Public Service (Cmnd. 1681), The Committee on Departmental Records (Cmd. 9163), and The Fulton Report on the Civil Service, Volume 5; *David Higham Associates Ltd.*, Masters of Indecision by G. K. Young; *Hodder & Stoughton Ltd.*, Anatomy of Britain Today by Antony Sampson; *Hutchinson Publishing Group Ltd.*, Keeping the Peace, and Not in the Public Interest, both by David Williams; *Longmans Green & Co. Ltd.*, More Power to the People: Young Fabian Essays edited by Lapping and Radice. From an essay by Donald Anderson, M.P., 'Constitutional Law' by Wade and Phillips; *MacGibbon & Kee* and *Granada Television*, The Future of the Press by Cecil King, and Privacy by Ernst & Schwarz; *National Council for Civil Liberties*, Privacy Under Attack, and Are You a Security Risk?; *New Society*, article entitled 'Land Commission: Too Big to Kill?' by W. Ricketts, from their issue of 15th August, 1968; *New Statesman*, articles entitled: 'Cybernetics and Society' by A. Wedgewood Benn, in the issue of 13th December, 1968, 'Brains versus Computers' by Nigel Calder, in the issue of 17th May, 1968, and an extract from the issue of 9th September, 1966; *The New York Times* and *Mr. Anthony Howard*, 'Exile to Washington from London', in the issue of 23rd October, 1966; *The Observer*, extracts from the issues of 28th July, 1968, and 14th July, 1963; *The Pall Mall Press Ltd.*, British Politics in the Suez Crisis by Leon Epstein; *Penguin Books Ltd.*, Freedom, the Individual and the Law by Professor Harry Street, and What's Wrong with Parliament? by Hill and Whichelow; *A. D. Peters*, The New Radicalism by Brian Magee; *Miss Sonia Brownell* and *Secker & Warburg Ltd.*, 1984 by George Orwell, and Ramshackledon by L. G. Pine; *Security Gazette*, Leading Article in the issue of April, 1968, Volume 10, number 4, page 156; *Charles C. Thomas, Publisher, Springfield, Illinois*, Industrial Personnel Security by Professor Leon Weaver; *The Times*, an extract from The Times Educational Supplement, December, 1966, an extract from a report on a speech by Lord Devlin in The Times of 29th January, 1964; *Time Magazine*, from an issue in 1968; *United Nations*, an extract from Bulletin on Narcotics entitled 'The Cannabis Habit' by Murphy; *University of California Press*, History and the Homeric Iliad by Professor Denis Page; and *George Weidenfeld & Nicolson Ltd.*, The Code Breakers by David Kahn.

Preface

When the idea for this book first occurred to me, it was my intention to view Britain's drift towards Big Brotherdom from a much narrower angle than I eventually settled upon. As research progressed, the scope of the book widened considerably. Even so, it will be apparent that numerous aspects of the subject have been left untouched, or touched upon only lightly. The topic is a vast one. Every reader will be able to compile a different list of just what additional aspects should have been included. To deal with it in its entirety would require either a whole series of volumes—whose contents would largely be out of date before they reached the presses—or treatment at a level so superficial as to be valueless.

Of necessity then, I have concentrated upon those trends which I personally find most disturbing. In dealing with them, I have tried hard for brevity without the distortion that abbreviation all too easily brings. This is notoriously difficult. But as Aldous Huxley wrote[1]: '. . . life is short and information endless . . . abbreviation is a necessary evil and the abbreviator's business is to make the best of a job which, though intrinsically bad, is still better than nothing.'

It is my sincere conviction that if ever the risks attached to compression were worth taking, they were worth taking in this case. Anyone with a year or so to spare can explore for himself, and in some depth, much the same territory covered in the research for this volume. Those with an inclination for the task will, I hope, find my footnotes and short bibliography useful as signposts. But of the many people worried by the encroachment of Big Brotherdom upon our society, few have time for more than a crash course on the subject. That is what I have done my best to provide, neatly bound up between two covers. I have attempted to exclude from it too many expressions of personal opinion, and in this I may sometimes have failed. But in the main I have allowed the facts to speak for themselves.

[1] In his preface to 'Brave New World Revisited', Chatto & Windus Ltd.

The World of Big Brother

> 'He tried to remember in what year he had first heard mention of Big Brother. He thought it must have been some time in the sixties, but it was impossible to be certain. . . .'
>
> *George Orwell: 1984*

The world of Big Brother is a world of total organisation, total control. Within the boundaries of totalitarianism, nothing is sacred. It allows no legal, customary or moral restraints upon its power. Its citizens have no inalienable rights; only expectations. The individual counts for nothing; the State, for everything.

Half of mankind already lives under Big Brother. In Britain, where the Communist movement is little more than a nuisance, and Fascism only a nasty memory, there is a prevailing smugness: a conviction that, short of a war, 'it can't happen here'.

But totalitarianism is not necessarily a thing of rallies and uniforms, of hysterical speeches and passionate ideologies. It can come into being quietly, almost imperceptibly, and from the best possible motives. We in Britain are much further along the road to Big Brotherdom than most of us realise.

The complexities of a modern technological society do not merely favour the centralisation of power—they impose it. Even in America, self-proclaimed champion of free enterprise and rugged individualism, the increasing power and intrusiveness of Big Government and Big Business has caused widespread alarm. The citizen feels himself caught between two fires.

Here in Britain, the intrusiveness of commercial interests is not so marked as it is in America. But this advantage is more than counter-balanced by the much higher degree of control which our government exercises over the economy and every aspect of the national life.

In many respects we are much more vulnerable to the drift towards centralism and the extinction of personal freedom than are the Americans. Not only do we lack a written constitution—we actually make a virtue out of it. In May 1968 Lord Shawcross, the former Attorney General, warned that if ever there was a time when we could afford to be complacent about the absence of a written constitution, that time is now long past. There is now, he said, a vital need for 'the most explicit guarantees of individual rights, the fullest protection against the arbitrary use of governmental or legislative power against the clear will of the nation, and a system of control over administrative abuses far more effective than that of our so-called Ombudsman'.

'Bitter experience,' he said, 'is showing that the old ideas of constitutional morality are going by the board, that governments are prepared, for instance by retroactive legislation, to alter the rules in the course of play, and to disregard the clearly manifested wishes of the nation.'

The Americans possess the written constitution which we lack; and their laws protect many more specific areas of personal liberty than our own. For example: the very *concept* of privacy is unknown to British law—which also tolerates instruments as dangerous as the 'Writ of Assistance'—an open and general search warrant which was so odious to the Americans that it provided one of the prime grievances behind the War of Rebellion.

Never before in our peacetime history has the government exercised such a high degree of control over every aspect of the economy and the national life; never in peacetime since the introduction of universal suffrage has the individual citizen felt so powerless to influence the course of events. The qualification of 'peacetime' is important: twice already this century Britain has been controlled by Big Brother. During both World Wars the government was cheerfully given a blank cheque by the electorate. It was heavily drawn upon. Whitehall took complete control over not only the means of production, distribution and exchange, but (through rationing) it controlled the fruits of production as well. It regulated and 'directed' labour, controlled prices and rents. Tribunals, exercising power in a fashion that was frequently arbitrary and almost always unsusceptible to effective appeal, enforced countless regulations covering everything from the minimum percentage of breadcrumbs in a sausage to the maximum permissible number of buttons on a man's suit. Judges became openly 'executive minded', interpreting the law (whenever room for doubt existed) in what they conceived to be the 'national interest'. The notorious Regulation 18B allowed for the imprisonment of anyone without trial 'where the Secretary of State has reasonable cause'. There were secret courts, and even secret executions. The mail, press and radio were subject to rigid censorship; all forms of telecommunications were intercepted and censored. Elections were suspended, and the Executive reached its decisions behind the thickest of security curtains. All complaints received a standard reply: 'Don't you know there's a war on?'

In other words, Britain was ruled 'for the duration' by Big Brother. When a country is fighting for its existence, no alternative to a rigid centralism exists. When some of the most objectionable characteristics of such centralism appear in time of peace, it is time to become worried. And many of them *have* appeared.

There is still ample time for Orwell's gloomy prophecies of life in *1984* to be fulfilled. It was not for nothing that he chose a British setting for his nightmare. He did so 'to emphasise that the English-speaking races are not innately better than anyone else and that totalitarianism, *if not fought against*, could triumph anywhere'.[1]

[1] From a letter written to Francis A. Henson, 16.6.49. Reproduced in Vol. 4 of 'The Collected Essays, Journalism and Letters of George Orwell'. Ed. by Sonia Orwell and Ian Angus, Secker & Warburg Ltd.

The Machine in Action

'"Don't you want to abolish state power?" Yes, we do, but not right now . . .'

The Little Red Book of Mao Tse-tung

A licence to breathe may not yet be a necessity for every British citizen. But to judge from the ever-quickening pace at which legislation has been churned out since the turn of the century, it is only a matter of time.

Of course, by no means all of that legislation has had the effect of curtailing the individual's freedom of action. Indeed, in recent years especially, shiny new hedonistic freedoms have been won. This has tended to obscure the fact that in the same period other and more basic freedoms have been lost. The so-called Permissive Society is permissive only in superficial ways, at the expense of the moribund 'protestant ethic'. The essential power of the state to control our lives has quietly continued to grow.

To see just how immense that power has now become, let us look briefly at the degree of direct control which the state now has over three vital areas: industry and employment; housing and land; and the national income.

The differing ways in which official statistics have been compiled over the years make it next to impossible to chart with any accuracy the inexorable rise in the numbers of those employed to run our lives on government-approved principles. To plot the rise of British bureaucracy is a task further complicated by a lack of general agreement on just what a bureaucrat *is*. The nearest set of genuinely-comparable figures concern the growth of the central government's non-industrial Civil Service. In 1900, the number of non-industrial Civil Servants was less than 150,000. By 1914 it had nearly doubled, and by the end of the Second World War had reached around 496,000. During the fifties there was a decline to around 380,000, but by 1969 it was nearing the half million mark it had failed to achieve during the peak period of wartime 'Controls', when almost every conceivable action had to be sanctioned by some official or other.

In practice, the 'bureaucrat' with whom the citizen most often has to deal is an officer of local government. If we add these to the total, and go on to include the Armed Forces, doctors and nurses, postmen and firemen, teachers, museum staff, police, librarians, dustmen, lavatory attendants—the list is almost endless—we arrive at a figure of almost four million: one in six of the employed working population. Nearly half of government spending, and three-quarters of local authority spending goes on wages and salaries alone.

Then there are the two million or so employees of the nationalised industries and other public corporations, who on their own make up nearly 8% of the employed working population. They bring the grand total of jobs directly provided by local and central government to a staggering six million: *almost one in four of the entire national labour force.* Also on the nation's payroll: some seven million pensioners and a half million or so unemployed persons.

Not only is the government far and away the country's largest employer: the size of the industries under direct government control dwarfs anything in the private sector. British Rail employs six times as many people as I.C.I., while the Electricity Boards spend on capital investment alone enough to build up a firm the size of I.C.I. every three years.

The *scope* of the nationalised industries is equally enormous. It covers not just steel, coal, airlines, railways, road haulage, power and similar basics: the government also runs one of the country's largest pub chains, publishers, travel agents, brickworks and hotel groups—even a cinema chain.

New candidates for state control (in one form or another) include natural gas, telecommunications, the ports, and water.

Already the nationalised industries account for over 10% of the gross domestic product. Yet this may be only the beginning. When steel was renationalised and the Transport Act became law, the state acquired sweeping new powers to 'diversify' the activities of the nationalised industries. Without any further reference to Parliament, the state can now set up and operate its own garages, repair shops, newspapers, hotels and breweries; and is free to manufacture aircraft, motor vehicles, chemicals, plastics, ships and engineering products of all kinds.

Where efficiency seems to warrant it, the nationalised industries can now move outwards, 'swallowing more and more industries down the line as customers, and up the line as suppliers, and sideways as manufacturers of equipment'.[1]

[1] Standing Committee D on the Steel Bill, 17.11.66 (Mr. P. Jenkin).

Thus the Coal Board, for instance, has been moving into the distribution of solid fuel and heating equipment, and buying its way further into brickmaking and the chemical industry.

Even without further expansion along these lines, industrial assets under the direct control of the state are already worth some £10,500 million, with new investment adding to this at the rate of about £1,500 million each year.[2] Half of this new investment comes directly from the taxpayers' pocket.

The mushroom growth of the nationalised industries has placed vast new powers in the hands of the Executive. As Brian Chapman has pointed out, 'It is clear that ministers have constantly intervened in their affairs in private without any semblance of public or parliamentary control.'[3]

This intervention can and does go far beyond the boundaries of the nationalised industries themselves. Where private enterprise is allowed to compete with a state-owned concern, as in road haulage or air transport, Ministers can often 'steer' the management of the private-enterprise concern by altering, or threatening to alter, the rules of competition half way through the game.

Even more effective as a means of forcing state-approved policies on privately owned firms is the influence the state is able to exert in its capacity as a major customer and supplier of funds for development projects. The computer and aircraft industries are among those which have been extensively reorganised as a result of this sort of pressure.

But of course only a fraction of the control which the government is able to exert over industry and employment stems from its position as manager of the nationalised industries. In pursuit of a fully state-controlled economy, sweeping new powers have been acquired through legislation.

By adjusting personal taxes, bank rate and hire purchase controls, it has long been possible for governments to affect output and employment right across the industrial spectrum. Through the new device of the 'Regulator', these adjustments can now be made at a moment's notice.

But the government is now able to make much finer adjustments than these. Since 1965 alone it has acquired a whole new kit of instruments with which to tinker with specific components

[2] *Vide* report of 1968 Select Committee on the Nationalised Industries.
[3] 'British Government Observed', George Allen & Unwin Ltd.

of the economy. For example: it can now promote manufacturing industries at the expense of service industries,[4] and large firms at the expense of small ones;[5] help firms using 'approved' manufacturing methods in 'approved' areas at the expense of those using *unapproved* methods in *unapproved* areas;[6] and participate in the control and profits of a wide variety of manufacturing concerns now in private hands.[7]

Quite apart from these measures the government also has at its disposal what Enoch Powell has described as 'that great legion of big Neddies and little Neddies, councils to advise on this and boards to promote that, headed by the great panjandrum itself, the Prices and Incomes Board'.[8]

With the introduction of the Prices and Incomes legislation, Britain took a giant stride towards a state-controlled economy. 'Free collective bargaining in this country has probably gone for ever,' said the *New Statesman*. 'So has the free market system for fixing prices . . . Once the machinery is operating, it is unlikely that any government will relinquish it, however dramatically our economic prospects improve.'[9]

Only a few years ago it would have seemed inconceivable that such machinery could have been assembled in peacetime Britain. Yet as we have seen, the Prices and Incomes legislation forms only part of a package of revolutionary measures which, taken together, have immensely strengthened the state's control over the economy.

The increase in state control over industry and employment, wages and prices, has been accompanied by a parallel growth in control over housing and land.

Of the six million homes completed in Britain from the end of the last war up to 1967, over 3½ million were built for local authorities. Only 2½ million were built for owner-occupation. The provision of new rented accommodation for the lower income groups has virtually ceased in the private sector, because of rent controls and the workings of the subsidy system. By 1968, one family in three was living in a home under local authority control

[4] Selective Employment Tax (1966), Regional Employment Premium (1967) and Industrial Development Act (1966).

[5] Corporation Tax (1965).

[6] Industrial Development Act (1966).

[7] Industrial Reorganisation Corporation Act and Shipbuilding Industry Act (both of 1967), and the Industrial Expansion Act (1968).

[8] 1.9.68.

[9] 9.9.66.

—which in fact means state control. The Exchequer pays the lion's share of housing subsidies (£100 million of the £130 million paid out in England and Wales alone each year) and so has the power to quash or modify local authority housing plans which run counter to government policy. This was shown quite clearly during the controversy over the sale of municipal housing stock to council tenants. Together with the battle over comprehensive education, it serves to underline the truth of the words spoken by the President of the Institute of Housing Managers at the Institute's annual conference in September 1968: 'Local government is developing into a sausage machine, with Government departments supervising the ingredients going in and tying-off and checking the sausages as they come out.'[10]

The total number of dwellings effectively controlled by central government includes not only the five and a half million council houses, but police and service housing; property on the Crown Estates; and that owned by the National Coal Board, which with 130,000 houses and 210,000 acres of land, is one of the country's biggest landlords in its own right.

But this may be only the beginning of the State's career as a landlord. In 1967 the Land Commission was formed with the intention that it should buy up and release for development such huge quantities of land that in time its price would drop, and house prices with it. In its first year of operation the Commission spent over £3 million in expenses and salaries for its 1,500 staff. During that time it acquired only 1¾ acres of land. But 3,245 acres were 'under negotiation', and a further 23,000 were 'under consideration'.

Land acquired by the Commission will not be *sold* to developers, but leased out under an entirely new form of land tenure—'Crownhold' (that is, 'State-hold'). Owners of homes built on Crownhold land will be obliged to give 'first refusal' to the Commission when they wish to sell their property, and if they have a 'concessionary Crownhold', the Commission will have the right to take over the property for re-development at any time, at a figure which may be well below the market price.

Some have seen in the institution of 'Crownhold' an admirable precedent for the nationalisation of *all* land. John Lee M.P., for one, points to the fact that in many tribal societies it is impossible for any one individual to own land. In such societies, all land is

[10] *Daily Telegraph*, 26.9.68.

the property of the tribe as a whole. Why, he asks, should we not pursue the same ideal, and abolish freehold altogether?[11]

Even without such extremist measures, the implications of the Land Commission's task are far reaching enough. In the words of one commentator: 'The commission's servants, if enterprising enough and with a sufficient amount of capital at their call, could come to control the land market.'[12]

Control of industry, control of land—these are sought by our political masters from the best possible motives, in the belief that they know what is best for us. The same belief explains why ever-larger slices of the national cake are taken by the state in taxation.

In 1900 public spending[13] was equivalent to less than 15% of national output. By 1950 it had risen to over 40%. In 1964 it was still at about the same level as in 1950. But by 1968 it had risen to over 50%.

This startling rise can only partly be explained in terms of the search for social justice. In its early stages, certainly, it served to redress grotesque imbalances between rich and poor. But the 'redistribution of income' has long ceased to be a Robin Hood affair of transferring money from the pockets of plutocrats to the pockets of the poor. As Professor Parkinson has pointed out,[14] in the ten years between 1938 and 1948, total taxes on incomes *below* £1,000 p.a. increased by 615%. On incomes above that amount, the increase was a mere 171%. Today the worker who earns £5 in overtime actually receives less than £3 after deduction of tax at the standard rate. If he spends the remainder on a bottle of cut-price whisky and a packet of cigarettes, a further £2.9.0d goes to the Exchequer in duty. So—in this admittedly extreme case—in real terms his £5 overtime payment is worth only ten shillings.

Of course, he gets many benefits from the state in return. Yet numerous opinion polls have established beyond doubt that the majority of people in this country would prefer to provide for themselves many of the benefits now doled out by the State. They recognise that the very poor, the sick, the aged and the unemployed must be provided for. But for themselves they would prefer lower

[11] 'Socialist Land Reform': essay in 'A Radical Future', ed. by Ben Whittaker M.P., published by Jonathan Cape Ltd.

[12] 'Land Commission—too big to kill?' by W. Ricketts. *New Society* 15.8.68.

[13] Capital and current, including transfers.

[14] 'The Law and the Profits', John Murray (Publishers) Ltd.

taxes and a greater freedom of choice over the services for which they must now pay whether they like it or not.

But taxes and social security contributions continue to spiral upwards. Why? Because those who collect and redistribute them firmly believe that only they are fit to decide how the nation's resources should be allocated, just as they are convinced that only they are fit to run the economy efficiently.

This point of view is, of course, a tenable one, in theory at least. Provided it pursues the right policies with skill and determination a rigid centralism can produce undoubted successes.

Some people regard such a form of government as a panacea for all Britain's economic and financial ills. They rightly argue that the present trend towards the concentration of more and more power in government hands does not necessarily and inevitably lead to Big Brotherdom and the extinction of all personal freedom. The outcome will depend on the character of our leaders and the maintenance of the traditional democratic safeguards.

It goes without saying that all politicians devoutly believe in their own integrity and fitness to rule. So what about the democratic safeguards? How adequate are they to cope even with the comparatively limited potential for the abuse of power that exists today?

The Rise of the Executive Coalition

'How cheerfully he seems to grin,
How neatly spreads his claws,
And welcomes little fishes in,
With gently smiling jaws!'
Lewis Carroll: Alice in Wonderland

The English, wrote Voltaire, are free only once in every five years—at election times.

That freedom, limited though it is, dwindles almost to vanishing point unless it can ensure the choice of men and policies truly representative of the electorate's wishes. Unfortunately, our archaic electoral system ensures nothing of the sort.

It is more than sixty years since any British government has been able to claim the support of so much as half those voters who actually went to the polls. The Labour government won its majority in 1964 after obtaining only 44% of the poll. In the 1922 election, the Conservatives achieved a majority on a mere 39% of the votes cast.

Perhaps the clearest indication of how badly in need of an overhaul the system is came in 1951. In that year the Labour party received the highest degree of electoral support in its history, winning 48.73% of the votes cast, to the Conservatives' 48.04%. Yet although many more people voted Labour than Conservative, it was the Conservatives who were returned to power—with a majority of 26.

The anomalies of the system go deeper than this. In the last election (1966) just over 13 million out of a possible 36 million votes were cast in favour of the winning party. Almost one elector in four didn't bother to vote at all. It is only surprising that this figure was so low. Too many constituencies have massive 'built-in' majorities, which foster apathy among the voters. As the Electoral Reform Society has pointed out, 'until Kemptown was won in 1964, no Labour vote ever cast in the entire county of Sussex had ever contributed to the election of an M.P. Most Conservative voters in Co. Durham are in the same position; in South Shields their failure to elect a representative of the party they prefer has been continuous since the first Reform Act of 1832'.[1]

In the 1966 election, on a country-wide basis, it took 36,000 votes to elect a Labour M.P.; 45,000 to elect a Tory; and 193,000 to elect a Liberal. Of course it has long been a polite fiction in this country that votes are cast for the man, not the party. This fiction is now to be abandoned, and party labels printed on the ballot paper beside the candidates' names. But what real choice does even the most open-minded voter have? Two or three 'semi-finalists', one from each party, are placed before him; men who have already run the gauntlet of their party's central organisation before they are finally selected by a small coterie of, at most, one hundred local party supporters.

Until Britain adopts a fairer and more rational method of electing its rulers (perhaps the 'single transferable vote' as advocated by the Electoral Reform Society), governments will continue to come to power on the votes of a minority, and large sections of the population will continue to lack an effective voice in Westminster.

But what of those who are entirely happy with the M.P. elected to represent them? Can they also afford to be happy with the *quality* of that representation? However slender their majority, successive British governments have shown themselves ready to take the most far-reaching and irrevocable decisions without further reference to the electorate. Plebiscites may be all right for the Continentals, but not, apparently, for us. So for a period of up to five years, the power of the ordinary voter is limited to the pressure he can bring to bear upon his M.P. That power is only so great as the power his M.P. can, in turn, bring to bear upon the Government.

Each M.P. represents an average of 56,000 voters (although the M.P. for Ladywood, Birmingham, represents only 25,000, and the M.P. for Billericay represents well over 100,000). Of the 630 M.P.s who go up to Westminster, only a hundred or so can hope for even the most minor post in the government. The rest must be content as back-benchers. As such, their power has in recent years sadly declined.

As J. P. Mackintosh M.P., has pointed out,[2] there are two rough and ready ways to measure this decline: the reduced degree of control which back-benchers are able to exercise over their time-

[1] Memorandum to the 1965 Speaker's Conference.

[2] In an essay contained in a collection edited by Ben Whitaker, M.P., 'A Radical Future', Jonathan Cape Ltd.

table and the business of the House; and the lesser extent to which they can call Ministers to account and extract information from them.

A hundred years ago government business received priority in the House of Commons on only two days each week. The remaining days were left free for M.P.s to discuss matters which they, as individuals, felt to be important. They could raise not only matters of particular interest to themselves, but any government business, including any amendments they felt to be necessary to Goverment-sponsored legislation. Since the beginning of this century, however, the Government has had complete control over M.P.s' timetables and, by the use of devices such as the guillotine, closure, and careful selection of 'suitable' amendments, it can determine exactly what is to be discussed, when it is to be discussed, and at what stage the issue will be decided in the division lobbies.

How far this process has gone was illustrated at the time of the so-called 'Back-benchers' Revolt' of 1968, when four massive pieces of legislation (Finance Bill, Prices and Incomes Bill, Race Relations Bill and Transport Bill) were, as a result of the 'Crossman reforms', being pushed through Parliament at one and the same time. Not merely did M.P.s have little opportunity to debate these measures, or to introduce amendments (as furious members from *both* sides of the House testified), but the pace became so fast that the government was nearly defeated on several amendments because M.P.s found themselves required to be in several places simultaneously.

Even more vital to the individual power of an M.P. than the right to arrange his own timetable or to introduce specific business to the House, is his power to call Ministers to account and extract information from them. Formerly it was almost unheard of for M.P.s to be refused access to any government information which they felt it necessary to see before making up their minds on any particular issue. Today the picture is very different.

Question Time, which has traditionally given M.P.s their best chance to exercise their role as watchdog, has now been so curtailed that it occupies less than an hour a day on four days a week —and then only in 'term-time'. In former days, an M.P. whose first question was evaded by a stone-walling Minister could continue to bombard him with supplementary questions until he was satisfied with the reply. Now the opportunity to ask these 'supplementaries' has been drastically reduced.

Donald Anderson M.P., from a wide experience both as a batsman and bowler in the Private Questions game, has written: 'A P.Q. may force a Minister to show his hand. Yet my own impression . . . is that an able, well-briefed Minister . . . can block with ease the heaviest bolts hurled at him at Question Time. He need disclose no more than he intends.'[3]

M.P.s do not merely have difficulty in gaining an opportunity to ask questions; even given such an opportunity, they have the further difficulty of asking the *right* questions. Lacking inside information as they do, it is impossible for them to be effective critics. Most back-benchers today are no better informed than any well-read intelligent layman.

Disturbing inferences about the decline of the M.P.'s influence as an individual can be drawn from an examination of Parliamentary handling of two military expeditions almost exactly one hundred years apart: the Crimean War of 1853-1856; and the Suez Expedition of 1956.

In 1853, before the war was well under way, M.P.s demanded and received all Foreign Office despatches pertaining to it, *as they were issued;* and before the war ended in 1856 they had forced a public enquiry into the incompetence of its handling. In 1956, as Leon Epstein made clear in his 'British Politics in the Suez Crisis',[4] M.P.s were kept completely in the dark. Epstein wrote: 'The much-cherished Question Time never succeeded in obtaining for M.P.s the crucial information on British military plans before the commitment was made or any confidential reports after the event—even long after the event.'

It is not merely the ministerial smokescreens swirling so thickly through its corridors that make the atmosphere of the House of Commons so oppressive—it is the chronic overcrowding. Most M.P.s have nowhere to work there; just a tiny locker in which to keep their papers. A few really lucky ones may have a desk in an office so overcrowded that it would bring the lowliest clerk in a commercial firm out on strike. Most M.P.s cannot afford a secretary; so replies to routine correspondence and the preparation of 'bread and butter' speeches for meetings in their constituencies and elsewhere can easily consume what little time is left to them by the Whips. In the library there are only eight graduate

[3] 'More Power to the People': a collection of Young Fabian essays edited by Lapping & Radice, Longmans, Green & Co. Ltd.

[4] Columbia University Press, New York.

research assistants to serve 630 M.P.s in their search for facts.

John Smith, the present M.P. for Westminster, claims that the cost of dealing with correspondence from his constituents alone exceeds the whole of his Parliamentary salary. Admittedly, Mr. Smith probably devotes far more attention to this task than the vast majority of his colleagues, being both willing and able to pay out of his own pocket for office and secretarial help. In his first year as an M.P. he wrote 18,000 letters—about 70 per day. He spends £25 a year on typewriter ribbons alone.

But even if M.P.s were to be provided with the best of working facilities and the fullest possible information on every issue, the character of the proceedings at Westminster would be altered very little. For M.P.s have their own private 'Big Brother'—the Chief Whip. His task, and that of his assistants, was described by Sir Martin Redmayne, former Chief Whip under the Tories, as follows: 'His business is to keep contact with (the M.P.s), and not merely to keep in contact with them, but to know them so well that in an emergency he is able to give an opinion as to what their opinion will be without even asking them.' Each Whip is allocated a group of M.P.s and Committees and keeps tabs on his charges: 'He is always ready to pick up anything which may be useful to the government . . .'

Nowadays the Whips are so effective that voting to 'conscience' is largely a thing of the past. In 1959 Christopher Hollis, M.P., wrote: 'Parliamentary Government has already very largely perished. The member is the obedient servant of the party machine. He tramps into the division lobby voting for or against he knows not what upon subjects which as a general rule no opinion save that of the specialist is of the least value.'[5]

Occasionally, of course, 'rebels' arise and immediately there is great speculation in the press as to whether or not the government will be 'brought down'. The synthetic nature of these periodic excitements is shown clearly by the fact that the last time any British Government was defeated by 'cross-voting' of normal supporters was in 1885!

Not that a single defeat would 'bring down' a government anyway, except possibly in a vote of confidence. Yet cross-voting is so rare (in the absence of a massive majority, at any rate) that in his introduction to Humphry Berkeley's book 'The Power of the

[5] 'Will Parliament Survive?' Hollis & Carter Ltd.

Prime Minister'[6] Norman St. John-Stevas chooses as an example of Mr. Berkeley's 'outstanding political courage' the fact that he voted against his own party on six occasions in seven years. St. John-Stevas then goes on to admit that he himself, though with 'some slight reputation for independent thought', has 'never voted against the party so much as once'.

If loyalty to party alone is not enough to bring the rebels to heel, self-interest often does the trick. For example: on 2nd March 1967, after a big rebel abstention on a defence vote, the Prime Minister, Mr. Harold Wilson, appeared at a meeting of the Parliamentary Party and announced to his rebels, 'Every dog is allowed one bite . . . but if the dog bites because he is vicious . . . he may not get his licence renewed.' Despite the uproar it caused, this clear threat hit home and there was no further trouble.

'If the Whips were in mid-season form,' wrote Hill and Whichelow,[7] 'they could tell you before an important debate exactly what the vote will be at the end of it. The debate—the arguments and the speeches—has no effect on the voting; it could, some would say, equally well be omitted.'

Most of the time the proceedings of the House bear a strong resemblance to an expensively mounted but very boring play. In the chamber the sound that really matters is not the drone of voices reciting prepared speeches, but the ringing of the division bell throughout the bars of the House and in the homes of those M.P.s who live within the 'six-minute radius' of Parliament. Those M.P.s who have not been 'paired' off one against another like pawns go through the archaic procedure of 'division'. And one more issue, settled long beforehand by the few men who really matter, is rubber-stamped by the Party machine.

Sometimes that rubber-stamp is applied to bills couched in such vague terms that M.P.s commit their country to projects of enormous importance quite unknowingly. They granted the money to make the atom bomb, for example, under such hazy headings as 'research'. Now the decision to create Britain's nuclear deterrent was not merely one of the most far-reaching ever arrived at by any British government—it was also one of the most expensive, costing the taxpayer well over £1,000 million from 1948 to 1963 alone. Yet this decision was reached entirely by the Executive

[6] Published by George Allen & Unwin Ltd.
[7] 'What's Wrong With Parliament?'—Penguin Special, 1968.

Coalition. *Parliament was not consulted in any way.*

Just how lacking in any real interest most parliamentary proceedings are is shown by the almost complete absence from the popular press of reportage on even the ablest of back-bench speeches. Only Ministerial announcements really matter, and it is instructive to note how frequently these are made not in the House of Commons at all, but at outside functions such as the opening of a flower show or a new school, and often to wildly inappropriate audiences.

In other words (those of Richard Crossman, M.P.), 'In a period when effective power in all spheres of life, economic, social and political is being concentrated in fewer and fewer hands, parliamentary control of the Executive has been steadily decreasing without being replaced by any other methods of democratic control.'[8]

Many prominent politicians will willingly admit the near-impotence of the ordinary M.P., and will publicly deplore it. (Although since it makes their own jobs infinitely easier, they may express themselves differently in private.) They will, however, undoubtedly point to the valuable work performed by back-benchers on Select Committees.

Of these there are four main types: Estimates, Public Accounts, Nationalised Industries, and Statutory Instruments.

It is true that sleuthing by these committees has turned up some ripe scandals from time to time. Defence expenditure has been a favourite target for criticism, on matters as varied as surplus boots (a million pairs, all size seven and under—enough to equip a whole army of dwarfs) and contractors' profits (Ferranti and the 'Bloodhound' affair). But however many blunders may be brought to the notice of the House in this way, M.P.s can rarely get at the man truly responsible for them. As a cock-shy for their disapproval, they must content themselves with the Minister in charge of the offending department. Under the doctrine of Ministerial Responsibility, he is of course obliged to take any blame that is going—but he makes a thoroughly unsatisfying target. M.P.s are well aware that the complexity of modern affairs ensures that he can never hope to grasp more than the broad outlines of business within his department, and must lean heavily upon his Civil Servants. When one of these servants blunders, he remains faceless, protected by the long tradition of anonymity of his Service. His Minister will courteously express regret to the House, but only

[8] In introduction to Bagehot's 'English Constitution', Fontana Books Ltd.

once in recent years has a Minister taken the doctrine of Ministerial Responsibility so literally as to actually *resign*—in 1954, when Sir Thomas Dugdale surrendered his office after the Crichel Down affair. If the pressure becomes too great, a Minister can always retreat behind an even longer-established principle: that of the collective responsibility of the whole Cabinet. At this point the pursuit normally ends. It would take a blunder of really unparalleled magnitude to goad M.P.s of a majority party into bringing down their own government.

The doctrine of Ministerial Responsibility was originally formulated in order to ensure that the right Minister was disciplined by the House. In practice this has now become a mere farce. In the case of the Ferranti scandal of 1964, not even the right *Ministry* took the blame, let alone the right Minister. Although it was really the Treasury's fault for employing unqualified and poorly-paid estimators, it was the Ministry of Aviation that was officially saddled with the blame.

In some cases, of course, the correct Ministry is easily identifiable, but since the Public Accounts Committee, for example, normally works on figures two years old, the Minister in charge at the time of any particular blunder has usually been moved on in a Government reshuffle, transferred to 'Another Place', or may even have left politics altogether.

Even so, for those ordinary M.P.s who serve on them Select Committees are the best means available for 'keeping tabs' on what the administration is doing. As a result of a hard-won decision of the 1880s, the Public Accounts Committee at least has the right to see relevant files and also—that rarest of opportunities—a chance to quiz individual Civil Servants face-to-face. Even then they cannot demand to see any Civil Servant they wish—only the 'Accounting Officers' representing the various departments.

The Civil Service smokescreen may lift a little for those M.P.s chosen for Select Committee work, but for the rest it remains impenetrable. Even if an M.P. is able to convince a Minister that something is amiss with his department, there is no guarantee that the true facts will ever emerge. Ministers lack any automatic power of entry even to the files of their own departments; nor can they directly question their own Civil Servants except 'through channels'. Handicapped as they are, it is hardly surprising that they sometimes do not realise what is going on under their noses.

And if Ministers can fail to break the cover-stories of their own permanent staff, what chance does the ordinary M.P. have? How can he then fulfil one of his most important roles—that of watch-dog over his constituents' rights? Every M.P. receives huge piles of mail from constituents who have become caught up in the toils of bureaucracy; all too often he finds himself powerless to intervene.

This particular problem was recognised by the institution of the Ombudsman. He was to supplement the waning power of the M.P. as champion of citizens' rights, and especially to watch for misuse of administrative power.

Some feared that the Ombudsman would be the death of the Sacred Cow of Ministerial Responsibility. Many even hoped he would be. In answer to these hopes and fears, 'Justice'[9] produced a Memorandum[10] which said optimistically: 'The truth is, we think, that the Commissioner (Ombudsman) would help to make Ministerial responsibility more effective. He would penetrate the screen which ministers interpose between members of Parliament and government departments, and he would keep Parliament informed about administrative practices which were open to criticism.'

Had the Ombudsman been endowed with the powers originally proposed for him, all these things might have come to pass. Which explains, perhaps, why the Executive Coalition took such pains to emasculate the office before it could become an embarrassment Here is a *partial* list of the spheres of activity from which the Ombudsman is specifically excluded: personnel matters in the Civil Service and Armed Forces; security matters; government contracts; police action; local government; the government of Northern Ireland; regional Hospital Boards; matters concerning foreign governments; and the public corporations.[11]

Not content with shutting out the Ombudsman from such fertile fields of administrative malpractice as these, a further limiting refinement was introduced. Citizens seeking redress cannot approach the Ombudsman direct. He can look only at cases referred to him by M.P.s, who act as primary 'filters', eliminating such complaints as are obviously frivolous or self-evidently

[9] The British Section of the International Commission of Jurists.

[10] Memorandum on Whyatt Report, 1962.

[11] *Vide* 'The Ombudsman', edited by D. C. Rowat, George Allen & Unwin Ltd.

outside the Ombudsman's terms of reference.

In 1967—his first year of office—849 cases survived this filtering process and finally reached Sir Edmund Compton. In 661 of them he could take no action whatsoever.

The Department employs at least 60 Civil Servants, and costs £250,000 p.a. to run. The high cost and heavily-restricted nature of the Department's role have led many former champions of the Ombudsman concept to write off the reality as an expensive Public Relations gimmick.

The Department's cost-effectiveness is undeniably low. But the Ombudsman possesses a unique power, won only after much bitter in-fighting behind the political scenes: the power to call for any information and any document (with the exception of Cabinet papers) from any department involved in his investigations. The reports published at the conclusion of each inquiry might therefore have been expected to throw new light on the workings of the Executive Coalition.

If this were so, every penny of the Department's cost might have been justified on this score alone. Unfortunately, though in the course of an investigation the Ombudsman may see evil and hear evil, like the third Wise Monkey he may speak no evil. The Minister whose department's secrets have been penetrated has the power to exclude any of them from the Ombudsman's report before it is published if he feels that their disclosure might in any way be 'prejudicial to the safety of the State or otherwise contrary to the public interest'.

We may be sure that Ministers will take full advantage of this opportunity for censorship. The Ombudsman may perhaps succeed in exposing a few of Whitehall's skeletons to the public gaze. But most will remain hidden, as before, in the obscurity of their standard-issue Ministry of Works cupboards.

If M.P.s no longer have much hand in the selection and shaping of the legislation they ratify, and if neither they nor the Ombudsman can much influence the manner in which this legislation is applied, what safeguards remain against administrative malpractice and the exercise of dictatorial power?

The Courts still provide some measure of security, of course—but that measure is uncomfortably small. In America, judges of the Supreme Court can and do declare statutes unconstitutional and are thus able to block much repressive legislation. British judges have no such power. Their job is merely to interpret the law as it stands. However much they may disapprove of Statute Law brought into being by Parliament, they have no choice but to enforce it, even when it flies in the face of age-old principles established in Common Law, or means passing sentence for an offence which, at the time it was committed, was no offence at all.

Clearly, governments must have the power to change features of the law which they dislike. But when it comes to retro-active legislation—punishing a man tomorrow for actions which are permissible today—this strikes at the roots of democracy.

So far, retro-active legislation has aroused little popular indignation because most of it has been directed at that most unpopular section of the community, the wealthy. The last Conservative government attempted to introduce retro-active legislation with respect to 'dividend stripping'. Labour's 1968 'Special Levy' on unearned income was retro-active in effect. *Both* major parties introduced retro-active legislation to overturn judgements in the Burmah Oil case. But a salutary warning that retro-active legislation can hit all sections of the community was provided by the Labour Government's attempt in 1966 to rule against the pay rise won by the Trade Union ASSET from Thorn Electric—a rise won *before* the legislation needed to block it (Part Four of the Prices and Incomes Act) had been brought into effect.

This trend has implications for everybody. In 'Government by Deceit',[12] Brian Reading points out that from the use of retro-active legislation it is but a short step to coercion through the *threat* of legislation (as used to enforce 'voluntary' wage restraint) and from here, 'it is only another, but very significant, short step to not bothering to change the law at all. Then we have a dictatorship.'

Can we at least be confident that in cases where executive interests conflict with those of an individual, the judges will be scrupulously fair? The independence of the judiciary is one of the most important safeguards against the advent of Big Brother. In all states where even a pretence of democratic rule is maintained, elaborate steps are taken to shield judges from political pressure. Just how well shielded are our own judges?

Once appointed, they are very well protected indeed. Until comparatively recently, judges were elected (under the terms of the Act of Settlement of 1701) for life. To reduce the possibility of having dotards on the bench, a compulsory retiring age has now

[12] Conservative Political Centre, 1968.

been imposed. But there is only one way to remove a judge before he has attained the age of retirement: through an 'Address to Her Majesty' by both Houses of Parliament. This has never happened, and the machinery for the procedure is not even clearly laid down. To stop economic pressure being brought to bear, judicial salaries are paid out of the Consolidated Fund, and thus need no annual Parliamentary confirmation. Theoretically it would be possible to reduce a judge's salary, but this, too, has never happened.

There is, however, one large loophole in the bulwark of judicial independence—the method by which judges are appointed. Obviously an 'executive-minded' judiciary would be of great use to the Government, and if the right appointments were made in the first place, it is highly probable that powers of removal or salary stoppage would never be needed. In the United Kingdom at the present time, *all judicial appointments are in the hands of politicians.*

The majority are in the gift of the Lord Chancellor, a senior member of the Cabinet who has invariably had experience as a barrister and, usually, previous experience as a Minister as well. In the words of P. G. Richards: 'Normally, then, the Lord Chancellor is a politician and the danger emerges that the judicial appointments he authorises will be made on a political basis. If this should happen, and if the same political party remained in power for a lengthy period, the independence of the judiciary could be undermined . . .'[13]

In 1921 a dreadful warning was provided by Lloyd George. In that year the Chief Justiceship fell vacant. Sir Gordon Hewart, the Attorney-General, coveted this post but, as a loyal supporter of Lloyd George, was too valuable to be moved from his current job. At the same time, Lloyd George was anxious not to deprive Hewart of the position he wanted so much. By way of solution he appointed Mr. Justice Lawrence as Lord Chief Justice *on the express understanding* that when Hewart wanted to take over, Lawrence would 'voluntarily' retire. These terms were accepted and fulfilled to the letter.

Political control of judicial appointments is, however, not the only danger. Judges are chosen from the ranks of barristers and, because barristers have a notoriously lean time for many years before becoming established, they tend (as Richards points out)

[13] 'Patronage in British Government', published by George Allen & Unwin Ltd.

to be drawn, like bishops, from a narrow stratum of society; to be born, in fact, into the Establishment.

It thus becomes all too easy for judges to identify themselves with the Executive. And this process is further helped along by the British practice of co-opting judges for tasks with political implications—Royal Commissions, Tribunals, and Government-sponsored enquiries of all kinds. The dangers implicit in this situation were pointed out by Harold Wilson from the Opposition benches in 1964. Speaking in debate upon the Denning Report, he deplored 'the recent practice of turning to the judiciary to probe matters which are properly the sphere of the Executive, the responsibility of this House'. There were risks, he said, of 'blurring the edge which marks the sharp definition of the functions of the judiciary, on one hand, and the Executive and the Legislative, on the other'. Despite his grasp of the dangers involved, since moving to the other side of the House Mr. Wilson has shown no noticeable reluctance to continue the practice.

Many of the criticisms levelled against the way in which the judiciary is selected can be levelled with even greater force against the magistracy. Most magistrates, like judges, are drawn from the same narrow stratum of society. The handful of stipendiary magistrates excepted, they are unpaid; often ignorant of the laws they administer; and display their prejudices with an astonishing frankness. In 'British Government Observed',[14] Brian Chapman wrote: 'It is impossible to know whether or not the British system (of selecting magistrates) offers any guarantee at all, except the guarantees provided by the integrity of Civil Servants in the Chancellor's office.' And even they, he wrote, are subject to subtle pressures 'which the outsider may sense but never document'.

The closer the links between politicians and judges, the blacker the outlook for the ordinary citizen. Naturally the court cases which attract the most publicity are the more dramatic criminal cases; but there is a huge volume of civil cases as well. As the Government net of rules and regulations spreads ever wider it catches larger numbers of ordinary law-abiding citizens, who are already handicapped in their battle with the Government machine by high costs and delays in litigation. One third of all cases heard in the High Court involve just one Government department—the Inland Revenue.

However ill-conceived or repressive an Act of Parliament may

[14] George Allen & Unwin Ltd.

be, no British judge can refuse to enforce it on the grounds that it conflicts with established constitutional principles. But he does have the option, where a statute is ambiguous, to choose the interpretation most favourable to the liberty of the subject. Too often in recent years, this golden rule has been broken. As long ago as 1942 a distinguished judge[15] spoke disapprovingly of colleagues who, 'with claims involving the liberty of the subject, show themselves more executive-minded than the executive'. More recently Lord Devlin was reported by *The Times*[16] as saying that, 'in the past fifty years the judiciary had changed their attitude towards the State. They had become more executive-minded—or perhaps less anti-executive'.

But there is a growing area of legislation where the attitude of the judiciary, pro- or anti-executive, makes no difference at all to citizens in battle with authority. This is the area of 'delegated legislation', under which a citizen in conflict with authority may be heavily penalised without the chance to appeal to the Courts at all. As long ago as 1887 the great lawyer Maitland was worried about the spread of delegated authority. 'We are becoming a much-governed nation,' he wrote, 'governed by all manner of councils and boards and officers, central and local, high and low, exercising the powers which have been committed to them by modern statutes.' Maitland would be a good deal more worried today; the system has mushroomed out of all recognition. Lord Chief Justice Hewart, in a book pointing out the dangers of delegated legislation, has christened it 'The New Despotism'. How has it arisen?

Parliament has delegated enormous powers to Ministers; Ministers in turn delegated them to the Civil Servants and 'all manner of councils and boards and officers'. These powers then acquire as much authority as if each decision reached by those holding them had been ratified by the House of Commons itself. Often the Act conferring the power allows those receiving it to alter not only the original Act (and therefore, to some degree the terms on which it was granted) but any other Acts having a bearing upon it. Many of the bodies receiving such powers become law-making bodies in their own right. For example: in 1952, for every piece of legislation created within the House of Commons, *nine* were created outside it.

[15] Lord Atkin: dissenting judgement in Liversidge v. Anderson, 1942 A.C. 306.

[16] 29.1.64.

One species of this extra-parliamentary legislation may even be kept secret. Lord Justice Scott pointed out that there is no necessity for 'sub-delegated legislation' ever to be made public: 'John Citizen may remain in complete ignorance of what rights over him and his property have been secretly conferred by the Minister on some authority or other and what residual rights have been left to himself. For practical purposes, the rule of law, of which the nation is so justly proud, breaks down.' Even the Emperor Caligula, who had his laws inscribed in very small letters at the top of the highest column in Rome 'the more effectively to ensnare his people', did not go so far as this.

Rarely do the Courts, or even Parliament itself, have any control over the way in which delegated authority is used. Thus another vast area of power has passed to the Executive Coalition. How vast that area is may be illustrated by examination of just one form of delegated authority—'Government by Tribunal'. This system was perfected in wartime, when its inequities could be justified on the grounds of expediency. Today, however, it is on the rise again. The Annual Report of the Council on Tribunals, published in July 1968, stated that over 200,000 cases were heard before tribunals from 1967 to 1968, arbitrating on matters as varied as the valuation of rates, industrial injuries, compulsory purchase, and whether or not an individual should be committed to a lunatic asylum. Some of these tribunals arbitrate between two private individuals—between landlord and tenant, for example, in cases brought before the Rent Tribunals. The vast majority, however, operate between the Government and the private individual. Whatever the issue at stake there is one factor common to all: a lone individual, probably with no experience at all in arguing a cause, faces entrenched and experienced opposition, usually without representation. Some tribunals do, in fact, allow representation. But legal aid is not usually applicable and so the majority must go without professional advocacy because they cannot afford its cost.

The Council on Tribunals of 1968 admitted this, and half-heartedly proposed a system of lay advocates. This would of course be better than nothing, but a still greater abuse continues to exist: the lack of effective means of appeal.

On this point L. G. Pine wrote: 'In Act after Act, there is ruling that in the event of an appeal against the Act, such appeal shall lie to the Minister of the department that is to administer the

Act. That a man should not be judge in his own cause has always been a principle of English justice. How can this be upheld when appeal is to be made to a minister against a decision of the civil servants of his own department?'[17]

Once a Minister has rejected an appeal against his own department's decision, an appeal to the courts is almost never possible. The only recourse of the aggrieved citizen is to persuade his M.P. to take up the matter himself in the House, or to refer it to the Ombudsman. The slimness of any likelihood of success through these channels has already been illustrated.

Tribunals, whatever, their faults, do at least afford a citizen aggrieved by some administrative decision the right to put his complaint through formal adjudication machinery. Many statutes put powers into the hands of officialdom without providing for such machinery. These powers may authorise official decisions differing not at all in principle from others which may in case of dispute be brought before tribunals whose decisions are binding on the relevant departments. In 1960 an inquiry[18] into this state of affairs showed up some glaring anomalies. If you are ordered by the G.P.O. to alter, or cease from operating, a domestic electrical appliance which is causing interference on your neighbour's T.V. screen, you can appeal to a tribunal against their demands. But if that same government department refuses your application for the telephone on which your business depends, you have no such right of appeal. If your child has been refused a grant or scholarship; or has been refused a place at the school of your choice—again you will find no tribunal to hear your grievances. Complaints against your National Health G.P. *can* be heard before a tribunal—complaints against a hospital for treatment received there cannot.

The report produced after the inquiry strongly recommended that the right to impartial adjudication should be extended to remove these and other anomalies. A decade later, nothing has been done.

It is beyond argument that the balance of power has passed from the Legislative to the Executive. What *is* the Executive? The text-books speak of executive power as 'vested by the Sovereign in Ministers of the Crown: a maximum of 36 men (as laid down in the Ministers of the Crown Act 1964) appointed by the accredited

[17] 'Ramshackledom', Secker & Warburg Ltd.
[18] Whyatt Committee.

leader of the majority party in the House of Commons'.

Too many crews have clambered into the political cockpit and pulled the levers of power with no result for anyone to believe that Ministers of the Crown can control the country alone, however well they may dominate the party machine. Obviously their decisions are swayed by many factors, both foreign and domestic; by bankers, trade unions and extra-parliamentary pressure groups of all kinds. But in its purest essence, power lies in the coalition between Ministers and the three thousand or so members of 'Britain's first Meritocracy'—the Administrative Grade of the Civil Service.

Under the terms of the 1968 Fulton Report, the Administrative grade (as an exclusive and separately-recruited section of the Civil Service) will disappear, and it will become easier for members of the lower grades to fight their way up through the ranks. The effects of this change on the realities of power are unlikely to be great. An able and well-informed Minister, with the full backing of the rest of the Cabinet, can always force through a policy in the face of opposition from his Civil Servants. But when it comes to getting schemes to actually *work*, this is quite a different matter. How many schemes in recent years, launched with a fanfare of publicity, have been later allowed to founder quietly as a result of this factor? As we have seen, senior Civil Servants have the edge over their Ministers in a number of ways. They can deny him access to their files and are able to present a united front because the Minister, going through the correct channels (as he must) to obtain his facts, may never get further than the top man who disagrees with him.

What sort of information may a Minister be denied? 'Some of it is planning work which is deliberately concealed from him, either because it might lead him to support policies which the department does not approve of, or even because it is being done in preparation for a future government of a different political colour. It is this secrecy which makes some Ministers tools of their departments a good deal of the time.'[19]

One way for Ministers to circumvent the Civil Service barrier is to call in outside experts. In recent years governments have tended to do this more and more. But since neither the Ministers nor the outside experts can get at the files, they are forced to rely heavily

[19] 'The Power of the Prime Minister', by Humphry Berkeley, George Allen & Unwin Ltd.

on evidence carefully selected by their 'opponents'.

So it is a foolish Minister who does not take good care to form the best possible relationships with his senior Civil Servants. If they can make life difficult for him, they can certainly also make it a great deal smoother. There is a great tradition of loyalty in the Civil Service: the criteria which it applies to a Minister's policies relate to practicability rather than ethics. Once convinced that a policy is workable, Civil Servants will do their utmost to make things run smoothly. An able Minister backed wholeheartedly by his staff forms a powerful coalition indeed.

As one senior Civil Servant[20] put it: 'We jog along not unduly worried by the assumption that Parliament is virtually excluded from the formulation of policy . . . In between elections the politically-conscious elements in the country can only fume in impotence over developments which displease them . . .'

We possess neither an effective Upper House nor a Judiciary able to rule against measures on the grounds of unconstitutionality. The Commons is so securely harnessed to the Party machine, and has delegated so much of its authority, that the Executive Coalition has only one thing to fear: publicity so bad that the stink of it will remain in the public nostrils right up to the next election.

That fear remains our best defence against Big Brotherdom. As we shall see, much has been done in recent years to remove it.

[20] As quoted in 'Masters of Indecision', by G. K. Young, Methuen & Co. Ltd.

Executive Secrecy

'Who controls the past,' ran the Party slogan, 'controls the future. Who controls the present controls the past.'

George Orwell: 1984

'Before the election of 1964, Treasury and other officials were carefully redrafting important papers, with political secrets omitted. This arrangement is by agreement with the incoming prime minister, who always agrees to it, knowing that when he in turn departs he will not want to bequeath his party's secrets; when ministers and advisers complain—as they have done—they are quietly referred to the Prime Minister . . .'

Anthony Sampson:
Anatomy of Britain Today

Of all the weapons in the armoury of totalitarianism, secrecy is one of the most powerful. Its deployment always follows a common pattern: the process of government is shrouded in secrecy; heavy penalties are levelled against government servants who dare to throw any light on its workings; and, to prevent such scraps of information as may still escape from becoming public knowledge, rigid press censorship is imposed. Thus the cruel apparatus of totalitarianism can be assembled behind a curtain of secrecy. The regime can build up a reputation for infallibility, because its failures and blunders can remain hidden.

Carried to its logical conclusion, the policy of executive secrecy can ensure that the government view will always prevail, because no evidence is ever available to contradict it. In Orwell's Ministry of Truth, 'All history was a palimpsest, scraped clean and re-inscribed exactly as often as was necessary'. Thus Big Brother is always right—and can prove it.

In Britain today, executive secrecy is maintained not by the falsification or fabrication of evidence, but by its destruction and suppression. This of course is not quite so effective. Big Brother can't prove he is always right—but at least no one can prove him wrong, either.

For centuries, the Executive Coalition of Ministers and Civil Servants has adhered to a policy of secrecy as one of the prime canons of good government. Never has it had such scope for putting that principle into effect as today.

The Official Secrets Act is one of its most useful tools. The first modern form of this Act was passed in 1911 *specifically* against espionage at a time when the country was in the grip of spy scares and war fever. Yet it has found applications so far beyond those envisaged at the time it was brought into being that: 'If every occasion when this Act is broken were to be the subject of proceedings in court, a tenth of the working population might find itself in gaol.'[1]

Section Two of the Act deals with 'wrongful communication' of official information to any unauthorised person, and it is Section Two that successive governments have found most useful in achieving Executive secrecy. It means that any Civil Servant or other person in contractual relationship with the Crown who passes on official information without official sanction does so in peril of prosecution. This applies not just to Civil Servants in office, but to *retired* Civil Servants as well. It affects not just those who wish to write their memoirs, but those who have in the course of their duty discovered blunders or discreditable facts, drawn them in vain to the attention of their superiors, and then resigned in order to make them public. It applies also to prison and police officers, all holders of government contracts (of whom there are many thousands), members of the Armed Forces and many, many other government institutions.

To assist in their specific purpose of preventing espionage, the various Acts were deliberately drawn up so as to be capable of the widest interpretation. As a result of this they can be applied to matters in which spying need not be involved in any way. Protests against this state of affairs have called forth justifications such as the following, voiced by a judge in 1919: 'The security and interests of the State are matters which affect every individual from the highest to the lowest, and, consequently, it was right that the statute should be wide in its terms and all-embracing.'

[1] Professor Hugh Thomas, in 'Crisis in the Civil Service', Anthony Blond Ltd.

Just how 'wide and all-embracing' can be seen from the prosecution in 1932 of a junior clerk at Somerset House. He had disclosed the contents of three wills to a journalist a few hours before they were due to be released to the Press anyway. Despite the fact that he was seriously ill, this Civil Servant was charged under Section Two of the Official Secrets Act and sent to prison for six months.

One single safeguard exists against the misuse of the Official Secrets Act: the Attorney General's consent must be obtained before a prosecution can be brought under the Act. But the Attorney General is a political appointee—a member of the Executive Coalition whose secrecy the Act has so often been invoked to protect. As Winston Churchill said of the Official Secrets Act in 1938: 'It ought not to be used to shield Ministers who have a strong personal interest in concealing the truth about matters from the country . . . I am taking the case that if there were a Minister who had strong reasons to believe he would be convicted of inefficiency, he would have a strong interest in preventing the disclosure of facts which would support that charge.'

In cases where even the wide terms of reference of the Official Secrets Act cannot be made to apply, Crown Privilege may be invoked instead. This gives the Crown the power to withhold documentary evidence in Court—even when it is one of the parties to the litigation. It applies not only to documents in the possession of the Crown, but to those held by others; the value of this privilege can readily be appreciated. When can it be claimed?

In the 'Thetis' case of 1942, Lord Simon ruled that Crown Privilege could be invoked 'where disclosure would be injurious to national defence, or to good diplomatic relations, or where the practice of keeping a class of documents secret is necessary *for the proper administration of the public service*'.

This last phrase can be made to mean precisely what those in charge of the 'public service' wish it to mean. How widely it can be interpreted may be seen from the fact that on several occasions the Crown has refused to produce documents in divorce cases involving Servicemen because to do so would be prejudicial to the 'maintenance of morale of the armed forces'.

The Crown may also, as a result of this judgement, refuse to produce a document not regarded as confidential in itself, but because it belongs to a *class* of documents regarded as such. This 'classes' rule may even be invoked when (as in the case of medical records) the person concerned *asks* for the documents to be produced. It has come to be a particular bugbear of judges, who have often made scathing remarks about it.

A recent House of Lords decision[2] offers a possible chink of light. In future, whenever a Minister claims that it would be in the 'public interest' to withhold a document not because of its contents, but because of the class to which it belongs, the Court will at least be able to call for further justification if that claim seems shaky; or even to examine the document in question privately. But will claims for Crown Privilege made on the basis of a document's *contents* still be as impregnable as before? This question has still to be resolved.

We have said that Executive Secrecy is defended in depth. The first line of defence attempts to prevent the escape of information concerning the workings of the government machine. The Official Secrets Act is very effective here, with its power to muzzle government servants and ex-servants, while Crown Privilege takes care of cases where government servants might be forced to testify indirectly in Court, through documentary evidence.

The second line of defence involves press censorship, to prevent such snippets as still escape from becoming public knowledge. 'The Press in Britain,' said Cecil King in 1966, 'labours under restraints greater in their effect than those of any other democratic society . . . The fact is that British journalists have always had to fight authority to get at the facts the people are entitled to know.'[3]

The Official Secrets Act has its uses here also: under Section Two, anyone who *receives* or even *asks* for, information covered under the Act, is liable to prosecution. (Thus, in the case already quoted of the Somerset House clerk, not only was he gaoled, but so too was the journalist.) Nor may a journalist protect either himself or his sources by pleading professional privilege.

In the cases of Messrs. Foster, Clough and Mulholland in the Vassall enquiry of 1963, refusal to name their sources of information led to all three being charged with contempt of court. Two were sent to prison.

The value of the Official Secrets Act as a tool of executive secrecy will be readily understood when it is remembered how many press exposés of incompetence or malpractice in any part of the government apparatus rely upon information from persons

[2] Conway v. Rimmer.

[3] 'The Future of the Press'. Second series of Granada Northern Lectures, reprinted by MacGibbon & Kee Ltd.

in 'contractual relationship' with the government. Governments have shown themselves increasingly bare-faced in perverting the Official Secrets Act to cover matters unconnected with espionage. They need simply state that it is in the 'public interest' to apply the Act. And who decides just what the public interest is? The Government, through their political appointee, the Attorney General. In 1965, a distinguished committee under the chairmanship of Lord Shawcross had this to say of the Official Secrets Act: 'It can lead to the protection of inefficiency and malpractice, stifle the needful exposure of public scandals, and prevent the remedying of individual injustice.'[4]

Journalists who fall foul of the Official Secrets Act cannot plead 'professional privilege' to protect their sources. But there is one form of 'professional privilege' which is frequently invoked to suppress evidence, and which cannot be breached by any Court. This is parliamentary privilege. In the sixteenth and seventeenth centuries it played an important part in the struggles of Parliament to assert its independence from the Crown. Once that struggle was won, much of the justification for the continuation of parliamentary privilege vanished. In one aspect alone is it still valuable: it allows M.P.s to speak freely in the House without fear of defamation proceedings. In its workings as regards the press it forms an unjustifiable gag on the freedom of speech. The value of parliamentary privilege as a tool of executive secrecy was demonstrated in July 1968, when Mr. Tom Dalyell, M.P. was found guilty of a breach of privilege and gross contempt of the House for providing the *Observer* with a copy of evidence given to the Select Committee on Science and Technology. The document contained a number of controversial facts about the Porton Down Research Establishment. Dalyell may have deserved to be pilloried for revealing this document. The *Observer* certainly did not. The paper's Assistant News Editor, Mr. Marks, received it from Mr. Dalyell with the assurance that he was free to report its contents, and that no question of parliamentary privilege arose. Mr. Marks even went so far as to clear the material with the chairman of the 'D-Notice' committee before publication to ensure that it involved no security breach. As Mr. Astor (editor of the *Observer*) told the Privileges Committee, 'If a newspaper obtains information honestly and believes that the motives for giving this information are

[4] Report of the joint working party of 'Justice' and the British Committee of the International Press Council.

honourable ones, and that the material is of public interest it has to find a reason not to publish. We did not see a reason not to publish it, having been given it.' Yet both Mr. Astor, and Mr. Marks were found guilty of a contempt of the House. Comparison of the original document with the 'authorised version' issued later showed very clearly that the government would have preferred to suppress certain facts not because it could damage the national interest to have them known, but because disclosure could be (and was) *embarrassing*. In the words of the *Guardian*, 'the reasons for exclusion would not have been security but to avoid political controversy'.[5]

Select Committees offer the ordinary M.P. his best chance to penetrate the barrier of executive secrecy; they chiefly exist, as Mr. Dalyell pointed out in his defence, for the purpose of getting information into the public domain. Yet the Executive Coalition is usually able to plug even this loophole in its defences by 'sidelining' sections of any Select Committee report which it feels would be too revealing. Mr. Dalyell over-rode this safety measure, and was chastised for it. In his case, parliamentary privilege was the rod most conveniently to hand. It was used despite the fact that Parliament's own Select Committee on Privileges had produced a report (whose contents were widely known, although not yet debated at the time of the Dalyell affair) denying any justification for parliamentary privilege in its present form. As it now stands, it can be claimed on the most trivial grounds, and (in the words of Sir Dingle Foot, M.P.) 'the person against whom . . . complaint is made is not necessarily heard in his own defence. He is not allowed to be represented by counsel and nobody knows whether or not he can plead justification, i.e., that his statements were, in fact, true.' Let the last word go to the newspaper whose report started the whole fracas: 'Privilege is valuable when, and only when, it protects the rights of M.P.s to speak freely and carry out their job: for example, to make exposures, like the one about scientology, which it would be impossible to do outside the House. In their own interests M.P.s would be wise to question whether it makes sense to use privilege to limit the freedom of others.'[6]

It will be noticed that although the editor of the *Observer* felt it would be in the public interest to publish the Porton Down disclosures concerning that establishment's link with the Universities

[5] Issue of 24.7.68.
[6] The *Observer*, 28.7.68.

he still checked with the D-Notice Committee before publishing. From the government point of view the D-Notice system is the best possible method of maintaining executive secrecy because it is *voluntary*. It allows a complete cover-up without risk of the sort of public disapproval so often aroused by the invocation of the Official Secrets Act, Crown Privilege or parliamentary privilege. And despite the great D-Notice scandal of 1967, there is still much public ignorance about how the system works: a fact which is surprising in view of the extent to which it governs the contents of the newspapers we read.

The D-Notice Committee first came into being in 1912, under the name of the 'Admiralty, War Office and Press Committee', as a consequence of the Official Secrets Act of the previous year. Apart from the period 1939-1945, when its task was taken over by the Ministry of Information's Press Censorship Department, it has operated in much the same way ever since. It acts as an 'early warning system' on 'naval, military and air matters, the publication of which would be prejudicial to the national interest'. Editors are free to ignore the Committee's warnings—but only in the knowledge that they do so in peril of a prosecution under the Official Secrets Act. Today the Committee's official title is that of the 'Services, Press and Broadcasting Committee'.

Requests for the issue of a D-Notice come from the Ministry of Defence and are considered by a mixed panel of Civil Servants and journalists. If approved, the Notice is circulated to editors together with a letter amplifying its meaning. The usual formula adopted runs: 'Dear Sir, The Services, Press and Broadcasting Committee request that in the interest of national security you will make no reference to the following . . .'

There is no doubt that the system has performed sterling service. But as Lord Balfour of Inchrye said in May 1963, he did not believe that there was a Minister in the government who could put his hand on his heart and swear that he did not know of instances where the D-Notices system and the public relations set-up 'have not been used to cloak individual or departmental failure'.

The Notices are worded in such vague terms that they are capable of very wide interpretation. As Colonel Lohan (Secretary to the D-Notice Committee at the time of the 1967 Cable Vetting sensation) remarked of one 'wretched' D-Notice, 'people say it can mean anything and everything'.

In cases of doubt, the government expects editors to take the widest interpretation and not print. After the *Daily Express* disclosures about cable vetting, it set up an inquiry under Lord Radcliffe to decide whether a breach of the D-Notice system had been involved. When the inquiry found that this was not the case, the government refused to accept its findings and produced its own White Paper on the affair. Lord Radcliffe took the opportunity in a Lords debate in July 1967 to reaffirm his views: 'When we have a system of our kind, with a free press, I think we are bound to recognise that security is one of the questions, and an important one, which always has to be weighed against others, in that free dialogue between press and people on which our public life is built up . . . Governments always tend to want not really a free press, but a well-managed or a well-conducted press.' And later: '. . . I do not think that it is the duty of the press to have complete trust in what is advanced to them by the government. I think that they ought to be suspicious and they ought to be aware of a certain tension between the respective functions and duties of the two sides.'

The Radcliffe Report stressed that the D-Notice system 'must not be subjected to overstrain'. Pushed too far—used as an instrument of political and administrative convenience rather than of national necessity—it will break down. Some form of compulsory censorship would then inevitably take its place.

The present system suits the Executive Coalition pretty well as it is. Again to quote from the Radcliffe Report: 'There have been cases of non-observance, but, according to our informants, such cases have been relatively few, more often accidental than deliberate, and they have never been persisted in after the Secretary has taken up the matter with the responsible editor.' As one distinguished commentator on executive secrecy has remarked, 'What more could compulsory censorship give?'[7]

In fact, what amounts to compulsory censorship already exists in a number of fields. For example: local authorities, when debating matters of the greatest public importance, involving enormous sums of public money, have far more scope for keeping their deliberations secret than does the House of Commons itself; while in the Courts, reportage on a wide variety of proceedings is forbidden on pain of swingeing penalties for contempt.

This last form of censorship is particularly worrying because

[7] D. Williams: 'Not in the Public Interest.'

the principle that justice must not only be done, but must be seen to be done, can only find true expression when details of court proceedings are made available to a far wider public than can be physically present in the Courtroom. Uncertainty about contempt of court has hampered journalists for years, and recent legislation has greatly increased that uncertainty. Some of the older restrictions on the reporting of court proceedings seem justifiable—the Judicial Proceedings (Regulation of Reports) Act 1926, for instance, which was prompted by salacious press reports on the juicier details of divorce actions; the restrictions on the identification of young offenders; or the provisions for holding certain cases under the Official Secrets Act wholly or partly in private. But more recent trends in the development of the law on criminal contempt of court, although prompted by laudable motives (the prevention of 'trial by newspaper'), have disturbing implications.

In 1968, stringent new restrictions on the reporting of committal proceedings came into force.[8] Almost simultaneously, the point in time beyond which the press can safely report on criminal matters was pushed back still further, as the result of the trial of Dr. Savundra of 'Fire, Auto and Marine Insurance' fame. Commenting on the roasting Dr. Savundra had received at the hands of David Frost during a television interview, Lord Justice Salmon said that 'trial by television' was 'not to be tolerated in a civilised society'. While recognising the right of the press and T.V. to dig out and publicise scandals, he went on to say: 'It must not be supposed that proceedings to commit for contempt can be instituted only in respect of matters published after proceedings have begun. No one should suppose that he is safe from committal for contempt of court if, knowing or having good reason to believe that criminal proceedings are imminent, he chooses to publish matters calculated to prejudice a fair trial.'

Now, when it comes to criticising judges, one must be very careful indeed not to fall foul of yet another form of contempt, the charge of 'scandalising the court'. So suffice it to say that if Lord Justice Salmon really felt it necessary to widen the scope for contempt proceedings so drastically, he might at least have been more precise in his choice of words. 'Good reason to believe'; 'imminent': these are words capable of the widest interpretation. It would seem possible to apply them to almost *any* situation

[8] Section Three of the Criminal Justice Act 1967.

where criminal proceedings might conceivably be taken up, and so for any press exposure to be labelled a contempt. As the *Guardian* pointed out, '. . . on some occasions exposure in the press (or on television or radio) may have been a necessary jolt to prod a laggard prosecuting authority into action. That, plainly, is in the public interest.'[9]

Lord Devlin, asked whether 'imminent' is to be taken as meaning no more than 'under consideration', was forced to admit that this interpretation would have to be tested in court first. He also gave it as his opinion that the whole *concept* of contempt as an 'affront to the court' should be done away with, and the issue narrowed down to the publication of material prejudicial to a fair trial or interfering with the course of justice. The sooner this is done, and the law redefined on this point, the better.

Despite the elaborate governmental apparatus for the suppression of embarrassing facts, a journalist who digs deeply enough occasionally combines with a courageous editor to print a story highly displeasing to the Executive Coalition. The standard reaction is then for the appropriate Minister to dismiss the story as 'sensationalised and inaccurate' or 'false and irresponsible'. Favourite phrases, these. They were, for example, used to describe Chapman Pincher's revelations on cable vetting in 1967. In his case they were followed (as is also standard practice) by a little judicious character assassination carried out under the cloak of parliamentary privilege.

Criticism of this kind is often excellent for a journalist's reputation. To turn a familiar aphorism on its head, 'With enemies like that, who needs friends?' But what follows is far from good for any journalistic career. Sources of official information tend to dry up and the reporter may be driven out into the wilderness. In an article in the *New York Times* on 23rd October 1966, Antony Howard describes what happened to him when he decided to abandon the traditional charades at Westminster and to concentrate on happenings in the real centre of power—Whitehall. Howard's 'Whitehall reporting' in the *Sunday Times* was deeply unpopular with officialdom. He was summoned to the Prime Minister's office and told that 'all conventional sources of information would remain shut off until such time as I was willing to return to the personally cosy but essentially sham game played out at Westminster'. He refused to capitulate and was 'exiled' to

[9] July 1968.

Washington. Small wonder that many journalists less able and courageous than Howard tend, like the accountant who values the interests of clients less than his comfortable relationship with the Tax Inspector, to heed what Lord Radcliffe has called[10] 'all the subtle arts of pressure, the nods and the winks, the joggings of the elbow, the smile at what is called the responsible reporter and the frown at the man who does not see quite clearly the government's point of view'.

All the measures discussed so far—the Official Secrets Act, Crown Privilege, Parliamentary Privilege, the D-Notice System, the 'drying-up' of sources of information—serve excellently to suppress information at the point in time when its revelation would be most acutely embarrassing to the 'Executive Coalition'. But just how long *can* embarrassing evidence be kept under wraps?

All important *documentary* evidence will, at least in theory, eventually end up in the Public Record Office. But the fact that a document is stored in the Public Record Office does not mean that it will necessarily ever become *public*. The report of the 'Committee on Departmental Records' (The Grigg Report) of July 1954 had this to say: '. . . the term "public" which was formerly used to denote accessibility, refers now to documents accumulated by the Central Government, irrespective of whether there is any general right of access to them.' Even when right of access is allowed, the material involved is by then usually of interest only to historians. The Executive Coalition believes that records, like good whisky, require several decades of 'aging' before they become fit for public consumption. The so-called 'Thirty Year Rule' serves this process admirably. This is the period for which even the most innocuous records are kept secret. More controversial documents may be hidden away for much longer. Indeed, certain Cabinet papers, and items, whose revelation might cause 'embarrassment or distress', are generally kept secret for at least one hundred years.

In cases where 'embarrassment' or 'security considerations' would make the suppression of evidence desirable even *after* the passage of a hundred years, it can always be destroyed altogether.

Some provision for the destruction of official records is obviously vital. The whole of Britain would otherwise end up knee-deep in foolscap. The War Office alone opens some 80,000 new files every year. When the Public Record Office was *partially* evacuated

[10] In the House of Lords, 6.7.67.

in the Blitz, the move involved some 88,000 containers and packages, weighing over 2,000 tons. Repositories taken over to house them ranged from stations on the Underground to the 'Casual Ward' at Market Harborough and the Duke of Rutland's castle of Belvoir.

In fact, for every document preserved for posterity, thousands are destroyed. The most confidential dust-carts in Britain—the little blue vans of Her Majesty's Stationery Office—collect around six hundred tons of Whitehall waste-paper every week. Independent contractors shred and pulp most of it under Stationery Office supervision. Some will find poetic justice in the thought that a substantial proportion of these pulped documents is exported to Germany for the manufacture of inferior toilet rolls. Others will be reassured to learn that only material classified as 'Restricted' (or lower) meets this fate. *Really* secret documents (and the typewriter ribbons and carbon paper used to produce them) are shredded and then burned by the Stationery Office itself.

Who decides which documents to destroy and which to keep? Five years after files have passed out of active use they are subjected to 'First Review' and those of no further administrative or historical value are destroyed. 'The responsibility for decisions at this stage,' says the Grigg Report, 'will be solely the Department's'—that is, the government department which created them. The chances are then, that when the 'Second Review' comes round twenty years later, all embarrassing material will have gone up in smoke under the special security arrangements made for the disposal of 'secret waste'. But just in case, at 'Second Review' an officer from the Public Record Office goes through the residue with the Department's own 'Record Officer'. A further 'Destruction Schedule' is drawn up and laid before Parliament for a period of 40 days. (Neither House has, in fact, any power to amend or reject this schedule.) Those files which it is decided to keep are then 'stripped' of material which will *never* be suitable for public inspection before they are sent on to the Public Record Office for storage.

What are the chances of some outsider seeing material embarrassing to a department *before* it is destroyed? The official 'Guide for Departmental Record Officers' is beautifully explicit on this point. Permission to quote the relevant passages in full has been denied ('in view of the possibility of the extracts . . . being quoted out of their context') but an idea of the Guide's flavour can be gained by anyone who rings up a government department and asks to inspect its files. If he perseveres beyond the first polite refusal, he is likely to hear the Guide quoted to him *in extenso*, or at least in paraphrase. However innocuous the material he wishes to inspect, and however eminent he may be in his field, the researcher will be told of three main objections to his request. These provide a fascinating insight into the bureaucratic mind:

The difficulty of sorting classified from non-classified material: in a bureaucracy where almost everything except the lavatory paper is stamped 'confidential', this is obviously valid. (The lavatory paper is stamped 'Government property—now wash your hands'.)

The danger of creating a precedent: again a valid point. As is well known, within the Civil Service the creation of a precedent is a crime only marginally less grave than raping a tea-lady on the Ministerial carpet.

Danger of 'Impairment of unselfconsciousness' among officials writing documents; in Sweden and Finland, where any citizen may walk into any Government office and ask to see the files[12] the self-consciousness of the staff is pitiable to behold. But they still seem able to run the Government machine efficiently enough.

The Fulton Committee had the Civil Service in mind when it said in its report in June 1968: 'We think that the administrative process is surrounded by too much secrecy. The public interest would be better served if there were a greater amount of openness.'

The alienation of the individual citizen from the processes of government; his helplessness in the face of the growing power of the Executive Coalition: these make 'a greater amount of openness' not merely desirable, but vital to the survival of what is left of British democracy.

[12] In both these countries, the only files closed to public inspection are those dealing with trade secrets; treatment of inebriates and the mentally ill; and those vital to national security, in the very strictest sense.

The Great Bumf Explosion

The obsessive secretiveness of the Executive Coalition is matched only by its equally obsessive curiosity about the lives of those under its control. And as that control extends to cover ever-greater areas of our lives, so does the scope of the government records.

There are still primitive societies where it is believed that the camera, by capturing a person's image for ever, also captures part of his soul. More sophisticated peoples are uneasily aware of an analogous but much more substantial threat—the myriad personal details captured forever in the files of bureaucracy.

Obviously no modern government can function efficiently without detailed knowledge of those it rules. The more complex an administration, the greater its demand for information. Record-keeping alone makes centralised government possible. As more efficient methods of information storage and retrieval have become available, so governments have become more complex and more intrusive. 'It was not until the development of the camera that the modern assault on privacy really began,'[1] wrote a distinguished American jurist. Other authorities have dated this assault from the invention of carbon-paper, the typewriter or the duplicating machine, all of which made the keeping of records so easy that their proliferation became inevitable. But a strong case can be made for going back much further—to the invention of writing itself.

The earliest-known form of European writing is 'Linear B'—a form which for decades resisted all attempts at decipherment. Buried under the ruins of Knossos for almost 3,500 years, the clay tablets inscribed with the 'Linear B' script finally began to give up their secrets in 1953. Scholars the world over hoped for epic poetry, philosophy, historical and religious texts. What in fact they found is described by Professor Denis Page[2]: '. . . the records of a comprehensive and pervasive bureaucracy, administering for hundreds of years a most elaborately organised society . . . It is as if everything done by everybody was open to official inquiry

[1] The late Judge Curtis Bok, in the introduction to 'Privacy—The Right to be Let Alone': Macmillan (New York).

[2] 'History and the Homeric Iliad'; Sather Historical Lectures, XXXI (Berkeley, Calif.: University of California Press).

and subject to official orders . . . One would suppose that not a seed could be sown, not a gram of bronze worked, not a cloth woven, not a goat reared or a hog fattened, without the filling of a form in the Royal Palace; such is the impression made by only part of the files for a single year . . .'

Which came first? The art of government or the art of writing? The chicken or the egg? And what was the reaction of those ancient Cretans when the 'Man from the Ministry' came round with his questions?

Similar, perhaps, to the reaction of Englishmen when William of Normandy's 'Commissioners' came knocking at their doors in 1085. A contemporary chronicler regarded this, the first great government inquisition ever to be held in these islands, with alarm and distaste. The king, he wrote, 'sent his men into every shire all over England and caused it to be found out how many hundred hides (of land) were in the shire and what land the king had, and what stock on the land, and what dues he ought to have each year from the shire. Also he caused it to be written how much land his archbishops, bishops, abbots and earls had, and though I may be somewhat tedious in my account, what and how much each landholder in England had in land or in stock, and how much money it might be worth. So minutely did he cause it to be searched out that there was not one hide or yard of land, nor even (it is shameful to write of, but he thought it not shameful to do) an ox, cow or swine that was not set down in the writ.'

It all sounds very familiar to anyone who has ever filled out the longer version of tax return supplied by the Commissioners of Inland Revenue. (Although even they did not go so far until the arrival of the Capital Gains Tax in 1966. Now they go further.)

In ordering the survey King William had one aim in common with our modern Inland Revenue authorities—the efficient collection of taxes, 'from each according to his means'. But he had another purpose as well—the compilation of a record that would set his administration like an iron collar around the necks of his new subjects.

Our ancestors reacted to the presence of the Royal Inquisitors with a spirit we might envy. Riots broke out all over the country, and there were so many false returns that the Commissioners had to return to many counties and do the whole job over again.

But at last the task was complete, and the returns collated (with an astonishing accuracy and thoroughness) into the great volumes of the Domesday Book.

The rot had set in. It has been spreading continuously now for almost nine hundred years.

The Domesday Book is Britain's first great monument to bureaucratic noseyness. But it is only one item in what is widely acknowledged to be the world's finest accumulation of administrative excreta.

The Domesday Book is on view at the Public Record Office in London's Chancery Lane. The vaults of the same building contain a collection of documents which make up a record of administrative history unmatched for its complexity and completeness. In 1961 it was calculated that the Public Record Office had in its care some 50 million documents, ranging from a single piece of paper to rolls of medieval parchment dozens of feet in length. It would take a very extraordinary man to examine them all. If he worked at top speed, the job would take him about 3,000 years.

The men who wrote the earliest records were members of the Royal Household in the fullest sense of the word. They travelled all over the country with the King, taking their files with them. The people who figure in these early records are those in whom the King took a direct interest (usually for taxation) and those who took an interest in the King (usually for privileges). But Parkinson's Law was already at work. The scope of the records increased steadily, and so did the number of clerks needed to produce them. It took little more than a century of bureaucratic effort before records became too bulky, and the staffs too numerous, for the entire governmental machine to follow the King around the country as he 'ate up his rents'. One by one the departments of state acquired fixed H.Q.s. In 1265 the Chancery found a permanent home on the site where the Public Record Office now stands; the Exchequer settled down even earlier, at Westminster Hall.

Where King William had dictated his orders direct to his clerks, by the fourteenth century the royal commands often passed through three separate departments, under three separate seals, before they could finally be despatched. Already there were complaints about red tape from those who were forced to plod wearily from one office to another, greasing palms all the way.

By the reign of King John the British genius for record-keeping had already shown the world that although carbon-paper may be officialdom's best friend, it is not indispensable. Where copies had previously been kept of only the most important documents, in the first year of John's reign the Chancery, for example, began to keep copies of everything. Not just land grants, accounts and so forth, but day-to-day correspondence and even inter-departmental memos were painstakingly copied down on parchment sheets which were then sewn together to make up unwieldy rolls, thirty to forty feet in length.

So minutely detailed did the records become that today we know how much King John paid the man who prepared his bath—and just how often he took one.

Through the centuries the records piled up steadily, until they became a real embarrassment to their custodians. They were thrust into crypts and gatehouses and derelict warehouses, piled in attics and cellars. When Samuel Pepys visited the Rolls Chapel in 1665, the Congregations sat not on pews, but on lockers containing a large part of the Chancery records. Any room in any building that belonged to the Crown and was useless for any other purpose became filled with 'chests, presses, cupboards, linen bags, bundles, chaotic piles of paper and parchment'.[3]

The records were subjected to trial by fire and by water. They were defaced by mildew and gnawed by rats. But happily for modern historians, it rarely occurred to anyone to throw anything away.

Eighteen thirty-four provided a disastrous exception to the rule. In that year it was finally decided to destroy several cart-loads of tally-sticks—formerly used in an archaic accounting system by which money paid into the Treasury was recorded by a series of notches cut into 'hazel or ashen wands'. Even in the thirteenth century the use of tally-sticks had been restricted to illiterates. Higher officials had evolved a sophisticated system of written accounts. But the British Civil Service is nothing if not conservative, and a further six hundred years passed before the Treasury awoke to the fact that the 'Three Rs' were no longer the mystery they once had been. In 1826 the tally-stick system was finally abolished by Act of Parliament. One question remained: what was to be done with the tally-sticks that had accumulated over the years? After an uncharacteristically brief pause for thought (a mere eight years) an uncharacteristic decision was reached: they were to be destroyed. In October 1834, two cartloads of tally-sticks were cast into the flames. Things got rather out of hand. By the

[3] 'The Record Commissions 1800-37' by P. Walne. Soc. of Arch. Journal, vol. for 1960-4.

time the fire was extinguished, both Houses of the Mother of Parliaments were burned to the ground.

An act of impiety had brought swift retribution. The moral was not lost on the custodians of the public records. Ever since the turn of the century there had been increasing agitation for a central record repository. The lawyers in particular were tired of searching through anything up to fifty different record offices scattered all over London. So a general amalgamation of archives began, and in 1851 the foundation of the present Public Record Office was laid in Chancery Lane. The files no longer required by our administrators have flowed here ever since, in an ever-increasing stream.

Examine the scope of those files over the centuries and it becomes apparent that until comparatively recently half the bourgeoisie and almost all the 'working class' could escape the government filing system altogether—if they could also escape the Law. In Professor Galbraith's[4] words: 'Generally speaking, the "Man in the Street" will only come into the records as a debtor or a criminal.'

Professor Galbraith was writing of the period prior to 'The revolutionary development of state activities which accompanied the democratic development of the nineteenth century.' Today *every* citizen is covered by the Records from birth to death, and his life charted in detail at every point in between. Record keeping has always been an occupational disease of Civil Servants, but today that infection has taken such a hold that it accounts for approximately a quarter of the entire cost of British administration.[5]

The flood of paper has become so enormous that each government department has a functionary whose special task is to keep it from engulfing his colleagues altogether. How necessary he is can be judged from the fact that if all the records produced each year by the 3,000,000 and more people employed by the Civil Service and other bodies covered by the Public Records Act were to be stacked together, they would build a tower of solid paper over one hundred miles high. Most of that hundred-mile stack of foolscap accumulated each year would of course make very dull reading to a non-specialist. But hidden within it are innumerable

[4] 'Studies in the Public Records', Oxford University Press Ltd.

[5] D. D. Wellman, in H.M. Treasury's quarterly *O. & M. Bulletin*, Aug. 1968.

personal details about each and every one of us—details which we would not dream of divulging to even our closest friends.

How many forms have you filled out within your lifetime? How many other official forms and documents have been filled out by other people with your personal details, but without your personal knowledge?

Hundreds, certainly; quite possibly thousands.

Here are just a few of the facts that a government investigator (with the correct clearance) could assemble about almost every British citizen, from an examination of standard official records alone: name changes made by affirmation or deed-poll; place and date of birth, and whether legitimate or illegitimate; complete 'family tree'; scholastic abilities and approximate I.Q.; complete medical history; criminal record (if any); complete employment history; professed religion; income from all sources. Whether owner of any of the following: land; buildings; stocks and shares; all 'tangible movable property' (jewellery, paintings, bric-à-brac, furniture etc.) with individual value of over £1,000; car; T.V. set; dog; firearm; garden hose; swimming pool; central heating system; telephone; servant (full or part time).

This list is deliberately prosaic and could of course be extended almost indefinitely. If you are a ham-radio enthusiast, fly private aeroplanes at weekends or keep a tiger in your back garden, these facts will also emerge from the standard records. But even from the most commonplace details of your life, the trained investigator can build a highly-detailed picture.

If he feels the need for still more facts, he can try more specialised official sources. Have you ever applied for a passport? Served in the Armed Services or Merchant Marine? Run your own business? Registered any patents? Attended pottery classes? Undergone treatment at a V.D. clinic? Had your home inspected by a Fire Prevention Officer? Reserved books on any special subject at your local library? Run for election to political office? Offered yourself as a blood-donor?

All these and ten thousand other human activities will have left traces on the official records. The handful of activities shown above, for instance, could yield such disparate scraps of information as your finger prints; your political leanings; a list of your 'sexual contacts' as far back as you can remember, a complete ground-plan of your house, and the name of your local vicar.

So far our investigator has tapped only official files for his information. Unofficial sources can prove just as fruitful.

For example—a man's attitude to debt can provide valuable 'pointers' to his integrity and general character. For a trivial fee, the United Association for the Protection of Traders can provide a subject's complete 'credit history', with details of H.P. and other credit transactions entered into, whether or not goods have ever been re-possessed, or a court order issued in respect of non-payment of any debt. U.A.P.T. has well over 14 million names on file. If by any chance the subject's name is not among them, there are many organisations of a similar nature where the investigator may be more fortunate.

Does the subject have a credit card? The records of organisations such as American Express, Barclaycard and Diner's Club could provide material for a fat dossier on their own, and throw up leads enough to fill a dozen more. In America it has for several years been thought rather eccentric in certain circles to pay for anything in cash where a credit card will do. Thanks to vigorous propaganda from the credit card companies, the same attitude is catching on here. A credit card user leaves a clear trail behind him wherever he goes. The hotels he uses, the meals he eats, the cars he hires, the goods he buys, even his haircuts—all show up in detail on the computerised records kept by the card-issuing company.

If the subject has ever applied for a responsible post with a large company, the investigator will really hit the jackpot. Manufacturing giants such as Unilever and Shell—even large service organisations like J. Walter Thompson, the advertising agents—are increasingly inclined to put a prospective employee through a battery of tests which may last several days and aim at providing a detailed profile of his aptitudes, personality and intelligence. In regular use are tests which purport to measure, to several decimal places, a man's 'loyalty index'; degree of 'radicalism v. conservatism' and 'toughness v. tenderness'; mental stability; perseverance; aggression; 'contentment index'; judgement (both practical and social); sexual proclivities; and even his sense of humour.

To assemble such a vast body of information from so many diverse sources would be a very time-consuming job. All the facts are there—but digging them out can be a costly business, even if the task is confined to just *official* records.

The earliest records, before they were broken up for storage, had a unity which their modern counterparts cannot match. Increasing specialisation in government business has resulted in a fragmentation of filing systems and caused inter-departmental rivalries. Giving evidence to the 1968 Fulton Committee on the Civil Service, an ex-Assistant Director to the Department of Economic Affairs said: 'The biggest shock I received was when I learned that files do not circulate between government departments, and that information is not automatically made available to a planning department which is relevant to its work. Departmental rivalries I expected, but I did not expect, in my naïvety, to find that British government is merely a United Nations.'[6]

Consequently the right hand of government often has no idea what the left hand is doing. Professor Galbraith again: 'What we miss in the modern departments is any organic connection with the records of other departments . . . The size of modern bureaucracy has meant extreme specialisation and this in turn means separateness. The Cabinet system, which has preserved an undivided sovereign power in government, has failed to preserve the unifying force of a single mind and purpose in administration.' This fragmentation and specialisation of records has two consequences for the citizen, one in his capacity as a private individual, the other in his capacity as a member of society:

First: to gather from all available sources all available facts about all citizens has so far been impracticable, on economic grounds alone. Thus dossier-building (one of the first essentials of the modern totalitarian state) has so far been kept within reasonable limits.

Second: the full *collective* exploitation by the Executive Coalition of the increased powers acquired by each government department *individually* has so far been prevented by the fragmentation of records and by departmental specialisation and rivalry. That vital 'organic link' between departments has been missing. No 'single mind and purpose' has been able to run the machinery of government (infinitely more powerful than ever before) to its full potential—so far.

[6] Mr. D. L. Munby, quoted in The Fulton Report on the Civil Service Vol. 5, p. 993.

Big Brother Computer

The missing link has now been found. The universal dossier system is just around the corner. Hear Mr. Anthony Wedgwood Benn, as Britain's forward-looking Minister for Technology. 'Beyond Parliamentary democracy as we know it,' he said at Llandudno in May 1968, 'we shall have to find a new popular democracy to replace it.'

Among the recipes he gave for that new 'popular democracy'—a new 'tell-all' computer system. The government, he said, should know more about the community, with improved statistical services, and computers to tell it more about every individual's means and needs. He forecast a time when taxation and social security systems would be capable of complete integration. 'Then we shall be able to decide politically what to do about means and needs on a personal basis, entirely free from anomalies . . .' Mr. Benn added cautiously: 'Precise information about individuals could be the basis for a new police state and a mass of new safeguards would be required.'

Rounding off this speech, Mr. Benn forecast that 'The pressures for changes on these lines are as inevitable as was the incoming tide that ultimately engulfed King Canute. These are among the main political issues that will be argued about in the 70s and beyond.'

The arguments started a lot sooner than he had expected. What the press promptly christened the 'Big Brother Computer' hit the headlines next morning with a crash that must have shaken Mr. Benn in his ministerial chair. Mr. Benn's mistake was in raising the spectre of a police state, then attempting to banish it with the magic formula of 'new safeguards'. Only a professional politician or administrator could believe that a 'mass of new safeguards', however well drafted, could nullify the threat implicit in a 'tell-all' computer system.

Where, up to now, the government dossier-builder has had to search through half a hundred different filing systems (both governmental and private), with the aid of a computer he could assemble a complete dossier on any citizen at the press of a button.

The Belgians are likely to be the first to experience the effects of such a system. By 1970 every citizen will be issued with a nine-figure number at birth. (Several countries already employ the 'electronic name' system together with a degree of computerised records keeping. But none, so far, have linked the computers of different departments to form a 'data bank' such as is described here.) Throughout his life his electronic 'name' will be used to draw together the records of every government department and State agency, from the T.V. licensing authority to the tax-inspector's office. Belgium has just under nine and a half million inhabitants. It is estimated that all essential administrative data for the entire population can be recorded on a dozen tapes. Installation costs apart, the system will be cheap to operate—with annual operating costs of around £450,000—and all public authorities, including the police, will be able to draw on its services right around the clock, through coded Telex inquiries.

In America, too, some twenty government agencies, including the income tax authority, are planning to set up a National Data Bank. Every citizen should, it is proposed, be forced by law to fill in lengthy questionnaires. The answers would then be fed into a giant computer and held ready for instant 'print-out' as required. The State of California already has such a system in operation for state administrative matters. Worry about the scheme has led to a demand for a new 'Bill of Rights'—the right for each citizen to see the entries on his record; the right to challenge entries on that record; and the right to know who has been given a peek at it. This worry is understandable, since Americans have much more to fear from a National Data Bank than the Belgians; much more personal information is already available there, much of it in computerised form. Estimates on numbers of employees in government and business who have been subjected to some form of 'security check' vary between 8 and 20 million. These checks are not confined to investigations into political leanings. Defining the points looked for by a 'good investigative set-up', the Security Director of one U.S. aircraft firm listed: alcohol usage; sex deviation; police record; falsified qualifications; concealed health hazards; bad attendance records; and drug addiction. This sort of check is applied not just to top executives in 'high security' posts, but to *every* employee down to the office cleaners. Some employers go much further than this, employing lie-detector specialists. Firms like 'Truth Verification Inc.' will, for a flat fee, run searching investigations into the darkest corners of a subject's mind. A favourite method—the 'E.P.Q.' (Embarrassing Personal

Question) technique, with questions such as: 'When did you first feel the need for sexual experience?'; 'When did you start to masturbate?'; or 'Have you ever cheated on your wife/husband?' Again, such tests are not confined to high echelon employees; cases are on record of their use on parking attendants and school bus-drivers. When firms first introduce a 'good investigative set-up', experience has shown that approximately 6% of existing employees will be found lacking in one respect or another. Personnel managers of firms running such tests frequently have 'gentlemen's agreements' with their counterparts in other businesses in the same district to supply one another with the names of those who have failed their tests. This saves the expense of re-testing sacked employees or applicants who have already been rejected by other firms. The 'gentleman's agreement' frequently includes the police. Firms 'checking out' a name can then do so with the help of police records, and the police in turn can call on the records of private organisations when *they* are investigating someone. This cosy arrangement also includes the computerised records of the 'credit rating' organisations which (in the aggregate) have data on about 100 million American citizens on file.

So far this trading of information has been on a personal and localised basis—'you scratch my back, I'll scratch yours.' But the *tradition* is already there. Soon one of the main difficulties to the extension of such favours on a massive scale (different makes of computer speaking different mathematical languages) will also be removed. The 'multi-lingual' computer has already arrived, and with it the possibility of complete record linkage—not just between firm and firm, or government department and government department, but between government and business.

The erosion of privacy and deprivation of job opportunity are not the only threats implicit in a nation-wide network of computers gossiping to one another. Computers have now been developed to the point where their information storage capacity is virtually limitless. They use integrated circuits so small that 6,000 would not cover a postage stamp; yet each circuit may have over 120 components. The Illiac IV computer now being developed by Burroughs is to be 500 times as fast as any now in existence.

Present machines are crude by comparison. Yet a management consultant (quoted in Anthony Sampson's 'Anatomy of Britain Today') is already able to claim that ' a big computer can put a giant corporation back into being a one-man firm . . . If a computer is properly exploited, a company must be 'bent round it' and the pyramid changed in quite painful ways.'

This degree of control is achieved by feeding into the company computer not just the personnel files, but *all* the facts and figures on which management decisions are based—material costs, economic forecasts, market research data and analyses and a dozen categories more. Given a sufficiently sophisticated computer, such a process could be applied to an entire nation. The 'personnel files' (a full dossier on every citizen) would be only one body of data fed to the government computer. The workings of the entire economy and the interactions of all its elements would then be reproduced in a detailed 'mathematical model'. 'It seems legitimate to me to suggest,' one expert has written, 'that by 1984, a computable model of the economy, covering all aspects of economic life and perhaps some aspects of social life, too, will be an established part of the machinery of economic organisation.'[1]

In an article in the *New Statesman*[2] Nigel Calder examined the possible consequences. '. . . mathematical models,' he wrote, 'which are hypotheses, may come to look like social laws; the "optimised" planning that computers make so easy is full of pitfalls; departures from predicted behaviour by individuals may seem perverse and anti-social under a carefully computed plan.' In other words, the citizen must be 'bent round' the computer. Just how painful that process could be would depend on who controlled the computer. Who would control it?

At present we are in the position of shareholders whose influence on the firm's policy is limited to the election of a new Board of Directors every five years. The Board may make a lot of very unpopular moves, but at least we can be fairly sure that some of its individual members will have the shareholders' best interests at heart. But if a big computer can turn a giant corporation back into being a one-man firm, what could it do to an entire country?

We may have the chance to find out the hard way—and long before 1984. Spokesmen for both the major political parties have sung the praises of a computerised Government Data Bank, although for predictably different reasons.

For the Left, Mr. Wedgwood Benn has talked of its value as

[1] Prof. Richard Stone, contributor to 'The World in 1984', pub. by Pelican Books Ltd.

[2] 'Brains Versus Computers': *New Statesman* 17.5.68.

a planning tool and as a means to reduce 'anomalies'. For the Right, the Conservative Political Centre has published a pamphlet advocating such a system for the economies it could produce in government expenditure: 'If the Government really wants to reduce employment in unproductive and service industries, it ought to start with its own staff. AUNTIE (Automatic Unit for National Taxation and Insurance) may be the answer to Parkinson.'[3]

Both arguments are impeccable when looked at solely from the economic viewpoint. The old free-market, laissez-faire economy kept inflation within bounds by maintaining unemployment at a level which would be politically unacceptable today. It is now received doctrine that the delicate juggling act of keeping employment and productivity up while at the same time keeping inflation down can only be performed under controlled conditions—*Government*-controlled conditions. Huge volumes of facts about every aspect of the economy are needed, and only a national data bank is equipped to store and process them properly. At the same time, a data bank would eliminate such grotesque examples of wastefully-duplicated effort as the application of 1,668[4] unique and separately administered means tests by Britain's local authorities alone. Add the rent rebate schemes run by the 1,413 different rating authorities, and we have a total of over 3,000 means tests, all of which virtually ignore each other. The cost can be illustrated by the fact that when Swansea's housing committee approved a rent rebate scheme in 1963, it was calculated that the cost of administering it would add 4/3 a week to the rent of every house the council owned.[5] The economic advantages of employing 'Auntie' to perform all these calculations on a national basis at the press of a button are obvious.

The choice of the name 'Auntie' for the machine to carry out the task shows a genius for public relations. The image it conjures up is a warm and cosy one, but even the computer experts feel it to be misleading. Auntie, they feel, could all too easily come under the influence of Big Brother.

We have already shown how the Executive Coalition has gradually extended its stewardship to cover almost every facet of the national life, and we have looked at the weakness of the controls designed to keep that stewardship responsible to democratic

[3] 'Auntie', by H. Sewill. Conservative Political Centre, 1966.
[4] 'Means Tests Galore', by M. Reddin. *New Society* 30.5.68.
[5] 'Honourable Estates', by J. Tucker. Victor Gollancz Ltd.

control. We have also described some of the ways in which a computerised data bank could lead to the concentration of even greater power in even fewer hands. That concentration may, of course, never reach the critical point at which tyranny begins. There is even a school of thought which holds that the computer could actually *reverse* the present trend towards a rigid centralism. 'For some purposes,' wrote Mr. Wedgwood Benn in the *New Statesman*, 'decision making will need to be more centralised to gain such benefits as could flow from that. For other purposes, computers will actually allow you to decentralise decisions that hitherto have had to be taken centrally. Provided that the whole system has been programmed to allow the parts to interact upon each other, and to take account of what is happening in other parts of the system, the scope for self-regulation will be much greater than we have enjoyed so far.'[6]

This interpretation is at first sight a heartening one. Looked at more closely, all it boils down to is that the administrative machine could be re-jigged in such a way that problems could safely be fed in at a lower level than is now possible, since the 'master programme' would ensure that only 'correct' decisions would be reached. And who would draw up the 'master programme'? The Executive Coalition, naturally.

Those who believe that a way can be found to wed power indissolubly to responsibility will see nothing sinister in this. After all, '. . . what is freedom? Rightly understood, a universal licence to be good.' But dodging the jackpot question of how you ensure the marriage will last, there are several other distinct problems to be solved before the programmers should be given free rein.

In 'Computers and Freedom',[7] a sub-committee of the Society of Conservative Lawyers examined these problems in some detail. They apply not only to any government data bank, but to privately-owned ones as well. They also affect many conventional record systems now in operation, but these, because of their fragmentation, and comparatively modest scale, suffer from them much less acutely. In every case, the committee found that existing legal and technical safeguards are inadequate to cope.

Erroneous information fed into a man's computerised record could, through cross-connection with other details of his life, cause him great damage, and not only where government records are

[6] 'Cybernetics and Society', *New Statesman* 13.12.68.
[7] Conservative Research Department. N.C.P. No. 8 of 1968.

concerned. An incorrect entry in the records of a credit-rating bureau (an entry supplied by a malicious shopkeeper, perhaps) could result not only in the loss of H.P. facilities, but in the refusal of a mortgage, or of insurance cover.

We are told that 'computer error' (of which we all have our favourite stories to tell) is almost invariably caused by the human factor. Even so, it leaves plenty of scope for errors which, if they appeared on any of today's individual record systems, could be damaging enough; but which on a man's *master* record could be nothing short of disastrous. 'Computers and Freedom' catalogues possible errors based upon 'incorrect or misleadingly incomplete factual material', or upon 'wholly or partly erroneous or misleading opinions, deductions or classifications' arrived at from such material, or 'arrived at mistakenly or misguidedly, or involving some wrong or misleading categorisation without requisite qualifications.' Not to mention old-fashioned typing errors made at the input keyboard.

Even if a man is lucky enough to learn that his computerised record contains erroneous information, it is at present almost impossible for him to enforce its correction or deletion. In certain very specialised circumstances the law of defamation could apply. But in most of the fields where computerised information is most in demand, even this legal remedy will be denied him because of the doctrine of 'qualified responsibility'. For example, 'as a general rule a credit-rating association would therefore probably not be liable for an unintentionally false and defamatory credit rating supplied to a member of the association'.[8]

To many people it is the *type* of information that could pile up in a data bank that is so worrying, not its veracity. A number of expert individuals and associations both here and in America have suggested that all data banks should (with certain exceptions) be obliged to provide any one on their files with a 'print-out' of the information held about him, together with a list of the purposes for which it is used and the names and addresses of those who have been allowed to see it.

If these proposals were adopted, data banks might almost prove a blessing in disguise. For the first time, everyone would be able to judge for himself the extent to which the personal details of his life are being documented by government and business. Such a storm of indignation would follow that our laws might at long last

[8] Ibid.

be changed to give some recognition to the concept of privacy.

Chiefly because so many of their customers are worried about industrial espionage, the computer manufacturers have devoted considerable ingenuity to defeating the 'electronic burglar'. Their machines can be supplied complete with input and output checks, scramblers, passwords, badge-readers and a variety of electronic and mechanical locks.

But against the man with the proper authority to use the machine, all these safeguards are useless. Not only might an operator find it profitable to pass along choice items of information to those willing to pay for them, from private detectives to blackmailers, but there is also the prospect of every petty official being 'in the know' about the most intimate details of his acquaintances' lives.

Present day filing methods make it relatively easy to confine different classes of information to the officials authorised to receive them. But cross-connect all the files in one computerised master file, and (to quote again from 'Computers and Freedom') 'one's doctor could know all about one's finances; one's neighbour, employed in the Inland Revenue, could know more about one's recent operation and illness than one did oneself'.

If a data bank is to work efficiently, an enormous number of officials from different departments and of widely varying seniority will have to be given access to it. It is theoretically possible to provide electronic locks capable of confining each one of them to information sectors and classifications appropriate to his department and seniority. But controls to provide this high degree of discrimination would have to be infinitely more complex than those designed to counter the 'electronic burglar' with no right to use the bank at all. At least one computer expert—Mr. Webb, of the London School of Economics—believes that they will never be fitted. Their cost, he says, would be prohibitive. So it seems likely that in the future a large proportion of Britain's half million or so members of the 'non-industrial' Civil Service are never going to be short of interesting lunchtime reading.

Sooner or later, the creation of a national data bank seems a certainty. We have looked at some of the problems which need to be given urgent consideration *now*, before that day comes.

Of these problems, that of discovering new ways to defend personal privacy is going to be one of the hardest to beat. But it is the *political* implications of a future data bank which deserve the closest attention. Not only would a data bank for the first time allow the machinery of government to be run to its full potential: it could be used to ensure that the same political crew remained to control it indefinitely—and in a deceptively familiar and wholly democratic way.

In our cockeyed electoral system, the balance of political power is determined by about three million 'floating voters'. At election times, each political party studies the preferences of this vital section of the electorate with anxious care, and (often at the expense of its traditionally-reliable supporters) adjusts its programme to cater for as many of these preferences as possible.

Pre-election manifestos are notoriously unreliable guides to what a party will do after it has actually achieved power. But right up to polling day the strength of the appeal its manifesto can make to the floating voter can be all-important to a party's fortunes. At present this appeal must be founded largely on guesswork. But in a lecture he gave to the World Liberal Union in 1967, Mr. I. W. Fotheringham (then on the staff of I.C.T.) showed how the computer could be used to analyse the preferences of the vital three million with an unprecedented accuracy: 'It can analyse the views of a cross-section of known . . . supporters, or the voting intentions of a representative cross-section of the electorate. Furthermore if the form of the questionnaire is suitably designed it can read this information into its store directly without requiring any punching of tapes or cards. The analysis could be supplied by the computer indicating the appropriate policy or area to be explored by further questionnaires. Questionnaires could be mailed directly and handled automatically on return . . .'

This idea opens up a most intriguing possibility. Such is the flood of government questionnaires today that a new one, if drawn up cleverly enough, would not seem very remarkable. (See Appendix, note 1.) Or the necessary information might be gathered from questions tacked on to such old favourites as the Registrar-General's pilot survey. This new information on individual preferences could be added to the vast store of personal details already contained in the data bank, and a mathematical model of the 'floating voter' constructed from it.

Such a model would have two uses. It would enable the government to construct an electoral programme of unbeatable appeal. It would also predict, with an accuracy guaranteed to turn today's pollsters and psephologists green with envy, the most favourable moment to put that appeal to the voters. Governments rise and fall in response to quite minor swings of public opinion, as can be illustrated by the fortunes of the Socialists since the war: 1945, 48% of the votes—a 2 to 1 parliamentary majority; 1951, 49% of the votes—out of office; 1964, 44% of the votes—back to office. So with a computer to help pick the right policy and the right moment to present it to the electorate at a General Election, a government would have to have a pretty black record if it failed to sweep the polls.

The defeated parties would scream that it was all very unfair. The victorious politicians would point out with justice that they had merely refined time-honoured electoral tactics in a praiseworthy attempt to offer the electorate what it wanted most. Magnanimously, they might offer their opponents the use of the data bank for the *next* election. But the trump card—the ability to call an election at the most favourable moment—would remain with the government. So would the ability to adjust their actions while in office to keep them in step with what the computer told them about shifts in public opinion.

All very democratic—but how would any opposition retain its vigour during endless terms of political impotence? Parliamentary democracy depends upon the existence of a vigorous opposition. The one-party system degenerates all too easily into tyranny, however auspicious its birth.

The possibility of permanent political control achieved through the use of sophisticated polling techniques and computer analysis could, paradoxically enough, be cancelled out by using those same techniques on an even wider scale. Electronics, which brought the threat of Big Brother Computer, could be used to strip the politicians of all power and hand it to the people.

'Possibly in a generation,' *Time Magazine* commented recently, 'polls may lead to instant national referendums. Every voter would have a small electronic box with "yes" and "no" buttons. The President could ask for public opinion on any issue . . . and the presumably informed electorate would flash back an immediate response. Technically, this is feasible right now.'

It is difficult to imagine any group of politicians voting themselves out of business. But what if they did?

Attitude surveys in many countries have forced social scientists to the sad conclusion that government by consensus would be illiberal, reactionary and violently intolerant of minority opinion.

Had such a government been established a couple of centuries ago, it is true that we might have retained certain freedoms now lost to us. Among them might have been the freedom to spend an idle hour gawping at the lunatics in Bedlam, or watching a criminal disembowelled at Tyburn.

Who's Reading Your Dossier Now?

'I'll be judge, I'll be jury,' said cunning old Fury;
'I'll try the whole cause, and condemn you to death.'
Lewis Carroll: Alice in Wonderland

In the future (perhaps the near future) dossier building and 'background investigation' may become a simple matter of pressing a button. But today it is still an expensive and time-consuming business, not to be undertaken lightly. The security of the State is however no light matter, and no security apparatus can function without the dossier system. At present it is within the security context alone that the State takes the trouble to assemble really comprehensive personal files on its citizens. Even so, the number of people involved is very large.

A high proportion of them have only themselves to blame. The Criminal Record Office at New Scotland Yard has the fullest possible details on every person ever convicted of serious crime in Great Britain. There are over two and a half million cards on file.[1]

The way in which the C.R.O. organises its material is well worth investigation; it shows the perfection to which even a non-computerised filing system can be brought. The secret lies in the cross-indexing. Has the *Gold Bar Trick* been perpetrated on a *Bank Official* by a *Bearded Man* with a *Stammer*, posing as a *Foreign Prince*? The Fraud Index has separate categories for each italicised feature. If the same man's name turns up under more than one of them, he will need a very good alibi indeed. But the days are gone when only the convicted criminal was afforded the doubtful privilege of a detailed government dossier.

Once upon a time a spy was a man found on a lonely beach at midnight, asking the way to London in a thick foreign accent. No Englishman would sell his country's secrets to a Foreign Power —at least in the popular view. There were a few cynics who believed

[1] Some of them refer to the same man. Wherever a criminal has used an alias in the past, a separate card is made out under that alias. The record is held by a man with 440 cards.

that a man of no family and without the advantages of a Public School education just might be corrupted, if offered enough money. Such men weren't usually allowed within a mile of 'official secrets' anyway. But a chap 'with the right sort of background' was above suspicion. A quick check around the old boy net, and he was 'in'.

This touching belief in 'background' (in this limited sense) persisted long after it was officially discredited. The Philby affair showed how the finger of suspicion could be waved aside when it pointed to a man with the right sort of antecedents. It also illustrated why years before it had been thought necessary to introduce to this country a system of 'security checks' which was found repugnant not only by those checked, but by those ordering the checking. Philby was in early youth converted to an ideology that knows no frontiers, and can over-ride the conditioning of class and education which to earlier generations had seemed treachery-proof. Clement Attlee had made the situation plain years earlier when in March 1948 he introduced to the House of Commons the first British political 'loyalty programme' of modern times.

'Experience, both in this country and elsewhere,' he said, 'has shown that membership of, and other forms of continuing association with the Communist Party, may involve the acceptance by an individual of a loyalty which in certain cases can be inimical to the State. The government has reached the conclusion that the only prudent course to adopt is to ensure that no-one who is known to be a member of the Communist Party or to be associated with it in such a way as to raise legitimate doubts as to his or her reliability, is employed in connection with work, the nature of which is vital to the security of the State.' Where such 'legitimate doubts' were raised, Mr. Attlee added, 'there may be no alternative to refusal of employment or dismissal'.

This was the start of the 'purge' procedure. Over the next seven years it led to the removal from their posts of 167 Civil Servants. Of these, 25 were dismissed, 24 resigned, 86 were transferred to non-secret work, and 32 were subsequently reinstated. Action was in many cases taken on the strength of information already in possession of the Security Services: proof that more stringent standards really were being applied.

But not, apparently, stringent enough. The 'purge' procedure is essentially negative in nature, merely being designed to ensure that 'nothing is known' against the subject from the records. It is the equivalent of the American 'National Agency Check'. In 1952 a new procedure was introduced to supplement it. The change in approach is underlined by its name—Positive Vetting.

Positive Vetting involves: a check with Security Service records for 'adverse information'; the completion of a detailed security questionnaire; and a thorough field investigation, which attempts (through interviews with such people as teachers and former employers) to build up a complete picture of the subject's life right back to his school days.

Perhaps in order to disarm as much as possible the inevitable criticism that was to follow its introduction, Positive Vetting in this early form applied to only about 10,000 posts: those involving possession of a *complete body* of knowledge of crucial value to an enemy or potential enemy; and those involving *any* access at all to Atomic Energy information. American influence was responsible for the stricter application to the field of Atomic Energy. It was required under the terms of the Anglo-American agreement for the exchange of information in this sector. The investigators were concerned only with 'subversive influences' on the subject's life, and the standard of proof required before a man could be removed from his post was fairly high.

Although American concern over possible security leaks was at least partly responsible for its introduction, Positive Vetting was at this stage nothing like so stringent as the detailed 'background' checks already in use on the other side of the Atlantic.

Two years later, however, in 1954 (when the fuss about 'witch-hunting' caused by what we may call the 'Mark One' procedure had died down) Positive Vetting 'Mark Two' was introduced. This was tailored very much to the American pattern:

Firstly: Positive Vetting was now to apply to *all* persons with 'constant and regular access to Top Secret defence information or material' as well as to those with even occasional access to Atomic Energy information.

Secondly: from March 1954[2] investigators were to look not just for membership of or association with 'subversive organisations', but for 'serious character weaknesses of a kind which might make a person liable or subject to blackmail'.

Thirdly: A much lower standard of proof was now to be required before 'guilt' was assumed.

The 'Mark Two' procedure is essentially the same as that in operation today; but since its introduction in 1954, it has become

[2] Annexe to Treasury Circular of 31st March, 1954.

more stringent in two respects. In 1956 the Conference of Privy Councillors specifically stated that in borderline cases, the balance of proof should be delicately tilted in favour of the State: and in 1962 the Radcliffe Committee recommended 'a more frequent resort to the purge procedure', which was now to apply to *all* sensitive posts. Furthermore, all departments were now at regular intervals to re-check all staff members holding posts covered by the Positive Vetting procedure. Up till then, only the Foreign Office and the Atomic Energy Authority had double-checked on staff in this way. With the other departments, Positive Vetting had up to now been a once and for all affair. (See Appendix, note 2.)

Not only was the coverage of the 'loyalty programme' vastly extended by the Radcliffe Committee in these respects—the list of fatal 'character defects' was expanded to cover even *suspected* 'insobriety, financial instability, untruthfulness, irregular sexual or marital relations, family connections behind the Iron Curtain, etc.'.

On the subject of character defects, the National Council for Civil Liberties has commented: 'If we are to exclude all those who have ever been drunk, had financial difficulties, told a lie, had sex outside marriage, or had a cousin living in Eastern Europe, who would remain?'[3]

Even if we are to admit the grim necessity for a system under which the private lives of tens of thousands of Civil Servants are combed for indiscretion as far back as their schooldays, we should at least ensure that it is administered with scrupulous fairness, and allow a suspected man every chance to defend his reputation. Unfortunately these elementary principles of justice are to some degree set aside when it comes to judging a man under the 'purge' or Positive Vetting procedures.

The Radcliffe Report of 1962 clearly states that under either of these procedures, a man may be found guilty on 'no more than a question of suspicion or risk'. He will be told of the charges against him in only the vaguest terms. If he chooses to deny them, he may usually appeal to the 'Three Advisers'. At his first appearance before them, he can bring a 'friend'—a lawyer or an official of his Union, perhaps. After that, he is on his own. He is given no particulars of the evidence against him unless it 'can be disclosed without prejudicing secret sources of intelligence'. This means that he is not only denied knowledge of the source, but often of the actual *substance* of the charge, since to reveal this would

[3] 'Privacy Under Attack': N.C.C.L. 1968.

frequently reveal the source as well—an informer perhaps, who insisted on secrecy as the price of revelation. He is not allowed to subpoena witnesses of his own (just in case he guesses the source anyway) and, finally, when the hearing is over, the 'Three Advisers' are specifically instructed to tilt the balance of judgement against him if any doubts remain in their minds.

A man's career therefore can be blighted not by an action, nor even an intention, but for a belief; and not necessarily for an actual belief, but for a suspected belief. He is deprived of the protection of the courts and the safeguards of legal procedure, denied the chance to face his accusers, and has the burden of proof thrown upon his shoulders. No doubt his judges act as fairly as they can within the terms of their brief. But the system embodies techniques which bear an unpleasant resemblance to those employed by the late and unlamented Senator Joe McCarthy, however different the spirit in which they are employed.

It is in fact most instructive to see how each development of the American security programme has tended to be reproduced in our own. The American Government now employs some 25,000 professional investigators (not counting those in espionage and counter-espionage); and around one in four of the American working population is subjected to some form of 'loyalty' programme. Our own programme is more selective, but now embodies almost all the characteristics of the American one. It differs only in scale. In America, as here, the inability of those under suspicion to confront their accusers is perhaps the most controversial feature of all.

'As essential as confrontation is to fairness in other proceedings,' writes an American authority,[4] 'it is doubly so in security cases. Security charges almost always relate to a period of time long past, and the untested remembrances of confidential informants cannot but do truth a disservice . . . Confrontation in the security field has never worked for the simple reason that it has never been tried. Precisely because the government has been able to use its secret informants against security defendants without confrontation, there has been no incentive to utilise informants in their historic role as providers of leads for witnesses who would testify openly. What we have in the security programmes today is a system based on *administrative convenience* rather than *security necessity*'.

The security watch on Civil Servants extends to their Unions

[4] 'Industrial Personnel Security Cases and Materials', Ed. by L. H. Weaver. Pub. by Charles C. Thomas, Springfield, Illinois.

and staff associations as well. 'We understand,' said the Radcliffe Report of 1962, 'that there is no evidence that the Communists have made any exceptional effort to gain control of these Unions. But they appear in fact to have achieved a higher degree of penetration here than in almost any other sector of the Trade Union movement. No evidence has been brought to our knowledge that Communist union officers have been detected in any form of espionage. Nevertheless, we regard this presumably deliberate massing of Communist effort in the Civil Service unions as most dangerous to security.'

The Report suggested therefore that any department should have the right, where secret work is concerned, 'to deny access to or refuse to negotiate (either by correspondence or face to face) with a named trade union official whom it had reason to believe to be a Communist under the definition used in the purge procedure'. To establish which officers should be 'named' involves extending the network of security investigations to cover the entire leadership of Civil Service Unions and Staff Associations. This is, of course, only one instance of the way in which the security web has been extended in recent years to cover an ever greater number of Civil Servants. But it is an instance with dangerous implications. Any private employer would give his eye-teeth for similar control over union leadership. Carried to its logical conclusion, it could allow an employer to remove from the bargaining table any opponent he found too able or intractable. It would not altogether transfer the selection of union leadership from employee to employer, but it would serve the employer's purpose almost as well. As things are, men are 'named' by the security service on the grounds of their supposed allegiance to Communism. But there is strong reason to suspect that mere militancy or radical socialist tendencies can be enough. The cases of seven Civil Service Trade Union Officers 'named' under this procedure were examined by the National Council for Civil Liberties. They found evidence to suggest that only one of the men was actually a member of the Communist Party. The other six were 'named' on vague evidence of the 'association' type.

Few people would altogether deny the need for detailed government investigation of convicted criminals and of Civil Servants engaged on highly secret work, although many might question certain aspects of such investigations. But these two very different classes of citizen are not the only ones drawn into the security net.

If you work in a factory engaged on government contracts of a secret nature (and many tens of thousands of British citizens do) you also are liable to be investigated thoroughly—and so are all your friends and relatives. All contracts for work involving acquaintance with 'Official Secrets' contain a security clause which entitles the government to full information on all those engaged on the work. Any breach of the terms of the clause also implies a breach of contract, which becomes liable to termination. Not surprisingly, contracting firms work closely with the Security Service and co-operate in any way asked of them.

The Radcliffe Report of 1962 gave a clear picture of how this co-operation is achieved:

'(a) They (contractors) are provided with a manual which gives both detailed and general guidance on security procedures.

(b) The Security Service runs special short courses for industrial Security Officers and occasional short courses for higher management.

(c) The Security Service employs a team of officers who act as agents for the contracting Departments, visit contracting firms to examine their security arrangements and to offer help or advice on any security problems that may arise.'

The Radcliffe Report recommended that the 'secret aspects' letter setting out the government's security requirements for each contract should be even more detailed and explicit in its terms, and that the team of security advisers should be strengthened even further.

Few contractors have any illusions about the degree of freedom they have, or care to ignore the 'help and advice' proffered by the Security Advisers. In 1956 I.C.I. was requested to dismiss from their staff an Assistant Solicitor whose only indiscretion had been to marry, five years previously, an *ex*-member of the Communist Party. And dismissed he was—although much against the inclination of his employers.

It is a mistake to think of the vetting procedure as something affecting only the higher echelons. Even the humblest employees of contracting organisations will be put through the vetting procedure when their work seems to warrant it. Contractors such as Costains are reported to have in the past sacked unskilled labourers whom the Security Service found politically unacceptable for work on certain construction projects. Charladies on the staff of Affiliated Cleaning Co. and other office cleaning firms are thoroughly investigated before they are cleared for contract work in government buildings.

Perhaps you have never worked for the government or for a firm engaged on secret government work; have led a blameless life, without so much as a parking ticket to your name; have no friends, relatives or associates whose own dossiers might contain details of your life. Perhaps. But you may still be 'on file'.

'Are you a Security Risk?' asks a pamphlet produced by the National Council for Civil Liberties. 'The mere fact that you answer "no" is neither here nor there. Was your wife politically active on the Left? Are you an active Trade Unionist? Have you ever been guilty of supporting C.N.D.? Or worse, the Committee of 100?' If you can answer 'yes' to any of these questions, the pamphlet warns, then you will be investigated thoroughly, *and so will all your friends and relatives.*

To be marked down and investigated as a 'political', it is not necessary to make rousing speeches, to organise rallies, or even to join a political organisation. Regular attendance at demonstrations (however varied their complexion) may be enough. Special Branch cameramen have long been a familiar sight at demonstrations (although the universal sporting of copies of the *Morning Star* by S.B. photographers at one demonstration in September 1968 was a new feature). If your face turns up often enough on the projection screen back at H.Q., discreet but thorough inquiries will be made about you.

The Special Branch is the nearest approach that we have in Britain to a political police. It was originally set up in the 1880's as an off-shoot of the C.I.D., to deal with an outbreak of terrorist activity by the Irish Republicans. Under the name of 'Special Irish Branch', it had great success in putting an end to the series of explosions which from 1883 to 1885 were directed—among other targets—against Nelson's Column; three Underground stations; Scotland Yard, the Tower of London; London Bridge; Westminster Hall; and (as a grand finale) the crypt of the House of Commons itself. When the emergency was over, the word 'Irish' was dropped from the unit's title, and it has remained in being ever since as the 'Special Branch'. Since 1886 it has taken a keen interest in the activities of organisations as varied as the Nihilists, the Anarchists, the Suffragettes, the Fascists, the I.R.A. and the Communists. The modern duties of the Special Branch are to gather information on 'subversive' or terrorist organisations and to pass it on to the Security Service; to guard against and investigate 'offences against the security of the State', such as treason, espionage, offences against the Official Secrets Act and the Public Order Act; to 'keep watch on seaports and airports for criminals and other dangerous persons'; and to 'make inquiries into aliens and so forth'.

In the words of ex-Commissioner Scott of the Metropolitan Police,[5] 'an interest in the byways of political thought and action is required of officers in this branch.' This interest has led them to an increasing concern with Trade Union leadership.

Speaking in the House of Commons on June 28th, 1966, the Prime Minister stated: 'The House will be aware that the Communist Party, unlike the major political parties, has at its disposal an efficient and disciplined industrial apparatus controlled from Communist Party headquarters. No major strike occurs anywhere in any sector of industry in which that apparatus fails to concern itself.'

Just over a year later, Mr. Ray Gunter (then Minister of Labour) warned that an 'unholy alliance' of Communists and Trotskyists was planning to disrupt the economy and undermine Britain's hopes of recovery.

Communist Party membership in the U.K. stands at just over 33,000. Whether or not the threat presented by the Party and its fellow-travellers is as serious as the 'unholy alliance' speech suggested, there is no doubt that an intensive struggle to gain control of the Unions has been waged by the Party for years. Mr. Ramelson, the Communist Party's National Industrial Organiser, claimed in November, 1967, that there was 'not a struggle in which Party members were not at the centre'. The Party's National Organiser, Mr. McLennan, referred on the same occasion (the 30th Congress of the Communist Party) to the 'widely acknowledged leadership of Communists in the recent industrial struggles'. The factories have long been regarded by Communists as 'the key centres of the class struggle', and the emergence since 1956 of a powerful Trotskyist movement has brought the battle for control of these 'key centres' to a new pitch of ferocity.

The S.B. and the Security Service therefore, have excellent reasons for their interest in all who become active in the Trade Unions, and must sometimes sigh for the days before the fragmentation of the Communist movement, when the byways of leftist thought were less tangled.

[5] 'Scotland Yard', by ex-Commissioner Scott, André Deutsch Ltd.

Nowhere of course is the political scene so confused as in those traditional centres of radical opinion—the Universities. Here too the dossier-builders are at work. The watch on the Universities first came into the limelight in 1952, when Mr. Butler told the House of Commons: 'investigations have . . . to be undertaken in the Universities from time to time to protect the security of the state. It would not be in the public interest to disclose the arrangements to carry out these investigations . . .'

Political convictions formed at University are often of short duration, but this is by no means always so, as scandal after security scandal in recent years has proved. Nowadays a degree is necessary equipment for most 'sensitive' posts. A watch on those still in the process of acquiring that equipment, in the unguarded atmosphere of academic freedom, can save a great deal of trouble later. With the new upsurge in student activism, and its links with events outside the university sphere, it can save trouble in the short term too.

In June 1968 the President of the Students' Union at London University charged the police with attempting to recruit informers from among the student body at the School of Oriental and African Studies. He alleged that a number of foreign students (chosen, he believed, because they were more likely to co-operate than native-born students) had been asked to establish the political opinions of fellow-students, and to obtain information on plans for demonstrations. A Persian student, Mr. Shahpoor Bazergan, claimed that he had been approached but had refused to co-operate. The police, he said, had been most surprised. 'They said that they had interviewed many students about the same thing and had never had a reception like this before. All they wanted were the names of any radical students known to me in the college, of any nationality, not just foreigners—and forewarning of any demonstrations or political activities.'[6]

By December 1968 the National Union of Students had become seriously concerned about the number of similar complaints coming in from other London colleges, and from provincial universities as well. A Union spokesman said it was known that the police were interested in the activities of militant Left-wing groups, but he 'deplored any situation where one student was asked in secret by the police to spy on a colleague'.[7]

In pursuing their task of compiling a master-file of the nation's

[6] *Daily Telegraph* 19.6.68 and 20.6.68.
[7] *Daily Telegraph* 19.12.68.

political dissidents, the S.B. and the Security Service have a great deal of ground to cover. The Labour Party's own list of 'proscribed organisations'—those whose members are debarred from membership of the Labour Party—runs to 44 entries, ranging from the 'British Soviet Society' to the 'British Youth Festival Committee'. New organisations are set up by the dozen each year; many of these are 'fronts' which are no sooner identified than they dissolve themselves, perhaps to pop up again a little later under a new and innocent-looking name. Then there are the perfectly 'respectable' organisations which become penetrated by extremists and are eventually taken over. The 'Young Socialists', for example, is now largely a Trotskyist body; the Labour Party has now been forced to rename its own youth movement the 'Labour Party Young Socialists'. Strenuous efforts are now apparently being made to take over the new organisation in its turn.

The official security forces are not alone in keeping an eye on subversive individuals and organisations. Britain's industrialists are anxious to help, and have set up four main organisations for this purpose. Just one of them, the 'Economic League', is backed by industry to the tune of about a quarter of a million pounds every year in its aim of 'exposing the intentions and strategy of subversive organisations and providing positive education to combat misrepresentation by industrial agitators'. Another, much smaller firm is 'Common Cause'. It has similar aims, but does not stick so closely to the industrial field. Then there is 'Aims of Industry' (with an annual budget of around £100,000) which confines itself to propaganda; and finally, 'British United Industrialists'—a firm which takes a close interest in front organisations and subversive groups and individuals of all kinds and whose revenue reportedly fluctuates between £200,000 and £400,000 p.a. The potential effectiveness of these four firms, can be judged from the fact that in an election year their total revenue is likely to come close to, or even exceed, those of the Conservative and Socialist parties *combined*.

The Special Branch is also assisted by local police whenever necessary—as it often is, because of the scale and time-consuming nature of so many of their inquiries. For example, it was on behalf of the Special Branch that a detective asked a staff-member of the *Nottingham Evening News* for the names and addresses of pseudonymous contributors of 'Letters to the Editor';[8] and Hert-

[8] *The Times* 16.12.59.

fordshire police helped them out by establishing the identities of people who turned up at a number of 'ban the bomb' meetings. Press photographers were asked for copies of pictures they had taken, and the registration numbers of cars parked at these meetings were noted down.

Sometimes the Special Branch must regret asking for local co-operation, however much finicking detail work this can save them. When the proprietor of a village shop in Surrey complained to a local Inspector in 1962 that one of his men had cleared all the customers out of her shop and quizzed her about the politics of her eighteen-year-old son, she was told, quite frankly, that it was part of a nation-wide scheme to list members of Communist and Fascist organisations.[9]

Any examination of the way in which Britain's 'Loyalty programme' has grown over the years must inevitably prompt the question: how much further will it grow in the future? Will the ideals of democracy ever become completely stifled under the security blanket? The 'Report of the Committee Appointed to Inquire into Security Procedures in the Public Service'[10] stated the problem neatly: 'It would be commonplace to say that the social and political system of this country is inimical to effective security. In considering any additional security measures to recommend, we have reminded ourselves that security weaknesses are part of the price we pay for having a social and political system that men want to defend.' Paradoxically, one of the most objectionable features of the present security system is that it does not go far enough. The past lives of tens of thousands of government servants, and of the servants of government contractors, are put under the security microscope. Great care is taken to exclude from 'sensitive' posts all those whose records hint at the wrong sort of political associations, or at circumstances which might render them amenable to blackmail. This goes for the Permanent Secretary as well as the charlady who cleans his office; for the Chief Designer as well as the builder's labourer who helps give his ideas material shape. But it does not go for the politicians who direct them.

'Some Hon. Members with possible ambitions to enjoy Government secrets would be denied them if the test of what political views they held when they were 17, applied to them,' W. Griffiths M.P. told the House of Commons in 1960. 'That goes for Hon.

[9] *Daily Herald* 15.10.62.
[10] Cmnd. 1681 H.M.S.O.

Members on *both* sides of the House.' The Security Service is probably right in assuming that men who flirted with Hitler early in their political careers present no real threat in today's world. But they have consistently treated any connection with Communism as a very real threat indeed.

Brian Magee, in an eloquent plea to his fellow-Socialists to rethink some of the basic assumptions on which their political thinking was founded in their youth, has pointed out that, '. . . almost everyone in the generation of Socialists that grew up in the 1930s was Marxist in outlook. The extent to which this is true can be illustrated by the fact that Anthony Crosland . . . (was a) thorough-going Marxist, Roy Jenkins only somewhat less so, and Denis Healey a member of the Communist Party'.[11] At the time of writing, Anthony Crosland is President of the Board of Trade; Roy Jenkins is Chancellor of the Exchequer; and Denis Healey is actually Minister of Defence.

No one would seriously question the 'political reliability' of these men, or suggest that they be removed from office because of beliefs and allegiances long since modified or outgrown. Yet surely there is both injustice and absurdity in a system that can countenance such appointments while at the same time blighting the careers of other men whose connections with the Far Left are infinitely more tenuous, and whose posts allow infinitely less scope for doing real harm to the nation? If the defence of Britain's dwindling store of secrets really demands the dismissal or transfer to other work of government servants who joined the wrong club at University; or who chose to marry someone who did so; or who were unfortunate to fall into enemy hands during the Korean War and may therefore have been subjected to brainwashing—then surely, what is sauce for the bureaucratic goose ought to be sauce for the political gander as well?

[11] 'The New Radicalism', Secker & Warburg Ltd.

MI5: Watchdog Without a Master?

> 'One could of course—the government of whatever complexion could—run a closely-controlled, almost a police state. If you want absolute security, you have to do that.'
>
> *Harold Macmillan*

Each year the Special Branch draws its net ever tighter over the Universities, the Civil Service and the Unions, over demonstrations and meetings; over spies, saboteurs and subversives by the hundred; over political and quasi-political organisations by the score. But many of the fish it lands are not of its own catching.

There are other, more shadowy organisations with specialised security functions of their own, which call in the Special Branch only when an arrest is to be made or a case prepared for trial. When that point is reached, they keep very much in the background.

Every government department engaged on secret work is responsible for its own internal security. Most departments have some work in this secret category; three of them have security responsibilities wider than the rest.

The Foreign Office is responsible for MI6. The H.Q. of this, the 'overseas branch' of Britain's Intelligence Service, is at 54 Broadway, London S.W.1—cunningly listed in the telephone book as a branch of the Ministry of Land and Natural Resources. *The Ministry of Defence* houses in its Whitehall building the Director General of Intelligence. He heads the combined intelligence staffs of the three fighting services, plus two 'non-military' units: one for technical and scientific intelligence, and one for economic intelligence. The Director General's title is somewhat misleading. There is no Supremo of British Intelligence, but three joint heads. The Director General of Intelligence is one. The head of MI6 is another. The third member of this select trio is, strictly speaking, responsible to *The Home Office*. Known on official minutes by the cryptic initials 'D.G.', he heads MI5—the Security Service—the organisation with overall responsibility for the 'Defence of the Realm' against subversive activity from within. Until 1952 'D.G.' reported direct to the Prime Minister. As the result of recommendations made in the Fulton Report, he may soon do so again.

The three separate services coordinate their activities through the Joint Intelligence Committee, which presents agreed assessments of defence problems to the Cabinet. From time to time, usually as a result of a serious security scandal, there have been suggestions that all Britain's intelligence services should be combined into one jumbo 'Ministry of National Security'. The idea has been rejected on the grounds that the creation of such a ministry would cause all the other government departments now responsible for their own internal security to sit back with a sigh of relief and 'leave it to the experts'. So the present tri-partite arrangement continues: three separate empires, three different heads, each free to do things very much in his own way.

Some years ago, the *Daily Mail* claimed to have tracked down the Security Service to its lair—Leconsfield House[1] in Curzon Street, Mayfair. This was in 1963, the year of the Profumo scandal. The Security Service was very much in the news. Its activities had always been shrouded in such mystery that when it seemed to have been prying into the morals of a Minister of the Crown, there was widespread public alarm. Lord Denning, in his report on the Profumo affair, went to extraordinary pains to calm these fears. Of the police, he said; '. . . it is no part of their duty to pry into the private lives of anyone, be it a Minister of the Crown or the humblest citizen . . . we are not yet a police state.'

Of the Security Service, he said: 'They are not to be used to pry into any man's private conduct, or business affairs, or even into his political opinions, except so far as they are subversive . . . it would be intolerable to us to have anything in the nature of a Gestapo or Secret Police to snoop into all we do, let alone our morals.'

The Service, he pointed out, had no special powers of search, entry or arrest. 'We would rather have it so, than anything in the nature of a "secret police".' In case anyone still wasn't convinced, he next emphasised how small the Security Service is. 'In some other countries there is to be found a massive organisation with representatives dispersed throughout the land. Whereas in this country it is and remains a small professional organisation charged with the task of countering espionage, subversion and sabotage.'

[1] Still part of MI5 today, but no longer its H.Q.

These efforts to convince the ordinary citizen that there was nothing to fear from the Security Service might almost have convinced a few unwary spies, saboteurs and subversives that they too had nothing to fear from the Service, so puny did Lord Denning make it seem.

It is true that compared, for example, to the American counter-espionage organisation, the British Security Service is minute. The F.B.I., its nearest American equivalent, is reputed to have over 14,000 employees, and to spend almost 147 million dollars p.a. out of a total national 'security budget' that tops four thousand million dollars a year. Half this grand total admittedly goes on 'electronic espionage', radar and radio monitoring, codes and code-breaking, aerial espionage by 'plane and satellite. But during the 1950s, Britain probably spent no more than £5 million a year on all her intelligence services combined. Even as late as 1963, Chapman Pincher set the figure no higher than £12 million p.a., of which overseas intelligence spending, he believed, accounted for about £7 million. On limited resources such as these, a 'massive organisation with representatives dispersed through the land' is obviously out of the question. Indeed, Britain's Security Service is actually believed to have fewer men on its staff than its counterpart in tiny Belgium. But as Lord Denning himself pointed out, 'Those absences (they are not deficiencies)—the absence of powers and the absence of numbers—are made up for by the close co-operation of the Security Service and the police forces.'

This co-operation sometimes breaks down. In May 1968 two Russian 'trade delegates' snooping in the neighbourhood of a mysterious Ministry of Defence installation in Battersea were arrested for 'loitering with intent' by two detectives—right under the noses of the MI5 agents who had been trailing them.

The premature arrest at Battersea was made by C.I.D. officers. Special Branch men would hardly make such a mistake. As Lord Denning emphasised, liaison between the Special Branch and the Security Service is very close indeed. The Security Service may have neither special powers nor a large staff. But the Special Branch has both, and can be called upon to provide auxiliaries, or to take over when an arrest is to be made or a case prepared for trial. The Security Service can thus remain cloaked in secrecy to a degree which a larger and more self-evidently powerful organisation could not hope to match.

In America, the Heads of the various intelligence services are publicly appointed, and their lives written up by the press in articles replete with homely detail ('Rear Admiral Souers, the nation's first Director of Central Intelligence, once headed up the Piggly-Wiggly stores in downtown Memphis . . .'). The C.I.A. actually produced a lavish recruiting brochure designed to attract the brightest University graduates to its ranks. Tourist buses stop outside the H.Q.s of the F.B.I. and the C.I.A. while their drivers reel off facts and figures which in this country would be kept in triple cipher under lock and key. Scores of books have appeared describing the workings of American security organisations in authentic detail: the American Espionage Statutes and Internal Security Acts have never been used to muzzle journalists and writers as British journalists and writers are muzzled.

Many of these books have been written by ex-employees from first-hand knowledge. The U.S. Government has no Official Secrets Act, and so cannot enforce silence upon its servants after their retirement. In contrast, an ex-employee of any of the British Intelligence Services who writes an account of his experiences without first submitting it for censorship at the manuscript stage is likely to suffer, as Sir Compton Mackenzie once did, both a heavy fine and the destruction of every copy of his book. Even when the material has already appeared overseas, the Official Secrets Act will sometimes be used to prevent its publication in the United Kingdom.

The American public, then, has a broad understanding of how its intelligence services operate and the sort of work they do. In the U.K. the very different attitude towards publicity has served to perpetuate an almost universal ignorance. Not only is the general public kept very much in the dark on the subject—so are its elected representatives.

'The Security service is, after all, a *secret* service,' Mr. Brooke blandly informed the Commons in 1963. 'This is part of its essence. Its cost is borne on the Secret Vote and one must bear in mind therefore that the number of parliamentary questions which could be put to me with any hope of an answer being properly given is very limited.' So who does know precisely what goes on inside Britain's intelligence services, other than those who actually man them? The astonishing answer seems to be—no one at all.

MI6, for instance, is theoretically controlled by the Foreign Office. Yet in 1968, Donald McLachlan (himself a former intelligence officer, and author of a standard work on naval intelligence) wrote: 'I was not amused, but somewhat surprised to learn lately from a former Foreign Secretary and from a former head of the Foreign Office, that they had known next to nothing of the organisation and assessment of secret intelligence for which some years ago they had been responsible. They had been advised that there was no choice between knowing almost everything and knowing next to nothing: being busy men they had chosen the latter course.'[2]

The same state of ignorance seems to prevail at the Home Office with respect to MI5. The Director General of the Security Service is personally responsible to the Home Secretary, and has the right of access to the Prime Minister 'on appropriate occasion'. On the official table of precedence, his place is pointedly set just below those of the Head of the Home Office and the Head of the Ministry of Defence. They hold the exalted rank of Permanent Secretary; his rank is equivalent to that of Deputy Under-Secretary.[3] But the Security Service is not *part* of the Home Office. It is a separate department, and its Head is specifically instructed to keep to himself all but an absolute minimum of information on its workings. This instruction is not chiefly designed to save the Home Secretary's time. The Denning Report of 1963 set out the directive which Sir David Maxwell-Fyfe (as Home Secretary) issued to the Director General of the Security Service in 1952. Its final clause reads: 'You and your staff will maintain the well established convention whereby Ministers do not concern themselves with the detailed information which may be obtained by the Security Service in particular cases, but are furnished with such information only as may be necessary for the determination of any issue *on which guidance may be sought.*' That 'well established convention' arose from a desire to save Ministerial embarrassment. In the course of its work, the Security Service is bound to do things which the Minister would rather not know about. Consequently the Head of the Security Service has an unparalleled freedom of action.

Sir Findlater Stewart's report of 1945 showed by implication how dangerous that freedom could be in the wrong hands: '. . . from the very nature of the work, need for direction except on the very broadest lines, can never arise above the level of Director General. That appointment is one of great responsibility, calling for unusual experience, and a rare combination of qualities;

[2] *Daily Telegraph* 26.9.68.
[3] Salary £6,300 p.a.

but having got the right man there is no alternative to giving him the widest discretion in the means he uses and the direction in which he applies them—always provided he does not step outside the law.'

So far as one can tell, the 'right men' do seem to have been appointed so far—at least in the limited sense that if any of them have stepped outside the law, they have covered their tracks remarkably well. It is to be hoped that the 'right man' continues to be appointed to a post which combines such a high degree of independence with such a low degree of accountability. The Denning Report tried hard to represent the Security Service as a small body of men working within tightly-defined terms of reference under Ministerial direction, and concentrating its activities upon a handful of dangerous men. But from the nature of its work in factories and laboratories engaged on secret work, and from the fact that the names of candidates for posts covered under Positive Vetting and 'purge' procedures are checked against its records for 'political unreliability' and 'character defects', it is obvious that the Security Service covers far more ground than Lord Denning's definition of their work would suggest. While its affairs remain blanketed by the obsessive secrecy so characteristic of the entire British governmental and administrative machine, public suspicion of the sort which rose to such a peak at the time of the Profumo affair will continue. The American intelligence system is no less effective than the British, despite its quite different attitude towards publicity. Britain's first Director General of Intelligence, who retired as recently as 1966, has himself written: 'It is undesirable and unhealthy that there should be no public debate or consideration of a subject that is of crucial importance in national and international decision-making, and to which after all public funds are devoted.'[4] The degree of independence enjoyed by Britain's intelligence chiefs, while innocuous enough in the right hands, could be disastrous in the wrong ones. As Thomas Jefferson once wrote, 'It should be remembered that whatever power in any government is independent, is absolutely so.'

[4] 'Intelligence at the Top', by Major General Sir Kenneth Strong, Cassell & Co. Ltd.

Public Enemy Number One

'To tax and to please, no more than to love and to be wise, is not given to men.'

Edmund Burke

Of all the long, sharp noses employed by bureaucracy to poke into our private affairs, 63,000 of the very longest and sharpest belong to the Department of Inland Revenue.

The Department's bill for wages and expenses already tops £87½ million p.a., and an intensive recruiting drive is adding about 2,300 new staff-members to the payroll each year. Even so, it can't separate the taxpayer from his money fast enough. Its myrmidons put in astonishing amounts of overtime—1¾ million hours in 1967, and over a million hours in just the first six months of 1968—yet at the time of writing, a backlog of over half a million individual items of business has mounted up. Despite their devotion to duty, or perhaps because of it, Britain's tax-men receive scant appreciation, either financially or in terms of public esteem. The head of the Surtax Department, whose efforts bring over £250 million a year to the public purse, is paid a miserly £4,500 p.a. An ordinary District Inspector of Taxes can earn as little as £2,970 p.a., after an arduous course of study which entails the mastering of such brain-twisters as the Income Tax Act (1,000 pages) and its 38 companion volumes (25,000 pages) of legal precedents.

Ordinary Clerical officers on counter duty are even less to be envied, not only because of their lower pay, but because they bear the full brunt of public fury. Assault is a common enough occurrence for their trade union to have taken out special insurance at Lloyd's. Claims for spectacles and dentures smashed by angry taxpayers are a routine matter. As the Estimates Committee of the House of Commons reported some years ago, '. . . the department is still in the view of many taxpayers "Public Enemy Number One".'

This is hardly surprising. As the chief supplier of the fuel on which the entire governmental machine runs, the Inland Revenue is provided with inquisitorial and punitive powers unmatched by any other department. Taken together, they constitute an attack on personal privacy that would have brought earlier generations to the point of revolution.

The first shot in a battle with the Inland Revenue is usually fired by the District Inspector of Taxes, in the shape of a polite invitation to talk things over at his office. If you employ an accountant, and the invitation is passed on to you through him, then probably nothing too nasty is in store. But if your accountant is bypassed altogether, and the invitation reaches you direct—then brace yourself. You can take it almost for granted that the Inspector believes you have deliberately been leading him up the garden path, and that in return, he is about to put you through the agonising process known as 'reconciling your capital', with an eye to establishing your 'omitted income'.

Strangely enough, there is no compulsion to accept the Inspector's invitation to walk into his parlour; or having accepted it, to answer any of his questions. If you refuse, you will simply be 'assessed' on the basis of what he thinks you ought to pay. Of course, without your cooperation, the bill will be calculated largely on the basis of guesswork. The sum demanded will be high. But pay it you must—unless you appeal to the Commissioners. Unlike the Inspector, these gentlemen have the power to issue 'precepts' requiring you under threat of penalty to produce any information they consider to be necessary.

So when the Inspector asks for a date, accept. Coyness really will not pay. But on no account go to the rendezvous alone. Take an accountant with you as chaperone. Let *him* do the talking. Restrict yourself to a courteous greeting and murmured remarks about the weather. Remember—at this stage the Inspector may have his doubts about your virtue, but probably no concrete proof. So in an effort to rattle you into making damaging admissions about your past, he will not ask openly for what he wants, but confine himself to vague innuendos about your affairs, and talk of the terrible penalties for holding out on him. Guilty or innocent, *do not be seduced.* Bear in mind the following words, written by a man hardened by years in the Revenue's service: 'The psychological effect on the taxpayer of an interview of this type is to induce a feeling of guilt. Few taxpayers are completely free from minor tax evasions, but the Inspector would not be particularly interested in these. . . . The taxpayer, however, will frequently jump to the conclusion that the minor evasions should be immediately disclosed and will thus lay up for himself a burden of trouble and worry that, with more mature consideration, could have been avoided.'[1]

In other words—*hold your tongue*. You are in quite enough trouble already, without making more for yourself.

Of course, it could be that the Inspector's suspicions are the result of some simple misunderstanding, which your accountant will be able to clear up very quickly. But supposing he can't? It may be that the Inspector is firmly convinced that your savings and/or spending are at a much higher level than your declared income would seem to explain. In that case, he will claim a 'discovery'—a word which suggests proof, but usually means no more than suspicion. He 'assesses' you on that discovery and presents you with the bill. It is now up to you to prove his calculations wrong.

This can be very difficult to do. A 'discovery' can be claimed at any time within six years of the event. Where fraud or 'wilful default' is suspected, a discovery can be claimed at any time at all. Thus an assessment relating to years long past and money long spent, can arrive out of the blue simply because your old inspector has been replaced by a new man, who considers you have been let off too lightly.

When the Inspector believes that you have not declared your full income over a period of years, he works on the simple proposition that your *total* income can be established by adding together your savings and your expenditure for the period. The income you have actually *declared* he obviously knows about already. What he is after is your '*omitted*' income, and to establish this he relies on a formula which any schoolboy could construct: savings + spendings − declared income = omitted income.

To get at the figures he needs to solve this formula, he will take you through a sort of financial strip-tease.

Where did the money come from for that holiday in the Bahamas? Why did you increase your wife's dress allowance? How could you afford to pay those school-fees? What insurance do you carry, and on what? How did you save the deposit on your house?

The process may take one or more interviews a week, and be spread over several months. If the Inspector goes back far enough, he is bound to strike something you can't explain. You may have

[1] 'The Back Duty Manual', by A. J. Roper, Butterworth & Co. (Publishers) Ltd.

forgotten just how you acquired that block of shares ten years ago; or you may know for a fact that a certain cash deposit made to your account in 1962 was the fruit of rich Uncle Charlie's generosity. But have you any proof? Documentary proof? This is often the only kind the Revenue will accept. Your win at Ascot in 1961—how do you prove *that*?

Many of the people who fall foul of the Revenue are small businessmen suspected of 'living out of the till'. The amounts involved each year may be quite small (although added together over a period of years, the final sum may be quite substantial). If yours is such a case, the Inspector will not just want to know about big items of expenditure—cars, fur coats, or lavish holidays. He will attempt to lay bare your whole pattern of living. The number of cigarettes you smoke, the size of your gas bill, the price of the new curtains in your drawing room, how often you visit the pub and what you drink there, the amount you put into the collection plate on Sundays—all these are grist to his mill.

The Inspector's suspicions may have been aroused by an informer —a jealous neighbour, a disgruntled ex-employee. Or he may be wondering how you accumulated your capital. The capital itself may be untaxable—but how did you put it together? You may have revealed its existence yourself—through the size of a dividend cheque scrupulously declared in your annual 'return'. Alternatively the Revenue's own intelligence network may have turned up the necessary clues. A spot check on a Building Society's records could have showed up your name as an account holder. Or your bank, in its return of interest paid out to creditors, may have indirectly given away the size of your deposit account. Possibly a Revenue investigator may have noticed a block of shares registered in your name at Bush House.

Although people who save their money come more readily to the attention of the Revenue than those who spend it, anyone who seems to be living above his income may also have some awkward questions to answer. The man with his own business is particularly open to suspicion. Expensive hobbies likely to attract newspaper photographers, or even grand weddings, can catch the Inspector's eye. Or one of the 'regulars' in your pub may be a Revenue employee who thinks your car is too large for your declared income. ('And of course,' says Sir Alexander Johnston in his book on the Department,[2] 'the staff of the tax office always keep their eyes open.') In this task they are backed up by a superb intelligence service run from Head Office in Somerset House. Information culled from a wide variety of sources is sent out from here to the relevant District Officers, who can also find out from the same source the answers to particularly knotty problems. To quote Sir Alexander Johnston again: 'The starting prices for a particular race meeting are easily provided but the section has been called upon, among other things, to supply information about the marriage customs of West African tribes, the transport of racing pigeons, the secondhand value of pin-tables, the grading of sausage skins and illegal trafficking in horses.' With staffwork of this quality behind him, the District Inspector makes a formidable opponent. To underestimate his abilities as a Private Eye could prove very expensive. But occasionally he will come across a case too big or too complicated to handle on his own. Then the Revenue's own private detective force will come into the picture.

The 'Enquiry Branch', as it is called, operates from Somerset House and twelve local offices. With a staff of sixty inspectors and twenty accountants, this hush-hush investigation team will work away at a case for months or even years if necessary. Britain's 340,000 *surtax*-payers have yet another group of financial sleuths to reckon with—the members of the Surtax's Office's own Enquiry Branch, who work in close liaison with their colleagues of the Income Tax department. Surtax payers who find the strain too much and fly abroad leaving the Department's bill unpaid, will come to the attention of the Collection Division. Tax evasion is a non-extradictable offence, but Britain's tax authorities maintain excellent relations with those of other countries (Switzerland is a notable exception). They may find that their tax problems, like Mary's little lamb, follow them wherever they may go. International co-operation in the tax field, as in a number of others, is based fairly firmly on the principle of the *quid pro quo*. Staff-members of the 'Secretaries' Office' at Somerset House, who are responsible (among other things) for negotiating tax agreements with other countries, have excellent contacts with foreign tax officials. A number of people who had thought their overseas earnings safely hidden from the U.K. tax authorities have found out

[2] 'The Inland Revenue'. One of the 'New Whitehall' series, George Allen & Unwin Ltd.

to their cost how easily the old boy net can stretch across national frontiers.

Smaller fry who try to shake off the Revenue without going into exile, by simply moving to another part of the U.K. without leaving a forwarding address, may come to the attention of the Assessments Division. This division specialises in extracting payment where a local inspector or collector has failed. It maintains a group of super-specialists to whom the tracking down of the most elusive defaulter is a routine matter. They can claim success in four out of five cases referred to them.

Some potential 'customers' attempt to avoid their bills not by running, but by taking care not to get on the Revenue's books in the first place. To deal with this gambit, local tax offices regularly check electoral rolls, telephone directories, and even the guest-lists of hotels and boarding houses. A new 'customer' may also be spotted if he takes up paid employment, however briefly. All employers are required to give the tax office details of those working for them.

Against those it suspects of wilful evasion, fraud or just simple negligence the Revenue is able to deploy a terrifying armoury of penalties.

A man suspected of fraud or simple negligence must, as we have seen, prove that he has not made the profits the Inspector claims he has made. The burden of proof lies on the suspect. If he fails to shift it—and it makes no odds whether he is innocent or truly guilty—he becomes liable to pay not only the back-tax but a penalty as well. The Revenue may choose not to exact the full statutory penalty, but invite an 'offer' in settlement. This will have to comprise the whole of the 'back duty' claimed, plus a penalty whose weight will depend upon the circumstances of the case. It can range from mere interest on the back-tax in the simplest cases of 'failure to notify liability', right up to 100% for serious fraud. In the majority of 'back duty' cases however, the Inspector will look for an offer of back tax plus 50-70% penalty, and will normally refuse to recommend a lower offer for acceptance by the Board.

There is of course no necessity for the taxpayer to accept the Inspector's judgement of his case. Every year eight thousand or so appeals against a District Inspector's judgement are heard before the General or Special Commissioners. A hearing before the Commissioners is a 'trial by tribunal', with many of the attendant drawbacks discussed earlier in this book. Most of the safeguards provided by a Court of the Realm are missing. The most spectacular departure from normal legal practice is the assumption of guilt in the absence of documentary proof to the contrary. In this respect the defendant is no better off than in his original dealings with the Inspector. But (as is not the case with most tribunals) a taxpayer who fails in his appeal before the Commissioners does at least have the right to go to the High Court. Few avail themselves of this right which is, in any case, confined to those cases where an actual point of law is in dispute. Those who do avail themselves of it are pitting themselves against a Department with limitless funds and armies of experts at its disposal, and which has proved itself willing to pursue the most trivial case—such as whether a toffee-apple is a sweet or a piece of fruit—through Court after Court. Not only does a court battle with the Revenue involve murderous expense—it forces a man to lay bare to public scrutiny the most intimate details of his financial affairs. Even if he should finally win his case, to a businessman such publicity could prove ruinous.

The Revenue will rarely exact the full penalty from a taxpayer who accepts their invitation to 'make an offer'. But up to 1960 the price for a man who fought them through the Courts before going down to final defeat was invariably very much higher than it would have been if he had paid up quietly to begin with. Until the passage of the 1960 Finance Act the Courts had no option but to impose the full statutory penalty. And that penalty was actually far more severe for simple negligence than for deliberate fraud. In cases involving £20,000 or more in tax (a total soon reached if the Revenue choose to go back far enough), a man who through simple negligence under-stated his liability by *one pound or less* was liable to a statutory penalty of twenty pounds plus three times the entire back-tax claimed. A man guilty of *deliberate* understatement was liable to a financial penalty of twenty pounds plus a mere three times the *difference* between what he paid and what he ought to have paid. So while a man who committed deliberate fraud might be prepared to fight a case in the High Court, someone who had been just plain careless almost certainly could not. The price of defeat was too high, since even the most sympathetic judge could impose nothing less than the full penalty. The Revenue, on the other hand, could. This has undoubtedly brought in enormous sums in 'settlements', and saved equally enormous amounts of the Revenue's time.

The Courts have at long last been given the power to reduce the penalties sued for in tax cases, and the penalties for fraud are twice as heavy as for negligence. Overworked as they are, Revenue staff must often look back with nostalgia to the days when strong men paled and reached for their cheque-books at the very mention of court action. But to outsiders it is one of the few examples in recent years of the Revenue actually losing a little of its grip on the taxpayer.

The normal trend is quite the other way, with ever-greater powers being conferred upon the Department.

For centuries the confidentiality of a man's relationship with his banker was held to be on a par with that of a doctor and his patient, or a lawyer and his client. It found expression in Roman Law as the Actio Iniuriarum, and in Germanic Law as the Lex Visigothorum. Italy, home of modern European banking, protected this relationship by statute. Throughout eighteenth century Europe it was so cherished that bankers submitted to the most ghastly physical torture at the hands of petty tyrants rather than abandon the principle.

Even today British bankers will only talk to the Revenue when they have to—but red-hot pincers are no longer necessary as 'persuaders'. As the result of a legal decision of 1924, banks can be forced to reveal complete details of a customer's account to the police or other authorities whenever so directed by a Court order or sub-poena; they may also break silence when it is in the 'public interest' for them to do so. Thus when Revenue officials want to peek at a man's bank balance, they may first plead 'public interest'. If this time-honoured gambit fails to work, then it is quite a simple matter to assess the tax-payer concerned for such an enormous sum that he will be compelled to appeal to the Commissioners, who acting within their power to demand any information they consider relevant, may then issue a sub-poena forcing disclosure by the bank. (The Special Commissioners are not of course alone in possessing this power: many other forms of Tribunal have it too.) But although the sub-poena method is fairly fool-proof, it is too cumbersome to provide the Revenue with details of more than a fraction of the country's millions of bank accounts. For years they pressed for wider powers, and for years successive governments refused to grant them, on the grounds that they would encroach too far upon the liberty of the subject.

In 1951 the liberty of the subject was in this respect found to be no longer 'in the public interest'. Since that year, banks have been compelled to disclose all interest payments over £15 paid out to their account-holders. From this information it is of course a simple matter for the Revenue to work out the size of a man's bank balance. The next assault on bank secrecy was delivered by the Finance Act of 1962, which gave the Revenue the power to require 'any person' to inform them about the disposal or acquisition of assets to which the short-term Capital Gains Tax might apply. *The Banker* mourned this as a precedent for 'bureaucratic inquisitions' into bank accounts. In fact it was simply the final blow to an already moribund principle. Bank secrecy in Britain, as in most other countries of the world, is now dead. One of the few exceptions is Switzerland, whose banking code forbids not only foreign tax authorities, but its own as well, to even inquire about the existence of an account, let alone its contents. To quote T. R. Fehrenbach[3] on this subject: 'Genuine democracy obviously has definite disadvantages for bureaucratic government that representative government does not pose.'

The Revenue won its next great victory over personal privacy in 1965, with the introduction of the new Capital Gains Tax. Up to that date, once a man had declared his income and paid tax upon it, what he did with the money after that was none of the Revenue's business—at any rate until he died, when the Estate Duty Office would enter the scene. But since the introduction of the Capital Gains Tax, if a man puts his money into jewellery, or vintage motor cars, or paintings, or antique furniture—into 'tangible movable assets' in any form whose individual resale value tops £1,000—then the Revenue will want to know about it in considerable detail.

In certain circumstances, they will also want to know about purchases of lesser value. It may take a lifetime's browsing round shops and salerooms to put together a fine collection of stamps, or snuff-boxes, or pocket pistols. Sell that collection to one buyer, or to several buyers acting together, and Capital Gains Tax will be levied on the total sum realised, even though the value of each individual item may be less than the £1,000 lower limit for the tax.

The temptation to evade the Capital Gains Tax on tangible movable assets is very strong. To deal with evasion in this field, the Revenue must use their inquisitorial powers to an even greater

[3] 'The Gnomes of Zurich', Leslie Frewin (Publishers) Ltd.

degree. Transactions made by dealers in *objets d'art* will be scrutinised closely; cheques paid into their accounts will frequently be 'traced' to their source. The problem will become vastly more acute when and if the threatened Wealth Tax comes into being. There will be a rush to convert funds at present invested in shares or land into less 'conspicuous' assets—a handful of gems, a priceless canvas. More and more transactions will be made in cash. What new step towards Big Brotherdom will the Revenue demand to counter this trend?

We need look no further than France for the answer. Since October 1968, French antique dealers have been compelled to note the names and addresses of all customers who make purchases of over 40 guineas in value. 'This makes us unpaid agents for the tax authorities,' one agent was quoted as saying. 'Can you see me asking the Prime Minister for his identity card?' asked another.[4] In this country, the answer would probably be 'yes'. After all, we already have a system under which dealers in television sets are required to pass on to the licensing authority the names and addresses of all their customers—prime ministers included.

The Capital Gains Tax in its present form sprang from the febrile brain of Nicholas Kaldor. If the 'Expenditure Tax'—another of his brainchildren—is ever introduced here, those who at present pay surtax can expect to have their *every* purchase monitored by Big Brother. This 'Pay-As-You-Spend' tax for the upper income brackets would involve its victims in the preparation of an annual 'Domesday Book', and give the Revenue an even more inquisitorial role than it now occupies. 'The Revenue would have powers to ask questions concerning a taxpayer's mode of living—the house or houses he maintains, servants kept, cars owned etc., or what he spent in the year on particular items or for particular purposes—and such evidence would be admissible in the Court in cases of disputed assessment.'[5]

Mr. Kaldor himself admitted that the 'Expenditure Tax' might seem too totalitarian in character for the British public to stomach. But the British stomach will take almost anything if the British palate is only given time to get used to the taste.

Not so very long ago, the inventors of another novel British tax quieted a storm of disapproval with a frank admission of the

[4] *Daily Telegraph* 21.10.68.
[5] 'An Expenditure Tax', by Nicholas Kaldor, Unwin University Books.

threat to liberty implicit in their ideas. Only the most extraordinary circumstances, they agreed, could justify proposals of such an inquisitorial nature. Once the present crisis was over, they swore, the whole scheme would be dropped for ever, and all the records of its brief existence destroyed.

And so the infant Income Tax was born.

Freedom of Speech and Assembly

> 'The way a society handles its dissenters is, perhaps, the best test of how civilised and democratic it can be considered.'
>
> *The Observer: 14.7.63*
>
> 'I disapprove of what you say, but I will defend to the death your right to say it.'
>
> *attrib. to Voltaire*

To ingenuous foreigners and a high proportion of native citizens, Speakers' Corner at Hyde Park is a living example of democracy in action. Speakers attacking hallowed British institutions with one breath and singing the praises of the various brands of Marxist-Leninism with the next are often met with the cry: 'You wouldn't be able to say that in Russia, chum!'

A warm glow of satisfaction sweeps over the audience. Its members all recognise the importance of free speech and assembly to the democratic idea. Few realise the extent to which these basic freedoms have been eroded.

They are not rights, but mere expectations, depending for their existence on the tolerance of authority. The policeman keeping a benevolent eye on the proceedings could demonstrate the point in a twinkling of an eye—by breaking up the meeting. He has wide discretionary powers to silence the speaker and disperse the crowd at any time he thinks it necessary, and he knows that the borderline between what the man on the soapbox may and may not say is very narrow indeed.

The man on the soapbox knows it too. If he is a 'regular', the police will already have approached him with a little fatherly advice and a polite request for his name and address. Like a court jester of medieval times, he is allowed to throw as many taunts and jibes at his audience as he wishes—just so long as the barbs don't actually penetrate the skin.

The Western democracies all pay at least lip-service to the 'rights' of free speech and free assembly. They are the basis for the one form of popular political expression that is cheaply and easily available to all. Rallies and demonstrations have proved powerful catalysts for change in the past, and the television camera has added immeasurably to their effectiveness.

Totalitarian regimes the world over openly recognise this fact by banning any kind of procession or meeting unless it is for a state-approved purpose—in which case attendance is usually 'by order'.

The most ardent democrat would hardly deny the state *any* power to regulate large-scale demonstrations. Clearly, there is a limit to the amount of inconvenience non-participants can be called upon to bear, and the inevitable hooligan element cannot be allowed to smash heads and shop-windows at will. Just how far should state control extend?

The Constitution of the United States of America specifically guarantees 'the right of the people peaceably to assemble'. In Britain we lack not only the safeguards of a written constitution; we have no 'right' of assembly at all. Public processions are held solely at the discretion of the authorities.

Limiting our freedom of speech and assembly are powers originally brought into being to deal with problems as widely spaced in time as those presented by unemployed fourteenth century archers[1] and militant twentieth century suffragettes[2]; with communal disturbances as varied as the battles between the Skeleton Army and the Salvation Army in the 1880s[3] and between 'Mods' and 'Rockers' in the 1960s[4]; and with ideological conflicts sparked off by groups as widely separated on the political spectrum as Mosley's Blackshirts and the Communists.[5] Where the problems have vanished (or appeared in a modified form) the powers hastily brought into being to deal with them still remain.

The 'right' to organise or join a procession is, predictably enough, the most circumscribed of all. The power most commonly called upon is that conferred under the Public Order Act of 1936, by which any Chief Officer of Police can impose upon those organising or taking part in a procession any conditions he feels necessary. He simply needs to have 'reasonable grounds' for suspecting that a procession may cause 'serious public disorder'.

He himself is the judge of what grounds are 'reasonable' and

[1] Justices of Peace Act 1361.
[2] Public Meeting Act 1908.
[3] Innumerable local bye-laws.
[4] Public Order Act 1963 and Malicious Damage Act 1964.
[5] Public Order Act 1936.

how 'serious' public disorder is likely to be. But perhaps the police may feel that nothing short of a complete ban on processions will do. In London, the Commissioners of the Metropolitan Police can, with the Home Secretary's approval, themselves impose a ban on all processions for a period of up to three months. (In the Provinces, such a ban may be imposed by the local council—again, with Home Office permission—on the request of the Chief Constable.) There is nothing however to prevent any chief officer of police applying for an *extension* to the three month period. During an upsurge of Fascist activity after the last war Commissioner Scott of the Metropolitan Police successfully applied for a ban on all political marches and meetings which, with sporadic gaps, ran from May 1948 to the Spring of 1951. It might have continued indefinitely but for vigorous Trade Union protests about the banning of their own traditional May Day celebrations.

Also available are powers to ban all processions within a mile of the Houses of Parliament on any day when either House is sitting; and numerous bye-laws and traffic regulations which can be used to restrict processions elsewhere.

What of the 'right of assembly'? Lord Hewart wrote: 'English law does not recognise any special right of public meeting for political or other purposes. The right of assembly . . . is nothing more than a view taken by the Court of the individual liberty of the subject.' Moriarty's 'Police Law' is even more explicit: 'There is no right to hold public meetings in any public place, as such places are for people to pass along. Every unauthorised obstruction of the highway is illegal either as an offence under some statute or bye-law or indictable as a common nuisance . . . An obstruction is committed even if only part of the highway is obstructed. However, meetings may be permissible in certain public places in accordance with local customs, but not usually as of right.'

It has for generations been 'local custom' to hold meetings in Hyde Park, or Trafalgar Square. You may be allowed to hold a meeting there yourself—although you will need a permit from the Ministry of Works first. But use a loudspeaker to address the crowd and you may be prosecuted under the Metropolitan Police Act 1839, or for committing a public nuisance, or under any one of a number of bye-laws. Carry a 'showboard or placard', and you risk police action under Section 54 of the Metropolitan Police Act 1839. Shout a slogan, and you may be prosecuted under the

Public Order Act or for using insulting language. ('Give us bread!' was once held to be insulting.) Distribute leaflets, or sell copies of a periodical relating to your cause, and you may be fined for obstruction of the footpath, even if you choose a 'pitch' where a regular news-vendor has operated undisturbed for years. Alternative charges for this offence include obstructing a police officer, conduct likely to cause a breach of the peace, and (in a surprisingly wide range of circumstances) contravention of the Race Relations Act 1965.

But suppose that you avoid all these pitfalls. Your audience may well contain an element intent on breaking up the meeting. The police may save them the trouble and break it up themselves, on the grounds that the presence of a hostile group made for a 'reasonable likelihood' of a breach of the peace. If on the other hand, the audience is solidly on your side, and (however harmlessly) demonstrates its enthusiasm, the meeting may still be broken up by the police—again because they feel there is a 'reasonable likelihood' of a breach of the peace.

As one authority puts it[6]: 'On one view it would seem that the so-called right of public meeting disappears if the suspicions of the policeman on the spot are roused.'

At the larger meetings, senior police officers of mature judgement are usually present. But the most junior constable has wide discretionary powers to break up meetings. The penalties for disobeying his orders to disperse can be severe. He may be panicked into action through inexperience, or because a crowd, although peaceable, is growing beyond the size he feels able to control should things take a different turn. There is no means of challenging his authority at the time, and in court afterwards magistrates have shown themselves most impatient with protests based on a civil liberties theme.

It was once possible to avoid police intervention at a meeting—by holding it on private premises. If disorder too serious for the organisers' own stewards to handle broke out, the police could then exercise their right of entry, and justly so. But a well-conducted meeting was normally safe from overt official surveillance. The police could of course try to smuggle a plainclothes man into the meeting, but there are snags to this time-honoured tactic. Whenever their man was caught, as happened for instance in 1920 (two Special Branch officers were discovered taking notes under

[6] Wade and Phillips on Constitutional Law, Longmans, Green & Co. Ltd.

the platform at the Communist Party's Central Committee meeting of that year) nasty remarks about 'police state methods' were sure to appear in the Press.

In 1934 this loophole was filled at last. The police can now quite openly turn up at any public meeting even when it is held on private premises, and can remain even when asked by the organisers to leave. They can afterwards justify their presence on the grounds that *in their opinion*, a breach of the peace was probable or seditious speeches or incitements to violence were likely to be made.

The judicial decision[7] which gave this power to the police carries with it an alarming implication which has yet to be thrashed out in the courts. 'The Court,' Professor Harry Street has written, 'held that because it was a public meeting the police were entitled to be there. But there is no doubt that, even though a general invitation is issued, the promoter can turn away particular individuals. Logically, therefore, this would seem to imply that the police have a right to attend *private* meetings in *private* houses where they believe the appropriate offences are likely to be committed if they are not there.'[8]

There are of course still meetings of interest to the police which they do not care to attend openly, whether they have the power to do so or not. (In 1961, for instance, two plainclothes policemen were found hiding behind a screen at a Scottish miners' conference on pit closures.) A meeting at which the police are known to be present may well take a very different tone. But whether they attend in uniform or plain clothes, a further problem remains: that of unobtrusively noting down the speaker's words. Quite apart from its effect on the audience, a speaker who sees that his words are being taken down is less likely to say anything actionable.

One way out of this difficulty is described by ex-Inspector Meek of the Metropolitan Police. In his book 'Private Enquiries',[9] he gives some recommendations based on a lecture he once delivered to a Sergeants' Promotion Class while still in the service. He advises 'a stiff notebook clipped to the trouser-leg and operated through a pocket-slit in the overcoat . . . Turn down each page as you complete it, so that you can locate the pages easily and

[7] Thomas v. Sawkins, 1934.

[8] 'Freedom, the Individual and the Law.' Pelican Books 1967.

[9] 'Private Enquiries—a Handbook for Detectives', Gerald Duckworth & Co. Ltd.

avoid covering the completed ones with fresh notes . . .'

Less dexterous note-takers need not despair. The Courts have frequently been known to convict a speaker on the strength of words written down by a police officer from memory alone, several hours after the speech had taken place.[10]

Just what can a speaker say without getting into trouble? What degree of censorship can the police impose?

There are two main pieces of legislation with a bearing here: Section Five of the Public Order Act, which makes it an offence to use insulting, abusive or threatening language; and the Race Relations Act, which provides heavy penalties for the incitement of racial hatred.

For a prosecution to succeed under the Public Order Act, it is only necessary to show that the words used were *likely* to cause a breach of the peace. This obviously involves a heavy reliance upon the judgement of the police officer on the spot. The flexibility of the charge can readily be appreciated when (as we have seen) the cry of 'Give us bread!' was once held to be insulting, while at Speakers' Corner on any Sunday afternoon speeches consisting almost entirely of insults, threats and abuse continue unchecked. Not for nothing has this charge become known as 'the policeman's friend'. But it is not in essence an instrument of censorship, although censorship may be a by-product of its use. It is concerned not so much with the contents of a speech as with a police officer's subjective view of its possible effect upon the audience.

A charge of inciting racial hatred however is very much concerned with the actual words of a speech. Its effect on the audience is immaterial. It provides heavy penalties for spoken or written words likely to stir up hatred against 'any section of the public in Great Britain distinguished by colour, race, or ethnic or national origins'. Wholly laudable in its intention, it could apply not just to white supremacists or to anti-semites, but to Welshmen who vocalise their dislike of the English, or Englishmen (like Doctor Johnson, perhaps?) who carry their distaste of the Scots into print. With the growth of Scottish and Welsh separatism, the Race Relations Act may in future years catch some very odd fish in its net. *The Times* talked of this section of the Act as 'an instrument of political censorship', and as making possible the 'legal harrassment of unpopular or officially deprecated opinions'. Its opponents

[10] A notable example of this practice emerged at the trial for incitement of Desmond Lock in July 1962.

believed, and still believe, that existing legislation was quite adequate to deal with the problem, and that the new statute, although perhaps valuable as a Public Relations exercise, presents a serious threat to free speech. Henry Brooke, a former Home Secretary, spoke for many when in June 1965 he said: 'The age-old battle in this country was not fought to say pleasant and fraternal and acceptable things. That is not what is meant by free speech. It was fought to win the freedom to say distasteful, unacceptable, provocative, antagonistic things.'

Sometimes a man's attachment to his cause is such that the police know he will not be deterred by the thought of later prosecution under the statutes we have discussed, but will go ahead and speak his mind anyway. In such cases they may 'bind him over' to be of good behaviour or to keep the peace.

If he cannot or will not provide the financial guarantees demanded by the Court, he will be imprisoned. If he does provide the guarantee, but persists in conduct of which the Court disapproves, he will lose his recognisance and run the risk of prosecution as well.

The binding-over procedure has proved very useful against demonstrators generally, but is particularly effective against their leaders. In recent years men and women of strong opinion have often refused to be bound over, and have consequently been sentenced to periods of imprisonment nicely calculated to end immediately after the rally they were to lead has ended.

Where the surety demanded is a reasonable one, the decision to go to prison rather than to pay rests with the individual concerned. Much more objection can be taken to the fact that it is open to the Courts to fix sureties deliberately high, as happened in the case of George Lansbury who in 1914 was imprisoned for three months because he could not and would not meet a demand for a personal recognisance of £1,000 and for two sureties of £500 each.

The selective way in which the binding-over procedure has sometimes been used has provided the impetus for two recent private members' bills to abolish it altogether. In his book 'Keeping the Peace',[11] David Williams has pointed out that 'in effect, the authorities are sometimes able to use the binding-over procedure as a means of "trying" political offences without having to have the issue thrashed out before a judge and jury'.

[11] Published by Hutchinson Publishing Group Ltd.

So far, only the most commonly used restrictions on free speech and free assembly have been discussed. There are several others which, though antique, are still serviceable. Among them are the charges of High Treason, Incitement to Mutiny, Incitement to Disaffection, and Sedition.

Of course, statutory weapons are not the only ones in the armoury of flouted authority.

Ask almost anyone when British troops last fired on British citizens on British soil, and you will be lucky to hear a guess within half a century of the truth. Yet it last happened well within living memory—during the police strike at Liverpool, in 1919. One man died. Not long before, crowds were dispersed by gunfire twice in one year—at Llanelly and Liverpool, in 1911. Four men died. From the wave of unrest that swept cities as far apart as Chicago, Paris, Prague, Tokyo, and Berlin, 1968 has been christened 'The Year of Protest'. London too had its share. The demonstration of October 27th, which involved 30,000 demonstrators and 7,000 police, achieved more publicity than any other domestic event of the year. Among its leaders were some whose main purpose was to re-teach the forgotten lesson of Llanelly and Liverpool: that the State's claim to control speech and assembly is absolute, and rests in the final analysis on the spilling of blood.

They failed in this purpose. So far as Britain is concerned, a significant outcome of the 'Year of Protest' was a hardening of public opinion towards demonstrators generally, and a widespread feeling that even greater powers were needed to control them. An N.O.P. survey made late in the year showed that 56% of all adults were against *any kind* of demonstration, and that 65% favoured the use of tear gas against those taking part in them.

The immensity of the discretionary powers already available to the police never became apparent during the demonstration of October 27th, because of the tact and restraint with which they were used. The lack of safeguards to prevent the abuse of those powers—safeguards other than the integrity of those to whom they are entrusted, that is—never became apparent either.

The dangers of relying too much upon the succession of men of integrity remaining unbroken are plain. As Aneurin Bevan said over 30 years ago: 'The whole essence of democracy, as I see it, is that when you give people power, you surround that power with all sorts of restrictions and safeguards in order that that power may not be abused. You do not defend yourself by saying that the man who is to exercise that power is a good and upright and scrupulous man, and therefore you do not need any safeguard.'[12]

[12] 30th October, 1934, during the debate on the Sedition Bill.

An Englishman's Home . . .

> 'There are now some 70 exceptions to the Common Law rule that a man's house is inviolate even from search under warrant. A warrant can be obtained to search in connection with matters as varied as offences relating to animals, explosives, public health, dangerous drugs, official secrets, and obscene publications. But the police have no power, nor can they get warrants, to search premises for the body of a murder victim or to secure a murder weapon.'
>
> *The Times:* 13.12.67.

Nowadays, it is in one respect easier than ever before for an Englishman to turn his home into a castle. The security business is booming, and any public library will have a copy of the Bible of the trade—'Hart's Security International'.

Here the security-conscious householder will find the names and addresses of hundreds of firms willing and eager to use every product of scientific ingenuity to keep intruders from his door. In the section on the U.K. alone, this invaluable directory lists some 1,189 entries, gathered under 71 different headings ranging from '*Armoured Car Services*' at one end of the alphabet to '*Whistles*' (presumably for use when all else fails) at the other. *Whistles* have only one entry—a comment in itself.

Many entries are of course duplicated. The same firms crop up again and again, under different headings and at different addresses. This is because the larger firms carry out many different kinds of work and have many different branches.

The larger organisations—giants such as Securicor, Security International and Factoryguards—will carry out advisory work anywhere in the country. So wherever he may live, the privacy hunted need not despair. Expert advice is always within easy reach.

As a first step, he might call in Platauer-Westwood to surround his property with an *electric fence*,[1] and Systems Control to fit a *remote control gate*,[2] watched by a *closed-circuit T.V. system*[3]

[1] FENCES, ELECTRIC—4 entries.
[2] GATES AND DOORS, REMOTE—3 entries.
[3] T.V. SYSTEMS—9 entries.

installed by Securitas Alarms. Abbey Wood Security will lend him *guard dogs*[4] to patrol the perimeter; if he prefers to buy his own animals, then the Stamford Obedience Training Kennels will *school*[5] them for him.

Once inside the perimeter, *detection beams*[6] set up by the A.F.A. group will monitor any visitor's progress to the front door. His arrival on the threshold will set off an alarm coupled to a *pressure-mat*[7] from Shorrock Developments.

The householder can now take a really close look at his caller through the 'Sentry' *door-viewer*[8] ('as used in leading banks'). If he doesn't like what he sees, he can use his A.E.I. *communicating system*[9] to send the man packing. He doesn't need to be polite about it either—even the angriest man couldn't get past a 'Home-guard' *steel door*[10] fitted with a Wadsworth *cypher lock*.[11] Not without explosives, anyway.

If the householder gets tired of calling off the dogs himself, and becomes bored with shouting insults at his visitors through his door intercom., then he can of course hire people to perform these tasks for him. Securicor is only one of the many organisations which will supply *guard services*[12] tailored to his needs. For good measure, he can always hire a bodyguard from the Ace *detective agency*.[13]

That still leaves him with chores like housework and keeping up with his correspondence. What he needs is a private secretary and a housekeeper—with carefully-checked references, of course. Management Investigations Ltd. ('specialists in *defence against industrial espionage*'[14]) will find the private secretary, investigating his or her background with fanatical care. As for the housekeeper —R.C.B. Security offer to supply 'security-screened cleaners'. From their extensive files they should be able to find at least one competent woman with a taste for the quiet life.

[4] GUARD DOG SERVICES—35 entries.
[5] GUARD DOG TRAINERS—4 entries.
[6] DETECTING EQMT.—5 entries.
[7] MATS, PRESSURE—5 entries.
[8] DOOR VIEWERS—2 entries.
[9] COMM. SYSTEMS—10 entries.
[10] DOORS, SAFETY—17 entries.
[11] LOCKS AND BOLTS—33 entries.
[12] GUARD SERVICES—32 entries.
[13] DETECTIVE AGENCIES—204 entries.
[14] INDUSTRIAL SECURITY—15 entries.

Webley and Scott will provide any *firearms*[15] that may be needed. And for the final touch—perhaps a few anti-personnel mines sown in the shrubbery? With their world-wide connections, Interarmco should be able to lay their hands on a dozen or so of these.

Electronic gadgets, ferocious dogs, armed men—the price of all these comes high. Just what kind of protection *can* money buy?

Leon Trotsky took similar precautions during his Mexican exile. As he discovered too late, the impregnable defence system has yet to be built. But O.G.P.U. hatchet-men apart, our householder should be reasonably secure against illegal intruders. So long as he lived a blameless life, never stirring outside his door—and provided he paid his bills and taxes—then he might well believe himself secure against official intruders as well.

Not so.

In Britain today there are over thirty different classes of National and Local Government employees with the legal right to enter private premises without permission. (Many of those thirty classes do not even need a warrant to do so.) They range from servants of the Forestry Commission to Defence Officials of the Board of Trade; from National Insurance staff to 'Waterguards' of H.M. Customs and Excise; and from alkali inspectors of the Ministry of Housing to investigation staff of the Ministry of Agriculture. There are even a thousand or so driving and traffic examiners and licensing clerks of the Ministry of Transport with this power—although they have been instructed never to use it.

The need to enforce the huge mass of controls and regulations introduced during the last war led to an unprecedented rise in the number of officials with the right of entry to private premises. But from 1948 to 1950, their number actually rose by over 50%. By 1952 the Tories were congratulating themselves on having reduced the number by 35%. Many M.P.s however were still dissatisfied. Inquiries initiated by Sir Fitzroy Maclean M.P. established a total of 16,744 officials with the right of entry to 'private residential and landed property'. 6,187 of them could exercise this power without even having to apply for a warrant.

Officials of the Gas and Electricity Boards, for example, needed no warrant to break into private homes. However wantonly this power was used, their victims had no means of redress, as a Mr. Charles Grove discovered when in 1952 he sued the Gas Board

[15] FIREARMS—2 entries.

for trespass and wrongful entry after officials had smashed glass in his front door in order to collect the sum of *twelve shillings* from his meter. Mr. Grove spent his life savings on the case—and lost.

The 1954 Rights of Entry Act was designed to prevent this sort of abuse. It made it necessary for Gas and Electricity Board officials to seek a warrant before entering private premises without the permission of the owner.

Officials impatient to carry out their work sometimes over-ride this safeguard. In 1965, for instance, a Mrs. Freda Laws complained to the N.C.C.L. about a gas-board official who had walked uninvited into her home while she was lying ill in bed. Her shock—she had thought him a burglar—having turned to indignation, she refused to let him read her meter. The next day, an inspector arrived from the Board. Far from apologising for the incident, he warned her that she had been 'obstructive'.

Such cases are fortunately rare. But even when the warrant procedure is adhered to, entry powers seem to be granted far too easily. In July 1968 power men broke into the home of a Mrs. Janet Price in order to cut off the supply. Mrs. Price had failed to pay her £4.7.0 bill because her husband's illness had kept her away from home for seven weeks.

Coincidentally, the following month electricity men forced their way into the home of yet another family named Price, again with the intention of cutting off the supply. The Price's three-year-old son was terrified when he was awakened by men climbing through his bedroom window. Mr. Price was understandably furious about the incident—the more so, since he had in fact already paid the bill in question.

Although there may be loopholes in the warrant procedure, it does at least stop over-zealous officials acting entirely on their own initiative, and keeps cases of abuse to a minimum. In 1961, Sir Stephen McAdden M.P. campaigned for the extension of the warrant procedure to cover *all* officials with entry powers.

Regrettably, his campaign failed. But he did at least establish that there were still 10,657 officials (see Appendix, note 3) with the right to enter private premises. No recount has been taken since, but when the topic was re-opened in the columns of the *Daily Sketch* in 1966, Sir Stephen said he believed their number had increased sharply in the intervening years. Shortly afterwards, it was revealed that entry powers had been granted to many more members of at least one government department—the Inland

Revenue.

The householder who obstructs an official armed with the right of entry will receive scant sympathy from the Courts.

In June 1963 a Mr. Smout lost his appeal against a conviction for assault upon a bailiff, whom he had hustled from his house as a trespasser. Mr. Smout complained that the bailiff had simply thrown open the door and marched into his house. Lord Justice Harman told him severely that the bailiff had been executing his lawful duty as an officer of the Court. The fact that the door was not fastened, he said, was *impliedly an invitation* by the householder for anyone having lawful business in the house to come inside.

Obviously, even a locked door forms no real obstacle to the official with the power to break it down. But the mere fact that an official *acts* as though he had that right to come in is often enough to secure him entry. A first-class row blew up in the Commons in October 1968 when Mr. Tim Fortescue M.P. reported on the case of a young divorced mother in his constituency who had been visited by two investigators from the Ministry of Social Security. She claimed to have been 'grilled' about her social life and men friends, reduced to tears, and then told: 'Remember—Big Brother is watching you!'

The Ministry of Social Security employs about 140 'special investigators', whose task is to look into cases of suspected 'benefit fraud'.

Sometimes this involves bizarre occupational hazards.

In February 1969, a divorce court heard the sad tale of a Mrs. Green, who had discovered in her husband's briefcase an address book listing what the judge called 'the proclivities and professional services of ladies of easy virtue'.

Mr. Green was one of the Ministry of Social Security's 'special investigators', and had in fact been given the book by his superiors, as an aid to his investigations into the call-girl business. True to his code of professional secrecy, he refused to give this innocent explanation to his wife when she confronted him with the address book. So Mrs. Green, in an effort to keep her husband by her side at night, slashed his shirts, soaked his trousers in a bucket of water, cut his ties to pieces and filled his hat with ashes.

Investigators like Mr. Green have no powers of entry, with or without a warrant. But many of the people they visit are ignorant of this fact. While investigating fraudulent claims for unemployment benefit by people who are really working, and cases of 'suspected cohabitation' (unmarried mothers, widows and divorcees who claim supplementary benefit while being secretly supported by a man) officials will sometimes follow suspects around and keep watch on their homes in order to see who comes and goes. But it has been claimed that in search of further proof, investigators have talked their way into people's homes; and once inside, have gone through cupboards and wardrobes looking for possessions that would indicate a man's habitual presence in the house.

Any over-zealous official who tries such tactics without lawful authority can be sent off with a flea in his ear. A smart kick in the pants is perfectly in order if a verbal refusal of entry fails to do the trick. But as we have seen, after a brief period of decline, the number of cases in which a demand for entry can be backed by a warrant is once again on the increase.

Not only is the number of officials with that power rising—the *grounds* on which warrants may be issued are also multiplying. And of course, in the vast majority of cases, entry warrants are issued not to some 'functionary' of local or national government, but to the police.

Of all police powers, the power to enter and search private premises has always been one of the most controversial. Contrary to popular belief, today that power can even be exercised without a warrant.

It has, for example, been ruled that 'a constable may break open doors where there are reasonable grounds to suspect that a felony has been committed and that the felon was present'. Naturally, everything depends on just what can be considered 'reasonable'. The circumstances in which the police can decide this for themselves are comparatively few. As a general rule, only a magistrate can give permission for private premises to be searched without the permission of the owner or tenant. From time to time the police have pressed for the power to issue warrants themselves. They claim that magistrates rarely refuse a request, but that the time consumed by the warrant procedure often loses them a 'catch'.

Over two centuries ago, Pitt the Elder could proclaim that: 'The poorest man in his cottage may bid defiance to all the forces of the Crown. It may be frail—its roof may shake—the storm may enter—but the King of England cannot enter—all his force dares not cross the threshold of the ruined tenement!'

The picture is very different today. Over the years, exceptions to the rule that an Englishman's home is his castle have multiplied to such an extent that the 16,000 lay magistrates of England and Wales can now issue search warrants on over 70 different counts.

Until recently, the trend aroused little public alarm. Most of the reasons behind a policeman's appearance on someone's doorstep with a search warrant were so obscure, and arose so seldom, that even those few people who knew of their existence saw little cause for concern. The few reasons which *were* well-known related to acts universally condemned as anti-social—theft for example, or cruelty to children. If warrants to acquire evidence of such acts were sometimes issued on rather flimsy evidence, few people were prepared to shed any tears over it. Again, if the police sometimes obtained a warrant to search particular premises, and then went on to search the homes of people *found* on those premises, or took away personal property on the suspicion that it had been stolen—it was generally felt that only members of the 'underworld' or their associates had any reason to worry.

Then in 1967 came the Dangerous Drugs Act, which granted wide new powers of search to the police. Hard on its heels came a number of cases which brought public apathy on the subject abruptly to an end. Now, it seemed, there was a real possibility of the police turning up to search the home of anyone, from a peer to a pop-star, on the slightest of suspicions.

The case which brought this home more than any other was that of Lady Diana Cooper. In February 1968 her home was searched after the police had assured the magistrate to whom they applied for a warrant under the 1967 Act that they had reason to believe, 'from a source believed to be reliable', that drugs would be found there.

Nothing was found. Lady Diana lodged a complaint, which was taken up in Parliament. The press had a field-day when the 'reliable source' turned out to have been an anonymous telephone call.

'Would it not be a good thing if the police could disclose whether information was based on an anonymous tip-off?' Lord Gladwyn asked the Lord Chancellor. 'Are we not opening the doors to the enemies of anybody to ring the police and say that they are hoarding drugs and that the premises should be searched immediately?'

Other critics pointed out a greater danger still—that if warrants to search for drugs could be granted so casually, the police might be tempted to apply for them when they were really looking for something quite different, and for which they could not properly obtain a warrant to search at all.

The official answer to this last criticism was that if both police and magistracy work as they should, a warrant to search for drugs is no more easily obtainable than any other. Before signing any warrant, the magistrate should ask if the man whose premises are involved has any past convictions, or any criminal associates. If he has neither, then the magistrate should probe more deeply. Is anything known against him other than the anonymous tip-off? In the case of a warrant to search for drugs—does the man have friends who are addicts? Has he been seen in suspicious circumstances—for instance, in a known meeting-place for addicts? The Cooper warrant, it was claimed, would never have been issued had the police not misled the magistrate when describing their source of information.

Many found this explanation unconvincing. The blame for the Cooper incident, it was felt, could not all be laid at the door of the police. They had certainly misled the magistrate who issued the warrant—but he had allowed himself to be misled, by not asking the proper questions.

Magistrates should not be 'rubber-stamping automatons for slap-happy policemen', trumpeted the normally-staid *Law Guardian*. 'It is just through such sloppiness, if allowed to go uncastigated that the English citizen can lose one of the freedoms his laws exist to protect—the privacy of his home.'[16]

The case for the defence was presented by the magazine *Justice of the Peace*, in an editorial which argued that anonymous tip-offs must be taken seriously if the police are to do their job.

'For example, it is not unknown for a parent to inform on his son or daughter in respect of drugs, with the intention that their lives possibly be saved, yet to keep anonymous in order not to lose their affection. It is by no means unknown that, completely unknown to an employer, a member of his staff may trade in drugs —therefore, to the police, it may not have seemed so outrageous as it does in retrospect for a search warrant to have been applied in a particular instance.'

In a final plea, *Justice of the Peace* explained that in densely-

[16] Issue for April 1968.

populated areas with a high incidence of crime, 'there must inevitably be less enquiry on the part of the magistrates than elsewhere, because the number of requests is likely to be so much higher'.

An estimated nine out of ten warrants issued under the Dangerous Drugs Act fail to lead to a court case. Pressure of business may be one reason why so many magistrates are apparently so bad at picking 'winners', but it certainly cannot explain the error of judgement in the Cooper case. The magistrate who authorised this search admitted that local police came to him during the night with a request for his signature 'three or four times a year'.[17]

Almost immediately after the Cooper affair was first raised in Parliament, certain 'adjustments' were reportedly made to the warrant procedure, in an effort to avert similar errors in the future. Then, five months later, it was announced that the Home Secretary had warned police chiefs to take 'reasonable steps' to check information before applying for warrants, and that the Lord Chancellor had warned magistrates to question the police more closely before signing them.[18]

At first sight, these steps to tighten up the warrant procedure seem most reassuring. But the police are still not required to identify their informants—only to satisfy the magistrate that they have additional information to back up any anonymous 'tip-off'. The difficulty is, any such additional information can often be only of the flimsiest. The warrant is itself frequently the only means of establishing the truth or falsehood of a report. Junior officers are now to consult their seniors in borderline cases. But the whole issue seems to rest very much as it did before—on the magistrate's judgement. The Lord Chancellor's 'caution' to the magistracy, which received so much publicity in August 1968, seems much less impressive when set beside his statement of the previous March, when he told the House of Lords that the Government had no power to instruct magistrates on how to exercise their judgement.

It will be a black day when any government acquires the power to influence the judgement of a magistrate in any particular case. But to impose more stringent *general* requirements which the magistracy would have to meet before issuing search warrants—nothing sinister could be seen in this. In New York, where the drug problem is incomparably more serious than in London, the

[17] *Daily Mail* 27.2.68.
[18] *Daily Telegraph* 12.8.68.

police must not only disclose the source of their information, but (when it comes from a regular informer) details of previous convictions obtained on the strength of information received from that source in the past. Even then, no warrant may be issued until the premises concerned have been kept under observation for a time. What is more, the officer to whom the warrant is eventually issued must return in person to report on the result of the search, even when this is negative.

If Britain's police were required to report back to the magistrate after each raid, in nine cases out of ten they would have to do so empty-handed. There is little doubt that such a requirement would quickly make the police as chary of applying for a warrant on inadequate grounds as magistrates would be of signing one. As things now stand, despite the tightening-up of warrant procedure that followed the Cooper case, the press has continued to report all too many instances of homes needlessly invaded.

There will always be overzealous policemen, just as there will always be careless (or just plain tired) magistrates. Until the law takes sufficient account of these facts of life, cases of abuse will continue.

It can, of course, be argued that the power to search private homes for drugs should never have been granted in the first place, however many new safeguards may be added to the warrant procedure in the future. After all, the sanctity of the home has always been regarded in this country as so precious that, even today, the police cannot obtain a warrant to search for the body of a murder-victim, or for the weapon that killed him.

Parliament granted the new powers of search because it was led to believe that if it did not, the drug problem would escalate to such a degree that the fabric of society would be threatened. Yet of the small percentage of searches made under the Act which prove successful, only an infinitely smaller percentage still results in the seizure of anything more harmful than cannabis—a drug which the Government's own 'Advisory Committee on Drug Dependence' called 'probably no more and possibly less harmful than alcohol', whose 'consumption in moderate doses has no harmful effects'.[19]

This report—the 'Wootton Report'—appeared in January 1969. Had it appeared two years earlier, it is arguable whether the

[19] 'Cannabis—Report by the Advisory Committee on Drug Dependence'. Published by Her Majesty's Stationery Office, January 1969.

Dangerous Drugs Act 1967 would ever have reached the Statute Book in its present form.

Although the Government rejected many of the recommendations set out in the Wootton Report, it did not quarrel with the basic assumption on which most of those recommendations were based: that no true picture of the extent and seriousness of the drug problem can be formed on the basis of figures which put cannabis on the same footing as heroin and other 'hard' drugs.

Yet it was *precisely* on this basis that the case for allowing private homes to be searched for drugs was argued when the Dangerous Drugs Bill came before Parliament. It was also on this basis that Lord Stonham persuaded the House of Lords to write into the Bill an amendment which greatly extended the 'stop and search' powers of the police with respect to drugs.

For over a century and a half, police in London have had the power[20] to 'stop, search and detain' any person or vehicle when they have reasonable grounds to suspect that stolen property will thereby be discovered. This power is of great value to the police, since it can be used without a warrant, and without the necessity for first making a formal arrest. They do not even have to tell the person involved *why* they intend to search him.

This power, with its wide opportunities for abuse, was granted to deal with the special problems faced by the Metropolitan Police. The police in a small number of provincial towns have acquired similar powers since, but Parliament had always been most reluctant to grant the power to search without a warrant on a generalised basis.

The handful of police forces with the ability to 'stop and search' for stolen goods had been accustomed to use it against persons suspected of carrying drugs long before 1967, although this was clearly contrary to the terms on which it was originally conferred. But when the Dangerous Drugs Bill of that year was originally drafted it was still not at first proposed to grant 'stop and search' powers to all police. The Bill had already passed the Commons and reached the committee stage in the Lords when Lord Stonham argued that without the power to search on the spot, police would have great difficulty in convicting the 'pushers' of drugs. In many parts of the country a search could still only be made after arrest, and arrest could only be made if there was good reason to suppose the suspect would abscond or fail to give his correct name and

[20] Under Section 66 of the Metropolitan Police Act, 1839.

address. So without an immediate search, Lord Stonham argued, the evidence would soon be destroyed.

In support of his views, Lord Stonham pointed to the 2,435 convictions for drug offences in the previous year (1966). What he did *not* point out was that these convictions related almost entirely to cannabis and the amphetamines. But his arguments were found convincing, and the amendment was carried.

The police in general welcomed their wide new powers to search persons and premises, but some of the more thoughtful of them have recognised that these powers are not an unmixed blessing. The drive against drugs has brought the police into collision with large numbers of young people quite unlike those with whom they have had to deal in the past. The rift between the police and the young is already wide, and has even led to the suggestion (in the inquiry 'The Police and Adolescents in a Changing Society'—a document given close consideration at Scotland Yard) that, as in some other countries, there should be special police for dealing with young people. Detective Superintendent Jones of the Hertfordshire Police, in his pamphlet 'Drugs and the Police' has stressed how difficult it is for police accustomed to coping with criminals to deal with young people on drugs charges.

In time, the police may develop for drugs suspects the same sixth sense which enables them, with surprising accuracy, to pick out from a crowd 'wrong 'uns' of a more conventional sort. But at present, many young people feel that long hair and unconventional clothes are quite enough to make them suspect. Because of the nature of the goods concerned, searches for drugs tend to be much more humiliating than the old-style 'frisk' for stolen goods or concealed weapons, and resentment caused by each unsuccessful search is considerable. When it comes to mass searches at coffee-bars, clubs and other places where large numbers of young people congregate, the damage to police public relations is incalculable. To be forced to strip naked behind improvised screens or in 'mobile police stations' is an experience not readily forgotten—the more so as whenever mass searches are carried out, nine out of ten of those involved are almost invariably found to be 'clean'—commonly *ten* out of ten.

Whenever drugs are found, not only do those in *possession* of them become liable to prosecution—so does the owner or manager of the premises. It took Miss Stephanie Sweet, an Oxford schoolteacher, eighteen months to clear herself of a conviction for 'being concerned in the management of premises' used for cannabis smoking, although the magistrates who originally convicted her in September 1967 accepted that she had not known that the farmhouse she had sublet had been used by her tenants for this purpose. Miss Sweet was not convicted under the Dangerous Drugs Act of 1967, but under the earlier Act of 1965. When she finally won her appeal, Lord Reid said that if the Act meant what the Divisional Court (to which she took her first appeal) said that it did, 'hundreds of thousands' of people who innocently leased premises later used *without their knowledge* for drug-taking, would become liable for prosecution. This would be 'obviously unjust', and he could assert with confidence that no Parliament within his recollection would have agreed to make such an offence absolute if the matter had been fully explained to it.

If the full implications of the 1967 Act had been properly explained to it, perhaps Parliament would not have accepted this later piece of legislation either. The fact is—the *scandalous* fact is —that not even the Home Office knows precisely how the police are making use of the powers granted to them under this Act.

'I am afraid that neither detailed nor approximate information about the numbers of persons stopped and searched by the police is reported to the Home Office, nor can we provide you with any figures about the numbers of search warrants issued to the police in connection with suspected drug offences,' admitted a Home Office spokesman, in reply to a request for guidance on these points. 'The Metropolitan Police keep some form of statistical account of the numbers of persons stopped in the street, and of the numbers of search warrants applied for and issued in the force area each year. The decision whether information of this sort should be disclosed to a member of the public on request, or instead be treated as confidential, is entirely a matter for the chief officer of police concerned, but you may be interested to know that the Metropolitan Police record information about persons stopped in the London area in such a way that it would prove a difficult and expensive task to isolate from the total those stops which are made under section 6 of the 1967 (Dangerous Drugs) Act.'

It is difficult to understand why these matters should be regarded as confidential, and downright impossible to see why the option of silence (which is invariably exercised) should be left with the police themselves.

'. . . no recent statute has opened the way to the abuse of civil liberties as widely as those concerning dangerous drugs,' said *The Times* in March 1968. Only God and the Police know how far that abuse has gone already. It is high time that somebody else was let in on the secret.

The Thought Police

> 'There was of course no way of knowing whether you were being watched at any given moment. How often, or on what system, the Thought Police plugged in on any individual wire was guesswork. It was even conceivable that they watched everybody all the time. But at any rate they could plug in on your wire whenever they wanted to. You had to live—did live, from habit that became instinct—in the assumption that every sound you made was overheard, and, except in darkness, every movement scrutinised.'
>
> *George Orwell: 1984*

Unpleasant though physical intrusion into one's home may be, there are more disturbing, though less obtrusive, ways in which one's privacy may be invaded by the State.

Countless people who have never read Orwell's gloomy forecast of the future are perfectly familiar both with the slogan 'Big Brother is Watching You' and the system of two-way telescreens which made that slogan a reality. Of all the horrors in the book, none captured the popular imagination so much as this. Its sheer nastiness is immediately apparent even to those who do not grasp its wider implications—that a tyranny armed with such a surveillance tool would be virtually indestructible.

Orwell's Big Brother was not concerned with monitoring the words and actions of everyone. There were no two-way telescreens in the homes of the Proles. He concentrated on the only group that could be dangerous to him: the Party, whose members occupied all the key positions.

Modern surveillance devices have been developed far beyond Orwell's imaginings. Darkness is no obstacle to the hidden watcher now, and to computer experts it is even possible to foresee (as to Orwell it was not) exactly how Big Brother could, if he wished, keep an eye on all of the people all of the time.[1]

But the likelihood is that any future Big Brother will be content,

[1] See Chapter 17—A Glimpse of the Future.

as Orwell's was, to plant electronic eyes and ears in the homes of a select group of potential trouble-makers. This is the system we have in Britain today. It differs from that of *1984* in two respects. Firstly in scale; and secondly, in that whereas Orwell's Party members were all too aware of the telescreen's presence, and could modify their behaviour accordingly, today's bugs and phone taps are planted in secret.

The distinction between a bug and a telephone tap is (except to the lawyers) somewhat unreal. There are at least six different ways of tapping a telephone, and three of them ensure that the instrument will pick up and transmit any conversation in the same room whether the handset is on its cradle or not. To a man whose private conversations are overheard and recorded, the mechanical niceties are unimportant.

'Telephone tapping,' said *The Times* in 1957, is 'with good reason . . . popularly associated with the worst excesses of the police state . . . and of all the means of detection it is the one most open to sinister and corrupt abuse.' This view is tacitly admitted even by those who nevertheless defend the practice on grounds of expediency. It can be applied with equal force to the secret interception of a man's correspondence, which provides the historical basis for the government's power to tap telephones.

Ever since Darius the Great introduced the first postal service in the fifth century B.C., governments have always kept a tight grip on the mails; partly because there has always been money in letter-carrying, but also because of its value as a source of Intelligence. In eighteenth-century Europe, postal interception reached wholesale proportions. In Vienna, 'crossroads of Europe', the government employed for this purpose a huge staff of translators, copyists, cryptanalysts and specialists in the fine art of opening and resealing letters without leaving a trace. Working in shifts around the clock, they dealt not only with letters to and from Viennese residents (foreign diplomats included) but with mail 'in transit' to other parts of Europe. Such was their speed and efficiency that mail delivered for 'processing' could be back at the post-office in less than three hours.

State interception systems took the invention of the telegraph in their stride. Telegraphic codes presented no real difficulty. Only 'authorised versions' could generally be used. Diplomatic cables were an exception that kept government code-breakers happily employed.

When the telephone and the wireless transmitter came into general use in the twentieth century, there seemed no reason to exclude these new forms of communication from surveillance.

Against this historical background it is easy to see why governments which had long asserted their right to eavesdrop on words committed to paper or the telephone should extend their claim to monitoring conversations committed to neither. It is in fact highly difficult to weigh up the comparative ethical demerits of telephone tapping and mail interception on the one hand, and the use of micro-miniature transmitters and long-range microphones on the other. And if the power exists to plant electronic ears all over a suspect's house or place of business, what greater objection can there be to the planting of electronic eyes as well?

Once interception becomes accepted practice, the temptation to enlist all the latest technical aids and use them to the full becomes almost irresistible.

Governmental interception of communications has in fact been part of the 'British Way of Life' for hundreds of years. A statute of 1657 proclaimed baldly that judicious interception was one of the best available means for discovering plots against the State. Later enactments, including the Post Office Act of 1711, reaffirmed this view. Two special sub-divisions of the Post Office were formed to facilitate the task of interception: the Secret Office, which handled foreign mail, and the Private Office, which dealt with domestic traffic. Originally operating under specific warrants, they later came to use general warrants, which saved time and red-tape. It has even been suggested that the concessionary rates for postcards and unsealed letters were introduced in the nineteenth century so that the authorities could the more easily keep tabs on the working classes, who were proving themselves so tiresomely revolutionary all over Europe. This is perhaps an unduly cynical view.

Diplomatic mail was opened as a matter of course, and where necessary, copies were passed to the 'Decyphering Branch'—used by Private Office and Secret Office alike. Then in 1844 public controversy arose over the interception of the correspondence of Joseph Mazzini, suspected of planning a revolution in Italy while resident in this country. In June 1844 the whole interception network was driven underground. Diplomatic mail, at least, was now allowed to leave and enter the country without being tampered with, and the Decyphering Branch was disbanded. But secret committees of both Houses of Parliament confirmed that the Executive, by virtue of long usage, did have the power to intercept communications whenever it was felt to be necessary.

Two world wars have put a fine polish on the techniques of interception, whatever the communication medium employed. In 1940 Britain had 1,200 mail censors in just one hotel[2]—the Princess, in Bermuda. In all, the British war effort deployed about 30,000 people in 'communications intelligence'. To minimise the risk of censors missing hidden codes, whole classes of message—crossword puzzles, Interflora cables, and many more—were banned. 'One letter containing knitting instructions,' wrote David Kahn,[3] 'was held up long enough for an examiner to knit a sweater to see if the sequence . . . contained a hidden message.'

The American authorities routinely opened, read and censored over a million pieces of overseas mail *each day*.

The staggering size of wartime censorship schemes shows how a government with a burning desire to know what people are writing and saying to one another, can effectively satisfy its curiosity. The value of the information to be gained even in peacetime from government sampling of the traffic carried by the G.P.O. can be judged from the following passage: 'Directly or indirectly, every man, woman and child, from the moment of birth, uses some service provided by the Post Office every day. A telephone call summons doctor or midwife to a mother's confinement. Maternity grants come through the post. Every ounce of food, every article of clothing, everything we use has reached the shops by virtue of letter or telephone; every piece of raw material for every factory has similarly been brought together by letter, telephone or cable. Modern living without the Post Office is unthinkable . . . we turn to it for everything from dog licences to the transmission of television, from the cashing of family allowances to looking after our savings.'[4]

We all of us from time to time commit confidential information to the Post Office. We have no choice in the matter, since the entire communications network is in the hands of a jealously-guarded government monopoly. It is important for all of us, then, to know what statutory restrictions exist to prevent government abuse of this very special position of trust.

[2] 'The Codebreakers', by D. Kahn, George Weidenfeld & Nicolson Ltd.
[3] Ibid.
[4] *Guardian* supplement of 28.10.68.

Regrettably, no statutory safeguards do exist. It is even doubtful if the government can *legally* intercept communications at all. The secret committees of both houses of Parliament which examined the legal basis for interception in 1844 could discover no statutory or even prerogative power to justify it, and were forced to fall back upon 'long usage'.

Yet since that date, successive governments have acted on the assumption that a prerogative power does exist. When a row blew up in 1956 after a controversial case of telephone tapping,[5] it seemed for a time as though the whole issue of interception might be given a thorough airing in Parliament, which has always been justifiably suspicious of governmental claims to prerogative. (In a sense, the whole history of Parliament has been one long fight to bring prerogative under democratic control.) To quiet the fuss, the government adopted the classic delaying tactic: it appointed a committee—the Birkett Committee—to look into the matter. It also followed the traditional gambit of drawing up for the inquiry terms of reference carefully designed to sidestep the most contentious aspect of the whole situation: the actual legal basis for interception. The Committee was not asked to decide whether the practice of interception was legal in itself, but only how and in what circumstances it should be carried out.

The resultant 'Report of the Committee of Privy Councillors Appointed to Inquire into the Interception of Communications'[6] found the whole practice of interception 'inherently objectionable' —but necessary. No further legislation was recommended.

This of course was excellent news to the police, the Inland Revenue, the Customs and Excise, the Security Service, the Home Office and the ten other government bodies which find interception so useful in their work. Even if the legal basis for the practice had stood up to Parliamentary investigation, it would undoubtedly have emerged hedged about with all sorts of irksome restrictions. Moreover, since 1947 no government department has had any cause to worry about the consequences of opening letters or tapping telephones: the Crown Proceedings Act of that year made it impossible for anyone to sue them for doing so. So whether it was legal or illegal didn't really matter.

Although the members of the Birkett Committee recommended no further legislation in the field, they did produce a number of

[5] The Marrinan case.
[6] Cmnd. 283 of 1957.

guidelines for the regulation of interceptions. These have no statutory force. (But then, neither does the government's claim to the power to which they apply.) A man's letters should be opened and his telephone tapped, they said, only on the strength of a warrant issued by the Home Secretary, who should first convince himself that:

(1) The offence under investigation is serious.
(2) Normal methods of investigation have been tried and have failed, or must, from the nature of the case, be unlikely to succeed if tried.
(3) There is good reason to suppose that an interception would result in a conviction.

In the case of an application by the Security Service:

(1) There must be a major subversive or espionage activity that is likely to injure the national interest.
(2) The material likely to be obtained by interception must be of direct use in compiling the information necessary to the Security Service in carrying out the tasks laid upon it by the State.

The only safeguard against abuse is therefore the soundness and impartiality of the Home Secretary's judgement. He must arrive at his decision *on the basis of information supplied by the body applying for the warrant*. Even if each case were presented to him with scrupulous fairness, so many applications are made that it would be impossible for the Home Secretary to give each one more than the most cursory examination.[7] Where the national security is involved—it will be remembered that the Security Service is specifically ordered to divulge only the minimum information on its activities.

Even if none of these objections applied, the question would still remain: should the Home Secretary, a key member of the Executive Coalition, really be entrusted with this delicate task? As Professor Harry Street has pointed out: 'Most European countries require the order of a judge before an interception is permitted. Would not a High Court judge be a more suitable person here?'[8]

Look again at the 'guidelines' produced by the Birkett Committee. The offence must be *serious*; other methods of investigation must be *unlikely to succeed*. There must be *good reason* to expect a conviction. The Security Service must believe that the

[7] *Vide* the *Sunday Times* article of November 1966.
[8] 'Freedom, the Individual and the Law', Pelican, 1967.

activity involved is *likely* to involve the *national interest*, and the material *likely* to be obtained must be of direct relevance to the Service's job.

It is difficult to imagine circumstances in which an investigating agency could not claim justification for a warrant on such grounds as these. So let us look at some examples of the way in which Home Secretaries have used their judgement on the matter in the past. It must be stressed that the cases on record represent only the tip of an iceberg. If the G.P.O. listens in at the exchange on a parallel plug; or having put your telephone out of order, waits for you to report 'a fault' and then sends round a man to 'repair' it—you will probably never know that your line has been tapped. And as a G.P.O. official is reported to have said to a C.N.D. supporter who was suspicious about the frequency with which she was finding 'Opened in Error' stickers on her letters: 'If the authorities had opened your mail, you'd never know they'd done it!'

Nevertheless, a fair amount of evidence does exist about the way in which the practice is carried out. Let us begin with *mail interception.*

A Brighton window cleaner placed an advertisement in a local paper offering, for a fee of ten shillings, to enrol applicants on a register of film extras. The police intercepted his mail. On the strength of evidence gained in this way, he was in August 1968 found guilty of obtaining money by falsely pretending to be connected with the film industry.

The penalty he received—a £60 fine plus £30 costs—proves fairly conclusively the elasticity of the phrase *serious crime*. But the room for manoeuvre left within the Birkett Committee's 'guidelines' is demonstrated even more conclusively in the security field, where interception warrants may be granted *in the national interest.*

Earlier chapters of this book have shown the freedom with which the Executive Coalition is accustomed to interpret this phrase. That this liberality should be extended to the context of mail interception is not surprising. What is surprising is the routine way in which 'blanket' interception is practised. Evidence of this has sometimes come to light in the most bizarre ways. In 1953, officials reading the mail addressed to a number of Communist leaders in Bristol replaced letters to two of them in the wrong envelopes. One was from the Bristol Town Clerk's Department, with its own special envelope, and so it became obvious that the two letters had been transposed in the post.[9] It has even happened that the official form authorising the intercept has been accidentally posted on to the victim. A representative of one of the organisations on the Labour Party's 'proscribed list'—the World Federation of Trade Unions—claims that not only was his name on the form he received in this way, but so were those of a number of other people, including a woman leader of a 'movement for political freedom in Greece'.[10]

In 1963 a Hampstead paper carried an intriguing article by a Mr. Nicholas Walter. 'When I worked at the Highgate sorting office in December 1954, the letters for Mr. Andrew Rothstein, the Communist writer, were sorted separately and then checked by a senior Post Office official before they came to me . . .[11] A week before this report appeared one of C.N.D.'s Group Secretaries received a letter (written anonymously, 'in view of the Official Secrets Act') from an official of the Board of Trade which confirmed suspicions—long held by the Group—that their mail was routinely censored.[12]

In February 1967 Eric Lubbock M.P. attempted to discover the extent to which routine interception was practised upon mail addressed to various political organisations. His interest had been aroused by the allegations of a former Post Office messenger, who claimed that during a security clamp-down preceding Kosygin's visit to the U.K., he had on a number of occasions carried packets of letters from a London sorting office to the G.P.O. headquarters in King Edward's Buildings, City. The letters, he said, were passed into a room containing photographic copying apparatus. After a short time they were handed back to him for return to the sorting office.[13]

When letters are opened under the Home Secretary's warrant, great care is normally taken to ensure that the addressee does not realise what has happened. A variety of discreet methods are available. Many countries use the 'twisting needle' technique. A needle is inserted through the flap of the envelope, just above the seal. It is then spun at high speed, winding the letter into a tight

[9] *Daily Express* 20.8.53.

[10] 'The Police and Civil Liberties', by S. Bowes, Lawrence & Wishart Ltd., 1966.

[11] *Hampstead and Highgate Express* 6.9.63.

[12] 'Privacy Under Attack' NCCL 1968.

[13] *Sunday Telegraph* 12.2.67.

cylinder which can be withdrawn without breaking the seal, then replaced, after examination, in the same way. But every year vast numbers of envelopes and postal packets are opened without subterfuge—by H.M. Customs and Excise.

In 1961 Mr. Anthony Barber, Economic Secretary to the Treasury, told the Commons that 'about' 300,000 letters had been opened in the previous year, under the authority of the 1947 Exchange Control Act. About £50,000 in currency had been discovered. M.P.s felt that the success rate of the exercise seemed too low to justify this wholesale interference with private mail. Mr. Barber was unable to say precisely what percentage of the letters opened had actually contained currency. The records, he explained disarmingly, were rather sketchy on this point.[14]

Six years later the *Daily Sketch*[15] reported that unofficial sources inside H.M. Customs and Excise had estimated that the number of letters opened under the Act had risen to a *conservative* figure of 500,000 a year. The increase was put down to the effect of the £50 travel limit.

No official spokesman could be found to confirm or deny this estimate, and so it is even more impossible to hazard a guess at the success rate than it was for Mr. Barber's figures for 1960. But it is easy to see why the authorities should be so reticent on this point. A proportion of British overseas mail is already passed under fluoroscopes and X-rays, both of which will unerringly pick out the metal strip running through all British treasury notes. If the enforcement of the 1947 Exchange Control Act really is the sole reason for this massive interception campaign, then there seems no valid reason why the success rate should not approach 100%. (Some people claim that a sheet of carbon paper wrapped around the notes will beat the machine. Belief in this theory can be a very expensive business.)

Some M.P.s however believe that 'Opened by Customs' stickers are sometimes found on envelopes intercepted for quite a different purpose. In November 1966 a number of allegations were made in the House of Commons that letters to and from Rhodesia were being opened for censorship purposes. The Postmaster General, Mr. Benn, categorically denied that letters were opened for this purpose, and then took shelter under the umbrella of the Exchange Control Act until the storm blew itself out. But by June 1968

[14] *Evening News* 30.3.61.
[15] 28.6.67.

M.P.s were again complaining about the number of letters which were arriving from Rhodesia with the red Customs sticker on their flaps. Patrick Wall M.P. claimed to have received half a dozen letters in this condition; another Tory M.P. stated that one envelope with a Rhodesian stamp had been opened although it contained nothing but a one-page circular. How could this, he said, possibly have contained anything of valid interest to the Customs?

What steps can you take if you believe your correspondence is being intercepted? You have no legal remedy against the Crown or its servants, and so cannot stop them reading your mail. But you can make it more difficult for them to lay their hands on it in the first place. One way would be to arrange for your letters to be sent to an accommodation address under a false name.

But the censors have a backstop here, in the shape of the ubiquitous Official Secrets Act. Section Five of the 1920 Act provides for the regulation of those offering the services of an accommodation address. A sub-section lays down penalties for anyone who 'furnishes any false information or makes any false entry'.

Those who drew up these provisions did so to facilitate the tracking-down of spies, and seem to have intended them to apply only to the *keepers* of accommodation addresses.

But as we have seen, when it comes to the interpretation of the Official Secrets Act, the intentions of the original legislators count for nothing. The Act can be neatly twisted to apply to cases totally unconnected with the national security, and can be used to penalise any *user* of an accommodation address who gives a false name. This was established in 1935 when a man advertising for a woman assistant was prosecuted for using an accommodation address in this way. At the first hearing he was acquitted on the grounds that only the keeper of an accommodation address could be held liable. The prosecution appealed, and won its case.

So it might be wiser, after all, to have even your most confidential correspondence sent to your known address in the normal way—but to make sure that it is written in code. 'Do-it-yourself' codes are unlikely to baffle an expert in the Foreign Office's 'Department of Communications' for much longer than it would take him to drink his morning cup of coffee. Much better splash out about £70 for a Hagelin-Cryptos Pocket Cryptographer—a neat Swiss coding machine the size of a packet of 20 cigarettes, which will code or decode about 40 letters a minute.

Heavy correspondents may find this too slow, and will need the typewriter-sized 'standard' model—a worthwhile investment at £200. Embassies and armies in over 60 countries rely on Hagelin machines, and so can you. The chances of anyone breaking your code will be about 24 quintillion quintillion quintillion against—odds to satisfy anyone.

Diplomats use Hagelin machines to encode not only their written despatches, but their overseas telegrams too. This however is a privilege reserved for them alone. Private individuals and commercial organisations must send such telegrams either 'en clair' or opaquely disguised under standard commercial codes, for which the G.P.O. holds the keys. So if you have secrets to send abroad, send them by letter. For one thing, you will then be able to use the code of your choice. For another, whereas the authorities open only a tiny fraction of the five hundred million or so pieces of foreign mail handled annually by the G.P.O., the 21 million overseas telegrams dealt with each year receive very different treatment.

Early in 1967, Chapman Pincher of the *Daily Express* touched off a major political row (The 'D.-Notice Affair') when he revealed that all overseas telegrams without exception are routinely vetted, and 'interesting' ones then passed on for detailed scrutiny by security men.

This treatment is not reserved just for messages put through the G.P.O.'s own overseas cables branch, but for those dealt with by the private cable companies operating in this country as well. The work is carried out under a general warrant from the Home Secretary. Before it received any publicity, it had quietly been going on for over forty years. *Selective* vetting has almost certainly been going on for longer still—probably ever since the first overseas telegram was sent.

The G.P.O. has had a very long time to perfect its system of mail and cable interception. The art of telephone tapping, although of more recent origin, has not been neglected.

The clicks and buzzes, the heavy breathing and the sudden fadings of volume which we all hear on the line occasionally may be signs that an inefficient telephone tapper is at work. The back-files of newspapers are stuffed with instances of such noises being cited by union leaders, journalists and officials of organisations such as C.N.D., as evidence that their calls are being officially monitored.

Most of these claims can be discounted. For the G.P.O., interception is a perfectly straightforward matter. If they want to monitor your calls, they will route them through an official 'listening post' like the one which is (or used to be) situated in two rooms on the second floor of Clive House, home of the Passport Office. Even more simply, they may listen in at the exchange with a parallel plug. Any technical hitches you then experience when using your telephone will probably be no worse than those the rest of us have to endure. The electronic hiccuppings of a dyspeptic telephone system, or someone making the most of the gift of a crossed line, are the likeliest explanations for any weird noises you may hear. It is true that Sir Tufton Beamish M.P. has claimed to have heard his entire conversation played back to him at the end of a call. If this was the error of an official phone-tapper, it must have been the exception that proves the old rule: practice makes perfect.

The G.P.O. have had a lot of practice. Until 1937, interception was an ill-regulated affair. Not even a warrant was required. The G.P.O. tapped telephones for the police, the Security Service and others entirely on their own authority. Today, the interception of telephone calls is bound by the same regulations that apply to mail interception. A warrant from the Home Secretary is required, and will only be issued when the offence under investigation is 'serious' or involves the 'national interest'.

Unfortunately (again, as with mail interception) the only evidence to show the spirit in which the Home Office interprets this requirement is indirect in form: the case of the young sailor, for example, who while absent from his unit without leave, rang his girl-friend to arrange a meeting—and arrived at the rendezvous to find an Assistant Provost Marshal playing gooseberry; or the case of the fake demonstration 'arranged' with the sole intention of discovering if an official snooper was on the line and which produced a clutch of policemen forlornly awaiting a crowd that never materialised.

It is evidence that tapping has been used in petty cases like these that has led Chapman Pincher and other observers to conclude that the practice is far more widespread than the available figures would suggest. These show a rise in the issue of warrants from a wartime peak of 180 in 1941 to 241 in 1955—the last year for which figures are available.

M.P.s have made numerous attempts to establish more recent

figures, but have consistently been told that it would not be in the national interest to reveal them. It is not clear why this should be so—unless of course the post-1955 figures would show an embarrassingly steep rise. But no one is even sure what is to be made of the figures which *have* been made available. On the surface, they suggest that telephone calls are intercepted on a very modest scale. How is it, then, that after all the truly serious cases have been catered for, there are apparently enough warrants left over to cover such minor cases as those instanced earlier?

There are two possible solutions. One is that much unofficial tapping is carried out. This is the favourite explanation; in April 1966, the *Daily Sketch* boldly guessed at 12,000 unofficial tappings a year. The other is that each warrant can cover several names. As we have seen, cable interception is carried out on the most massive scale without the necessity for individual warrants. Perhaps warrants to tap telephones are issued on the same principle.

In fact, there are cases where no warrant is required at all. All Ministries with work in the defence category, for example, run a system of spot checks on calls going through their switch-boards, in an effort to spot loose-tongued staff members. There is also nothing to prevent a policeman or security officer (or anyone else, for that matter) listening in on a party line; or having first obtained the consent of one party to the conversation, using an extension handset.

There is only one privileged group which can—in theory, at least—count on immunity from official telephone monitoring. In November 1966, Harold Wilson revealed that he had placed a ban on the tapping of M.P.'s telephones as soon as he took office.

This new piece of parliamentary privilege is as anomalous as the freedom M.P.s enjoy from the rigours of the 'loyalty programme'. But not long after Mr. Wilson had given his assurance, at least a dozen M.P.s from both sides of the House were protesting that their telephones were still being tapped, while others claimed that they had suffered in this way in the past. Sir Tufton Beamish—one of whose telephone anecdotes has already been related—claimed that in 1961 no fewer than 15 Labour M.P.s had been shadowed, and their telephones tapped. This, he alleged, had been at the request of their own Parliamentary Party, then in Opposition. The intention had been to smoke out concealed Communists masquerading as loyal Socialist M.P.s.

One of the most unattractive features of telephone tapping is that its tentacles extend to cover not only the man named on the warrant, but numerous other people as well. The potential for abuse that exists here was shown in 1956, when the Bar Council was investigating charges of professional misconduct laid against a barrister named Marrinan. It so happened that the police had been monitoring the calls of a criminal suspect with whom Marrinan had spoken on the telephone. Although Marrinan was not himself a police suspect, the Bar Council was given transcripts of these conversations, for use in their purely domestic inquiry.

The storm raised over the Marrinan affair was such that the police are unlikely to pass such evidence to the private sector ever again. It is however, wholly possible that evidence gained by *unofficial* telephone tapping may be passed in the reverse direction. Although the police may not themselves tap telephones without a warrant, they are perfectly free to use in court recordings of telephone conversations made by someone outside their ranks. In March 1968, a man was found guilty of 'attempting to pervert the course of justice' on the strength of tape-recorded evidence obtained over a party line by a private individual. His defence counsel claimed that this evidence was inadmissible, since for the police to use it in court would breach the parliamentary undertaking given on the subject. Lord Parker disagreed. The Crown's undertaking, he said, applied *only to its own servants.*

It is difficult to see how the Home Office could ensure that those given official facilities for phone-tapping never worked without a warrant—unless, while the tappers were tapping, they were to be tapped in turn. Perhaps this does happen. In November 1957, the *Daily Express* reported: 'During a recent drive against Communists in secret Post Office departments, the men who tap people's telephones had their own phones tapped—and didn't know it.'

But in a Home Office store at Welwyn, Hertfordshire, is a collection of gadgets which make telephone tapping look positively old-fashioned. Maintained for the use of the police and other 'authorised bodies', this collection is rumoured to contain every device that even the most sophisticated electronic eavesdropper could desire. The use of modern listening devices enables surveillance to be carried out to a depth unattainable by traditional methods. There are gadgets to suit every situation—'tracers' which once fastened to a suspect's car, make it impossible for him to shake his tail, and an awesome variety of micro-miniature transmitters and tiny microphones which can be hidden in his bedroom, office or even his favourite pub, and will eavesdrop on his every whisper. For situations where the concealment of such equipment would be difficult, there are laser-guns, 'shotgun' and 'spike' mikes to pick up his words at long range.[16]

Listening devices have obvious advantages to the police and security forces. But there is a further advantage which is less well-known: their use is not regulated by the safeguards (such as they are) laid down by the Birkett Committee for mail interception and telephone tapping. While it is true that Home Office permission is normally required before bugs can be used, this can be given by a permanent official. No warrant personally signed by the Home Secretary is needed—indeed, he need know nothing of the request. In certain circumstances, bugs may be used without Home Office permission in any shape or form. In special cases, a Chief Constable may give his permission on his own authority.

This astonishing departure from the pledges made by successive governments with respect to mail interception and telephone tapping is explained by the Home Office view that bugs are 'different'.

Indeed they are. Intrusive though the use of these other forms of surveillance can be, bugs are infinitely more so. There is no limit to the range of activities which they can monitor. A man whose bedside conversations are tapped will reveal more of himself than he would wish. But when that phone is turned into a permanent microphone—standard drill for the electronic eavesdropper—the world of 1984 seems suddenly very close.

It is not just the range of activities that can be electronically monitored that is so frightening—it is the massive scale on which the process can now be carried out. In the old days, a man with his ear pressed to a partition wall or window-pane could often eavesdrop quite effectively. But to keep up a 24-hour watch on just one suspect called for a whole team of men. Police-state tactics were limited by sheer considerations of manpower.

Thanks to the tape-recorder, mass surveillance is now an economic possibility. The conversations of a great many people can now be monitored by just one man. Modern machines even save him the boring process of running through long sections of blank tape, since they start up automatically only when there is something to record.

During the last war, American security men are believed to have

[16] See Chapter 16—The Tools of the Trade.

bugged every bedroom in any hotel of note within a wide radius of Chicago, Washington and other cities. To aid plant security in factories and laboratories engaged on top-secret projects, not only were working areas bugged—so were lavatories and rest-rooms. Now that Britain's police and security men have been given the green light, how far will the use of bugs develop here.

When the restrictions on the use of such equipment were eased late in 1968, the police themselves were surprised at this sudden shift in official policy. They were however directed to use bugs not as a means of gathering *direct* evidence, whose source would later become apparent in court, but rather as tools to uncover leads which might provide proof of a less controversial sort.

These instructions guarantee that the full extent to which the police and other bodies may come to rely on listening devices will never be revealed. It is highly unlikely that the Home Office will ever issue statistics on the subject, while the police will only admit to using bugs when they have no alternative.

Sometimes of course no alternative does exist, the transcript of a bugged conversation being vital to the prosecution's case. In 1966, in the case of 'R. v. Maqsud Ali', the police admitted that they had left two suspects alone in a room in the police station, and then recorded their conversation through a hidden microphone. In 1968, it emerged at the trial of the Kray brothers that a 'special apparatus' had been used in a nursing home to eavesdrop on a conversation between Ronald Kray and one of the witnesses at the trial.

If bugging can ever be justified, then it can be justified in both these cases, which involved the most serious of all crimes—murder.

But where should the line be drawn? How far down the scale of crimes should the use of bugs be allowed? In May 1967 a man and his wife were charged with 'demanding money with menaces' after a detective crouched in the boot of a car had used a microphone hidden in an umbrella to record a conversation in which £50 had been demanded.

Blackmail is an undeniably nasty affair. But what about bribery?

In October 1967 a housing officer employed by Hackney Borough Council was charged with 'trying corruptly to procure' a 'Miss X' to have sexual intercourse with him. He had offered her furniture and money if she would go to bed with him, and threatened to turn in a bad report on her fitness for permanent council accommodation if she would not. The police used a hidden microphone to overhear the whole affair.

Police also used hidden microphones to trap yet another housing officer—this time employed by the Godstone Rural Council—who was brought to trial in February 1969 on a charge of indecent assault. By some oversight, the police were not able to use the tape recorder they had brought with them, but listened through earphones as the accused promised a young housewife that he would use his influence to obtain a council house for her, if only she would go to bed with him. By careful timing, the police were later able to surprise him in a compromising position in the bedroom, where he had been taken by the housewife to 'look at the damp'.

From murder down to blackmail, from blackmail to bribery, and from bribery to indecent assault—this takes us a considerable way down the scale of crimes for whose detection bugging devices have obvious advantages. On purely practical grounds, the police could make out an excellent case for extending their use even further. So, no doubt, could many other official bodies.

The American Inland Revenue Service, for example, has found it worthwhile to run its own training school for electronic snoopers, and at one time had concealed microphones installed in its offices in over twenty different cities. These were so placed that officials could leave a taxpayer and his financial adviser to 'talk things over privately', and then eavesdrop on their conversation from another room.

If our own tax authorities were to adopt similar tactics, it would be to the great benefit of the public purse. After all, to eavesdrop on the privileged conversation between a man and his financial adviser is no more unsavoury than to eavesdrop on a conversation between a man and his legal adviser. Yet in May 1968, Peter Jackson M.P. alleged that solicitors' interview rooms at Brixton Prison had been bugged so that police could do just that.

From drunken driving to tax evasion, and from murder to petty theft, crime takes a vast toll in human misery and financial loss. A really thoroughgoing universal surveillance system might cut that toll almost to nothing—yet still be far too dear. Senator Long, who has spent a lifetime in the defence of the 'right to be let alone' has likened the temptations presented by bugs and similar devices to those presented by a far older short-cut to law enforcement—torture. He draws this parallel not for the sake of cheap dramatics, but in sober warning, and quotes in its support an example drawn from our own judicial history.

During a discussion on the Code of Criminal Procedure for India in 1872, a civil officer of great experience was asked why it was that the police would occasionally torture a prisoner.

'There is a great deal of laziness in it,' he replied. 'It is far easier to sit comfortably in the shade rubbing red pepper into a poor devil's eyes than to go about in the sun hunting up evidence.'

Short cuts offer the devil's own temptation to the zealous and overworked as well as to the lazy, and should be fenced off with strong laws. At present, too many of those fences stand badly in need of repair.

Peeping Tom

> 'Always the eyes watching you . . . asleep or awake, working or eating, indoors or out of doors, in bath or in bed—no escape. Nothing was your own except the few cubic centimetres inside your skull.'
>
> *George Orwell: 1984*

If the state's willingness to tamper with the individual citizen's privacy continues to grow at the same rate as the armoury of devices to make that tampering possible, we are on a very slippery slope indeed.

Old loopholes have been left in the law, and new ones added, through which personal privacy may be sniped at in the 'national interest'. But the 'right to be let alone' is not merely under fire from the government. Many of these loopholes are taken advantage of by private individuals and organisations as well.

Only one law designed for the protection of personal privacy as such has ever been passed in this country. It made it an offence to be caught eavesdropping—found so suspiciously near your neighbour's window or key-hole that, had it been raining at the time and the guttering in need of repair, drips from the eaves would have fallen outside the spot where you were standing.

This law was repealed as obsolete in 1964. Today a policeman catching a snooper in the act might think it worthwhile to arrest him on suspicion of vagrancy, or for loitering with intent, or even for conduct likely to cause a breach of the peace. But the concept of privacy, as such, is unknown and unprotected by English law. There are many situations in which remedy can only be obtained as an almost accidental by-product of laws designed for quite another purpose: the protection of property.

In the past, judges have sometimes bent the property laws where they could to meet deserving cases. In 1962, for instance, damages of £1,000 were awarded against a photographer who had sold to the newspapers pictures taken by him at a wedding which took place shortly after the murder of the bride's father. The publication of the pictures caused no financial loss to the newly-married couple. But it did cause them severe distress, for which the judge was able to compensate them solely because the copyright of the pictures was technically their property.

It used to be possible for the law of trespass to be bent in the same way. In cases where the real issue was one of privacy, judges made awards which were sometimes far in excess of any real damage to property caused by the trespasser. But in 1964 the House of Lords decided that 'exemplary damages' could no longer be awarded in such cases. Today, the intruder who is careful to commit no damage can spy upon you in the comfortable knowledge that a conviction for trespass can carry only a light penalty.

If you catch an intruder in your house or grounds, you are entitled to use 'reasonable force' to eject him. This is so even if the intruder is a policeman, provided that he cannot show lawful authority for his presence. As we saw in the last chapter, he can now claim such lawful authority in a far wider range of circumstances than formerly. But without it, he can be treated exactly like anyone else who had thrust his way uninvited onto your premises. In 1963, Sir John Townley broke the nose of a policeman who had refused to leave his house. Sir John won his appeal against the conviction for assault which followed, because it was held that the policeman had no right to be there. 'If a householder is not to submit to his liberty being infringed in his house,' said Lord Parker, 'I cannot see that to hit out with his fist is an unreasonable use of force.'

The use of the words 'householder' and 'his house' is significant, and underlines the extent to which any expectation of privacy must depend upon property ownership. A private detective may burst into an hotel bedroom and take compromising photographs for the divorce courts, or an insurance investigator or reporter pester some accident casualty lying helpless in a hospital bed, without fear of legal reprisals from the victims. Only the owners or managers of the premises can take up proceedings. The victims of such tactics lack any property interest, and so have no legal remedy at all.

Even when a property interest does exist, it is often impossible to obtain redress for the grossest forms of privacy invasion. The man who comes onto your premises in order to spy upon you can be asked to leave, and forcibly ejected if he refuses. But if he spies upon you just as effectively with a pair of powerful binoculars he can do so with impunity so long as he keeps off your land. Your only hope is to prove 'unreasonable interference' with the enjoyment of your property.

Just how difficult this can be was dramatically illustrated by the case of the Balham householder who complained that his neighbour had constructed an ingenious arrangement of mirrors which enabled him, from the comfort of his own premises, to see exactly what was going on next door. The court found that the defendant was perfectly entitled to carry on with his snooping for as long as he wished.

If such an apparently clear-cut case as this could find no remedy, what hope have those subjected to more subtle ways of spying? The armoury of devices now available to the electronic spy has made a mockery of what little protection English law once gave to personal privacy. Indeed, in one respect the law almost goes out of its way to encourage their use—by making material gathered by such clandestine means admissible in the courts *even though the law was broken while collecting it.*

The snooper who hides a radio bug in your home may have committed trespass to plant it there, and by operating a transmitter without a GPO licence be liable to prosecution under the Wireless and Telegraphy Act. But the mere fact that he broke the law on two counts in order to gather his evidence will not make that evidence inadmissible.

If he taps your telephone, and is stupid enough to be caught at it, the G.P.O. can proceed against him under the Post Office Act. You however will be unable to prosecute him if the G.P.O. fail to do so, since you have no right of property in your telephone.

The chances of a telephone tapper being caught in the act are actually fairly slim. Modern methods are so sophisticated that even an expert cannot guarantee to detect a tap without checking every inch of the line—perhaps not even then. But if the snooper wants to reduce the chances of prosecution to zero, he may be able to listen in quite legally—on a party line.

Until recently, evidence gathered by illicit telephone tapping was useless inside a courtroom. But Lord Parker has now made life easier for the electronic eavesdropper. As a result of a judgement he handed down early in 1968, this form of illicitly-gathered material is also classed as admissible evidence.

The investigator who steams open correspondence or extracts a letter from its envelope with the twisting needle technique can be prosecuted for interfering with the mails. But if he X-rays your letters, or uses a telephoto lens to photograph them through a window as they lie on your desk, the law cannot touch him, nor prevent him bringing the results of his researches into court.

Peeping-Tom neighbours and litigants in search of material to sway a court-room battle in their favour are not of course the only ones to be grateful for the blind eye which British justice turns towards violations of personal privacy. From the industrial spy to the journalist in search of sensational copy there are many others with a professional interest in challenging 'the right to be let alone'.

English law, biased as it is in favour of property rights, might be expected to take a very dim view of the man who makes a living by rifling other people's confidential papers for saleable material. But in the words of Mr. Bumble: 'the law is a ass—a idiot!' The man who merely *photographs* your top-secret papers commits no crime by doing so. If he actually takes documents away with him, he can, it is true, be charged with theft. But although the purloined papers may be irreplaceable, and their loss cause your financial ruin; and although they may contain secrets worth tens of thousands of pounds—the man who makes off with them can be charged with stealing only *the value of the paper they are written on.*

If the stolen material is covered by copyright, then you will be able to obtain an injunction to prevent its unauthorised use. But much material of immense value to a business rival is not protected in this way. Small wonder, then, that industrial espionage is a flourishing trade.

In November 1968, Sir Edward Boyle introduced a Private Member's Bill to the Commons which aimed to make industrial spying an offence punishable by a fine of up to £1,000 and/or up to two years' imprisonment. It was adjourned at the Second Reading, and so for all practical purposes can be considered dead.

In 1961, another Private Bill designed to counter a different aspect of privacy invasion—an aspect capable of arousing distress more acute than any mere financial loss—was also killed off after its Second Reading. This was Lord Mancroft's 'Right of Privacy' Bill.

No single piece of legislation could hope to safeguard privacy in *all* its aspects. The aspect which Lord Mancroft chose to champion is perhaps the most basic of all: a man's right to keep to himself such details of his personal life and conduct as could not fairly be claimed to be of 'legitimate public interest'.

In America, where the concept of privacy as such is well defined in law, it has been recognised that as society becomes more complex, so 'solitude and privacy have become more essential to the individual; but modern enterprise and invention have, through invasions upon his privacy, subjected him to mental pain and distress, far greater than could be inflicted by bodily injury'.[1]

From this view it follows logically that a legal code which provides redress for injured flesh should provide redress for injured feelings as well.

The same view is widely held in this country. The difference is, that whereas the Americans have backed it with legal force, we have not.

Lord Mancroft hoped to do so, by giving a person a right of action 'against any other person who without his consent publishes of or concerning him in any newspaper or by means of any cinematograph exhibition or sound broadcast any words relating to his personal affairs or conduct if such publication is calculated to cause him distress or embarrassment'.

To safeguard the rights of the press, Lord Mancroft proposed that certain categories of person should still be considered fair game: public figures—such as actors and politicians—who had placed themselves in the limelight of their own free will by their choice of profession; and figures temporarily in the public eye—such as criminals or people who had suffered some calamity—whose activities might justly be said to be of 'reasonable public interest'.

These proposals came under fire from various quarters. The Bill, it was said, would be unworkable; or would lead to a rash of speculative lawsuits and severe restrictions on the freedom of the press; or that it was not needed, because the law of defamation provided adequate safeguards already.

The newspapers were particularly worried about the definition of 'public interest'. In view of the way in which the Executive Coalition has interpreted this phrase as it touches public affairs, their anxiety was perfectly understandable.

'At what point,' asked *The Times*, 'do the personal affairs of parsons or film stars end and their pastoral work or their publicity begin?'[2]

Speaking for the Bill, Lord Goddard pointed out that 'in libel actions at the present time, judges have to rule over and over again what is a matter of public interest'.[3]

[1] 'The Right to Privacy.' 4 Harvard L.R. 193. [2] 13.3.61.
[3] 229 H.L. Deb. (5th ser.) 622 (1961).

The test that ought to be applied, said Lord Mancroft, was: 'Is this mud the public ought to know about, or is it mud for mud's sake alone?'[4]

The critics who claimed that the courts would be overwhelmed by speculative lawsuits were invited to look to American experience. The same fears had been expressed when legislation on the lines of Lord Mancroft's Bill had first been proposed there, but in the event had proved groundless.[5]

As to the law of defamation providing adequate safeguards already: while the Bill's champions would readily concede that a man who brings another into 'hatred, ridicule or contempt' might certainly find himself wriggling on one of the twin prongs of the law of defamation—libel and slander—mud could all too often be slung for mud's sake, and afterwards be justified as fair comment, if the facts as stated were actually true.

Just as the law of copyright can (as in the example cited at the beginning of this chapter) sometimes be bent to provide redress in a case where the real issue is one of privacy, so a sympathetic judge can occasionally bend the law of defamation in the same way. But apart from it being highly dangerous for the fabric of the law to be strained in this way for lack of a more specific remedy, there are circumstances which no amount of bending will allow the law to accommodate.

In America, the 'appropriation of a person's likeness or character' for purposes of advertising or trade is an actionable matter. In this country, an advertiser with a clever lawyer to advise him could spread your name and picture across every billboard in the country without your permission—and do so with impunity.

In England, any newspaper running a 'Where Are They Now?' series can dish up as many ancient scandals as the editor pleases, blighting in the process the declining years of forgotten celebrities who had thought the past lived down. Where no scandal exists, it can sometimes safely be invented—English law holds that you cannot libel the dead. (See Appendix, note 4.)

In America, the case is very different. Once a person has passed out of the limelight, it is extremely difficult to represent discreditable events from his past as of 'reasonable public interest'. Thus a reformed prostitute who had for many years led a quiet and blame-

[4] 229 H.L. Deb. (5th ser.) 613 (1961).

[5] *Vide* 'Recent Developments in the Law of Privacy,' by Feinberg. 48 Colum. L. Rev. 731 (1948).

less life was able successfully to sue a film company which exhumed her past and revealed it to her friends, many of whom had been ignorant of it. In this country, the film company would have had no case to answer.

Publication of a photograph showing a dead, deformed child; of details concerning a woman's 'male characteristics', and of another's venereal disease—in America these have all led to successful court actions. They could not have done so here. The Press Council might perhaps have rapped the knuckles of an editor who sanctioned the use of such items, but that is all.

The House of Lords evidently felt that the victims of tactics like these should be entitled to consolation of a more tangible sort—a thumping sum in damages. They passed Lord Mancroft's Bill at its Second Reading by a substantial majority. Nevertheless, the Bill was withdrawn—largely because of government opposition.

Even those who drafted the Bill admit that it had some minor blemishes. At the time of withdrawal, they consoled themselves with hints that the government would later introduce its own Bill on the subject, with these blemishes removed.

Eight years later, those hints have still come to nothing. The proliferation of electronic and optical gadgetry since Lord Mancroft first framed his Bill have made his proposals seem absurdly modest now. The 'Right of Privacy' Bill could not by itself have provided an adequate shield against the much more serious threat that exists today. Yet by giving the *concept* of privacy some legal reality, it would at least have provided a foundation on which to build.

Sadly, it is as if the Mancroft debates had never taken place. The indifference of officialdom on the subject of privacy was well illustrated by an exchange which took place in the House of Commons on the 28th March, 1968.

Mr. Gardner, Member for Rushcliffe, asked if the Home Secretary would introduce legislation to regulate the use of 'long-range cameras and television equipment to penetrate homes and offices'.

Answering for the Home Secretary, Mr. Taverne (Under-Secretary) said that he was 'not persuaded that there was an urgent need for legislation', but that the Home Secretary was naturally 'keeping this problem under review'.

Mr. Gardner persevered. 'It is possible,' he said, 'by the use of modern equipment, to keep a constant watch into people's homes and offices and even to read documents if necessary. Is it not time we had a new law to provide privacy?'

'This is a very difficult question because it depends on what kind of law one would want,' answered Mr. Taverne wisely. 'There could either be a general law to deal with privacy or a particular law to deal with certain kinds of equipment.'

Baffled, Mr. Gardner gave way to the redoubtable Mr. Hogg (Member for St. Marylebone) who, after mentioning a recent seminar on privacy, asked: 'In view of the widespread interest in this subject, when can we expect a Government announcement on the matter?'

'This is a complicated question which involves the freedom of the press as well,' Mr. Taverne informed him. 'At the moment there is no great evidence of abuse.'

It would be interesting to know what evidence would qualify as 'great' in Mr. Taverne's estimation, and if the tale of the little Dutch boy and the dyke was among the stories he heard at his mother's knee.

Even the magazine *Security Gazette*, which later—and for obvious reasons—applauded the skill with which Mr. Taverne had 'thrown the ball back' to his questioners, felt bound to admit: 'That privacy is under increasing attack cannot of course be denied. Respect for the individual has declined in a way that would astound even the late Victorians.'

Orwell could at least believe that the citizens of the world of 1984 would still be able to find some measure of privacy in the woods and fields. ('Are we all right here?' asks Winston Smith. 'Yes,' answers Julia. 'Look at the trees . . . There's nothing big enough to hide a mike in.') But telephoto lenses and long-range microphones are already so efficient that it is now possible to violate a man's privacy in the open as easily as Orwell's two-way telescreens were able to do in the home.

The use of such equipment has been so readily accepted by the public that it can even be exploited for its entertainment value.

When I.T.V.'s 'Candid Camera' team set out to involve passers-by in embarrassing situations and then filmed them unawares, the people concerned were given the choice of whether or not they would appear on the screen. But this choice was by courtesy of the television company. It is not a legal *right*, as in America. The B.B.C. ran no risk of prosecution whatsoever when they showed to millions the faces of those queuing to buy 'Lady Chatterley's Lover' on publication day.

Sometimes of course clandestine filming is carried out in the spirit of a crusade.

In 1968 the B.B.C. secretly filmed and recorded the reactions of landladies faced with coloured applicants for lodgings. In the same year, I.T.V.'s 'World in Action' team turned the tables on a private detective by first employing him—through a 'cutout'—to plant a bug on the premises of an Islington factory, and then using hidden cameras to film him in the act.

From cameras hidden in the cause of entertainment, we have already progressed to cameras hidden in the cause of law enforcement. Remote-control cameras at rooftop-level have already been used by police in Liverpool, Coventry, Lowestoft and (in London) Croydon, Hatton Garden and Soho, in highly successful experiments in crime detection.

The more such tactics are used, the more they become accepted. And they are being used on an ever-increasing scale. It is one thing to have cameras hidden at the deep-end in swimming baths, or watching over children's playgrounds; it is quite another to place them in the changing rooms of big stores to catch shoplifters. But where does one draw the line?

It is undeniably difficult to frame legislation that will guarantee some measure of personal privacy without unduly hampering law enforcement, or restricting the freedom of the press. There will always be border-line cases. But unless the border is fixed *somewhere*, and soon, it will be too late.

Today, the concept of privacy goes unrecognised by English law. Orwell forecast a time when it would go unrecognised by the English language as well. Subversive concepts such as privacy—and justice, and freedom, and love—will be eliminated, because in 'Newspeak', the language of the future, there will be no words to express them.

'We're cutting the language down to the bone,' says Syme, one of Newspeak's architects. 'In the end, we shall make thoughtcrime literally impossible.'

After centuries of unbroken despotism, the Russian people have no word in their enormously rich language to convey the concept of privacy as we understand it—as something desirable. Their nearest equivalent is 'uyedineniye'—an abnormal state of isolation, solitude, loneliness.

It could happen here.

Private Enterprise at Work

> 'The Private Detective works against Cheats and Bullies in the main, assists and often brings about the end of suffering and cruelties. Why does he not get due credit for his value to the Community? The answer is simple—all our Public Relations have been negative and damaging . . .'
>
> *The Association of British Private Detectives: Open Letter*

The assault on what little privacy remains to us is pressed home not only by the swelling armies of bureaucracy, but by the shock-troops of commerce as well. Never before in history has the minding of other people's business been so profitable. The affluent society has spawned whole new categories of informer and spy. Some work for pin-money: the delivery roundsman who sells snippets about his customers' home lives to the credit-rating bureau; or the employee of the big firm who acts as a head-hunter's talent-scout on the side, passing on information which will enable the brightest of his fellow-employees to be wooed away to rival organisations. Others are in the business for kicks; any full-time operative in any branch of the snooping business has on his books the names of freelancers eager to take on assignments not so much for the money—which can be derisory—but for the thrill of acting like real-life James Bonds or Mike Hammers. Then there are the specialists—'repo' men, industrial counter-intelligence experts, bugging technicians. But the vast majority—the 'G.P.s' of the snooping trade—are playing an old game brought up to date with new trimmings. These are the 'private investigators'; men who will tackle almost any job going. No one knows precisely how many people there are in this category. Anyone can set himself up as a trained investigator, and for a guinea or two have a nicely-framed diploma on his wall to prove it. Correspondence courses on the arts of the private eye have been offered by such 'experts' as bus-drivers, ex-railwaymen and shady solicitors' clerks. It is even rumoured that at least one ex-convict has made use of his hard-won personal knowledge of the detective's skills by 'putting up his plate' the day after his release from prison. There are also shoals of hobbyists and old-age pensioners advertising their services. In fact, if everyone calling himself a private detective were to be taken at his word, then the total number of operatives in the field might be set as high as fifteen thousand or so.

The two main bodies representing the field—The Association of British Detectives and the Association of British Private Detectives—strenuously contest this figure.

The A.B.P.D. estimates that there are probably no more than 2,700 full-time private investigators in the country, plus about 2,000 'status enquiry agents' and specialists in writ-serving. Of the 2,700 or so full-time private investigators, they claim that only about 1,000 are truly worthy of the name—and possibly as few as 500, depending on how strictly one interprets the qualifications needed for the job.

There is no doubt that the best private investigators are very capable indeed. As yet there is no single professional hallmark of competence by which they can be picked out from the rest. The various handbooks listing practitioners in the field show numerous discrepancies. Some of the most highly trained—although not necessarily those with the most integrity—are not listed in any handbook at all.

The A.B.P.D. and the A.B.D., as the two main representative bodies, spend much of their time fighting those who bring the profession into disrepute. Much of the rest, they spend on fighting each other—a fratricidal conflict springing from divergent views on how to win public esteem for their trade.

The A.B.P.D. claims to have closed down any number of disreputable firms—by gathering evidence of malpractice and then threatening exposure or legal action—and devotes much of its subscription income to firing off letters of exhortation to members and non-members alike, calling for higher standards, a new sense of corporate identity and pride. In the meantime, they plead: 'Stop mud-slinging! Learn to say "I am a Private Detective" without adding "Although not one of the crooked ones!"' The thunder of A.B.P.D.'s barrage falls mainly upon deaf ears. Members of the rival A.B.D., in particular, feel the evangelical approach, without effective sanctions to back it up, is totally useless. They concentrate instead on putting their own Association's house in order, and are inclined to leave the rest of the field to go to the devil in its own way. In an effort to give real weight to the words

'Member of the Association of British Detectives', they vet applicants very carefully, have set up a disciplinary committee, and are planning a tough professional examination. Although they regret the recurrent scandals involving P.D.s who have given way to one or another of the many temptations to which their trade exposes them, they feel that bad publicity may serve a useful purpose—by teaching members of the public to be more discriminating in their choice of firm. On one point, though, the A.B.D. is in total agreement with its rival: in opposing legislative restrictions on the field. Nevertheless, legislation is in the wind.

In the U.S.A., most States have long run a licensing and bonding system for P.D.'s. It is generally administered by State police, and medium-to-large firms must find (usually through an insurance company) a surety averaging out at about $50,000 for each branch office. Should an investigator be prosecuted for trespass or any 'infringement of civil liberties', then funds are always available from which damages can be met.

English law provides far fewer opportunities for the victim of an over-zealous private eye to obtain redress than would be open to him in America. But pressure for a system modelled on American lines has been increasing for some time, and in February 1969 the A.B.P.D. reacted with alarm to the news that a Private Member's Bill had been proposed which would require all P.D.s to apply to the police or County Courts for a licence to practice, and would further require a surety of £1,000 each.

'If this was to reach the Statute Book,' the A.B.P.D. warned its members, 'it would simply move us nearer the Police State and would eliminate our work as a field.'

This is highly doubtful. Changing moral attitudes on issues as varied as shop-lifting and divorce have thrown up more work for the P.D. than ever before, while new technical resources and commercial intelligence networks have made his role more effective. The prospect of easy pickings has attracted numerous fly-by-nights, many of whom would certainly be put out of business by legislation on the lines proposed. But although the shysters and incompetents are a menace to the unwary individual, and often employ distasteful or downright illegal methods, they are no real threat to society as a whole. This position is reserved for that small minority of thoroughly professional, adequately capitalised firms capable of giving their clients not just good value for money, but *frighteningly* good value. Many of these would actually welcome legislation. Mr. Colin Finlay, vice-president of the Council of International Investigators, sees it as the only way to clean up the profession and safeguard its reputable practitioners. 'As the law stands at present,' he says, 'anyone can start up a private detective agency. Some of the many agencies that have sprung up in recent years have done untold harm. The people who run them don't really know what they're doing and are just getting money under false pretences.'[1]

The A.B.P.D. fulminates about 'the continuous bleatings of the illiterate, and the ill-trained, and the unintelligent, in our Field who know not what they do when they keep on singing the song "We want legislation."' But the truth is that many of the most capable P.D.s support legislation for hard-headed commercial reasons. They know that it would send their way much business that now goes to small firms operating on a shoestring basis, at cut-price rates. Increased turnover and higher profit margins would accelerate growth and efficiency, and make possible the employment of better-qualified staff backed—on the American pattern—by superb head-office facilities.

The weeding-out of small, undercapitalised (and often inefficient) P.D. companies and the creation of new opportunities for highly efficient medium and large firms will not seem very sinister to the reader who in his mind's eye sees the investigator as a man in a shabby trenchcoat with his ear to a bedroom door. Of course, many P.D.s do fit the popular stereotype very closely indeed—although nowadays they are more likely to do their eavesdropping with the aid of a listening device from the comfort of a parked car, rather than at a draughty keyhole. Bugging and recording devices (often secreted under a mattress or behind a headboard) are used in 'matrimonial' work far more frequently than the number of press reports featuring their use would suggest. Often the couple concerned never realise they have been bugged at all ('It astonishes me how often they think it was just pure chance that we burst in at the right moment,' one P.D. reminisced). On other occasions, recordings will be used solely as a lever to extort a formal signed confession, and the subsequent divorce will go through on the undefended list. Either way, the fact that eavesdropping equipment was involved will never emerge in court. This type of operation can be highly profitable. For planting a tape recorder under a bed, one P.D. (Mr. Barrie Quatermain) is reported

[1] *Evening Standard*, 27.5.68.

to have netted £500. But such plums are rare. On a time basis, the average charge for a full day's work is about ten guineas plus expenses—hardly exorbitant when office overheads and 'idle time' are taken into consideration. A straightforward 'faithfulness check' runs out at about £20-£30, payable in advance. Because so many suspicious wives are unable to save enough out of the housekeeping to pay the whole amount at once, at least one P.D. has been forced to take this sort of case on a hire-purchase basis—£7 down and the balance by weekly instalments. Even less profitable are those matrimonial cases which involve tracking down an absconding husband who has left his wife and children to the care of the National Assistance.

A high proportion of divorce and 'missing persons' work only reaches the P.D. through a solicitor's clerk, and as often as not is paid for at legal aid rates. The A.B.D., for example, estimates that each of its five hundred or so members is called in by a solicitor upwards of a hundred times each year; the larger firms may be retained in this way six or seven times as often. Where the case is covered by Legal Aid, the P.D. can reap as little as five shillings an hour for 'keeping observation'; perhaps twelve and sixpence for serving a writ (which can be more difficult and time-consuming than the layman could believe). Fees for other types of work under the Legal Aid scheme are in proportion, and are often settled months in arrears.

Ill-paid though it often is, the sheer volume of the 'domestic' work available can keep an investigator supplied with his bread and butter. For his jam, he must search further afield: looking not to private individuals but to commercial organisations. For some, this search has been so successful that they can afford to be contemptuous about matrimonial work, and will not touch it at all. Others continue to undertake it merely as a supplement to their more profitable commercial work, which provides an increasing percentage of their turnover.

The private investigator finds two main categories of work in the commercial field.

The first—stemming from banks, finance companies and other such sources—includes credit investigation, writ-serving, repossession and debt collection. Top-notch investigators consider it rather low, almost on a par with matrimonial work. It is discussed in the next chapter ('The Blacklist Business').

The second category—industrial security work—is much closer

to conventional police work. It runs from 'screening' a job applicant to sending in an undercover agent to track down a troublemaker; from the provision of store detectives to trapping an embezzler.

P.D. firms operating in this area are forced to compete with the specialised industrial security organisations, many of which run detective divisions as an ancillary to their main guarding and cash-transit activities. Some P.D.s, carrying the war into the enemy camp, have started to offer guarding and cash transit services of their own—although on a very modest scale. But there is more than enough business for all. A mounting crime rate and the spread of 'security neurosis' from America have seen to that.

Industry loses far more to its own dishonest employees than to hijackers, wage-snatchers and other outsiders. 90% of industrial thefts are carried out by employees. In a factory turning out easily-disposable items such as radios or cameras, 10% of stock can be drained off by pilferers, and of 300 factory break-ins a day, about 80% are performed by employees who return after hours. To deal with the problem, more and more firms are writing search clauses into their contracts of employment. A system of spot checks can be particularly effective when—as is sometimes the case—a concealed microphone is used to pick up the conversations of those about to go through the checkpoint.

But personal searches cause much ill-feeling among employees. They can also lead to bad public relations. A London underwear factory received much unfavourable publicity in 1968 when a female security officer armed with a mirror was brought in to check on the arrival and departure of its women workers, many of whom were suspected of leaving the factory wearing several pairs of stolen panties after arriving at work wearing none. A union organiser described this check as 'indecent and deplorable', and the press agreed with her.

Casting around for an unobtrusive way of combatting pilfering, management will frequently call upon a private detective or security firm to supply an undercover agent. Slipped into the organisation as a 'new member of the staff', the investigator will then pursue his enquiries right under the noses of his suspects. To sustain his cover, he may need training in anything from accountancy to welding. But for most assignments, the ability to master a simple manual task is enough. Any ex-C.I.D. man is a 'natural' for the general run of undercover work. Examples of cases solved by this approach include: ending a spate of baggage thefts by porters at a major airport; uncovering a swindle in which a wholesaler's despatchers and drivers had collaborated to smuggle stolen goods out of a warehouse in the firm's own lorries; and identifying a disgruntled employee who had been polluting the output of a flour mill with foreign bodies. While going about his main task, the undercover man will also keep his eyes open for instances of poor discipline, irregular timekeeping, the falsifying of job sheets and other such matters.

In 1963, Security Services Ltd. (an associate company of Securicor) was suggesting that its undercover specialists could be used to report on 'any person who may be suspected of causing dissension or inciting employees to disaffection'. Today the big security companies steer clear of anything that smacks of politics or strike-breaking—it can too easily involve them in public controversy. But there are plenty of small concerns eager to take on this sort of assignment.

In 1968 a small family firm of sub-contractors called in an investigator to explore the motives behind a seemingly senseless strike in one of its departments. The management was inclined to attribute it to sheer bloody-mindedness, but the investigator had other ideas. Among the many items manufactured by the firm was a small but vital component for an armoured fighting vehicle. Quantities of these were being sent to Nigeria for the Biafran confrontation—of which two of the twenty-four men working in the strike-bound department violently disapproved, on political grounds.

As with any other spy, the undercover man's greatest fear is of being 'blown'. For him, it will lead to abuse and even physical violence at the hands of the colleagues he has deceived. For the management which engaged him, it will bring trouble with the unions. In April 1968, for example, a Lancashire engineering firm placed an overalled undercover agent on the shop-floor to track down metal thieves. He gave himself away—and 200 men walked out.

In fact, the undercover agent's greatest problem is not so much to escape detection while actually on the premises, but to leave when his task is complete in such a way that no hint of suspicion remains behind. A sudden resignation followed by vigorous management action would give the game away. An elaborate cover-story is usually needed. Some years ago, a Securicor spokesman was heard to say, 'We have even faked arrests to get them out.' In 1963, a perfectly genuine arrest put an end to the activities of one undercover agent, who had been recruited by a security officer at B.M.C.'s Bathgate works in Scotland. Tried on a charge of attempting to frame a number of his workmates by planting machinery on their lorries, he was found guilty and sent to prison. Although there are obvious risks to using an undercover agent, managers in many industries find them worth taking. The undercover technique is of particular value in a counter-espionage role.

Only a few years ago, most British firms thought of industrial espionage as unreal—even as something of a joke. Companies taking that attitude today are in danger of finding that the joke is on them.

In the last five years, an extraordinary variety of British firms have lost top-secret manufacturing or marketing plans for products as varied as toothpaste, self-suspending stockings, paint and crush-proof shirts. In the first few months of 1968 alone, cases of industrial espionage in the home news embraced plastics, computers, chemical plant, meat products and a new form of electronic landing device for aircraft. Yet the reported cases form only the tip of the iceberg. No firm which has suffered in this way likes to admit it. An admission may suggest new lines of approach to its rivals, or reveal to a thief the true value of his prize. It will certainly bring recriminations and charges of incompetence from shareholders.

By 1966 the Board of Trade had become sufficiently worried about the effect of the problem on the country's competitiveness as a manufacturing nation that it undertook an official investigation; in 1968, the Institute of Directors (hardly an alarmist body) produced its own handbook on the subject.

In America, where losses from industrial espionage have been estimated to exceed those from fire and embezzlement *combined*, industry is willing to pay handsomely for protection—to the tune of £18 million each year.

British private detective and security firms envy the rich pickings of their American brothers, but are confident that before long they too will have a counter-espionage boom on their hands. Business is already brisk; there is even enough of it to enable several firms to concentrate exclusively on this work. Three of them—Security Counter-Intelligence Agency, Management Investigations and Counter Espionage Services—are particularly well-known for specialities of their own.

Counter Espionage Services Ltd. features an astonishing selection of undercover agents—technical experts of all kinds, accountants, even a doctor. They are especially proud of their team of women agents. Hand-picked for their looks, they have demonstrated conclusively that the Mata Hari approach works as well as ever it did.

Management Investigations Ltd. has acquired renown for its background investigations and interrogation techniques. To pinpoint weaknesses among a client's staff, key personnel are put through a modified 'third degree', with highly detailed questioning covering home life, hobbies, friends and financial affairs. Hesitation in answering any question, however personal, is taken as a sign that further investigation is needed. This frequently takes the form of a Field investigation modelled on Security Service lines. A highly derogatory report on the methods used by Management Investigations has been circulated among M.P.s.

The third organisation—Security Counter Intelligence Agency Ltd.—specialises in bugging and counter-bugging. Mr. Arthur Johnson, one of the firm's directors, travels about 2,000 miles every week 'sweeping' premises for concealed microphones and transmitters. Mr. Eric Cooper-Key of Security Express created quite a stir in June 1968 when he revealed that from a sample of twelve boardrooms swept by *his* company, three were bugged. Mr. Johnson claims an even higher ratio: positive results on three out of every seven sweeps.

Most counter-espionage firms have at least one electronics expert on the payroll. His main task, of course, is to find bugs planted by others rather than to plant them himself. But his skills are always at the disposal of any client who wishes to eavesdrop on an employee suspected of dishonesty. One investigator, Mr. Peter Merken, even brought in closed-circuit television to spy on office staff employed by one of his clients, who suspected that details of tenders were being leaked to a rival firm. Mr. Merken kept up his watch for ten days—and eventually spotted an executive photographing confidential material.

From the use of electronic surveillance devices in isolated instances—to catch a definite suspect red-handed—industrial security firms are now promoting their use in a wider context. In America, there are already factories where buzzers warn the production manager the instant any machine falls idle on the shop-floor. Remote-control T.V. cameras then zoom in on the operator to check on his reason for stopping work. There are offices where every word spoken and every action performed can be monitored by a managerial Big Brother. As Vance Packard and others have explained, these tactics are usually 'justified' as a means of 'helping' employees who may be having 'difficulty' with some aspect of their work.

Slowly but surely, we in Britain are following the same path. The signposts are there for anyone to read, in hundreds of department stores and supermarkets up and down the country—signposts ranging from the dignified 'For security reasons, closed-circuit T.V. is installed on these premises' to the flippant 'Smile please, darling —there's a man downstairs watching you.'

1968 was breakthrough year for the security firms selling T.V. systems, two-way mirrors and other mass-surveillance equipment. Where they had previously counted their sales in hundreds of pounds, by Christmas they were counting them in tens of thousands.

The most spectacular of the many available gadgets is the Photoscan. With its five T.V. eyes peering out on stalks in every direction, it looks rather like a sea-mine. It was only introduced late in 1967, but twelve months later had already been installed in over 100 stores. Its distributors believe the market has barely been scratched as yet.

Retailers can install equipment such as this without opposition from their staff because they can claim quite plausibly that it is solely intended to deter shoplifting customers. The equipment salesmen are more honest.

'Imagine a device that gives you sequence pictures every few seconds, all day long, of the movements of your customers and employees,' urges the brochure for Cam-Eye, another popular surveillance device. 'Pilferage by employees disappears when Cam-Eye is on the job. Customers get better service because employees realise that they are under the scrutiny of this all-seeing eye. Cam-Eye can be installed without offending personnel because it is obviously needed to discourage customer shop-lifting. Like the modern cash-register, Cam-Eye protects the honest employee . . . encourages the ambitious, painstaking employee who serves each customer cheerfully and efficiently.'

Of course, cameras can and do cut shop-lifting losses quite dramatically. Shortly after installing a T.V. system the manager of a Carnaby Street boutique reckoned that he had saved the hire-charge 'in one afternoon, on sunglasses alone'. But of the £120 million or so lost by British retailers each year, an estimated 62% is pocketed by dishonest employees. Much of the pilfering goes on behind the scenes, in stockroom and loading bay. But a king's ransom is stolen by dishonest assistants out in the public areas, at the cash registers. The knowledge that Big Brother is watching on his telescreen can have a very salutary effect here.

That retailers are beginning to devote as much attention to spying on their own employees as to keeping a wary eye on their customers is borne out by the upsurge of the new-style store detective services. Traditionally, the store detective has been a full-time employee of the retailer himself. Although anonymous to the store's customers, he was obviously well known to the other staff. If they were so minded, they could simply wait until his back was turned before dipping into stock or till.

Nowadays, the go-ahead retailer hires his detectives by the day or the week. Scores of private detective agencies and security firms offer this service. Store detective work is a recognised training ground for investigators, and at Christmas (when the 'five finger discount' rate goes up by about 60% on *both* sides of the counter) hundreds of part-timers are drafted in to meet the demand.

Big firms like Store Detectives Ltd. and Factoryguards Ltd. field whole teams of highly-trained men and women who move from store to store, mingling unobtrusively with the crowds. Indistinguishable from ordinary shoppers, they browse around the shelves keeping one eye on the customers and the other on the staff. Before their faces become familiar, they move on to another store.

One leading security firm—Lodge Services—runs a hugely successful 'test-marketing' scheme to cut down on cash pilfering by assistants. Going in as anonymous purchasers, Lodge detectives work their way through a shopping list, pay for the goods and leave. The following day, clients are asked for the relevant sales dockets and cash-register rolls. These are then checked to see if the assistant had recorded the correct amount. Lodge Services has 2,000 British clients. In the first three months of 1968 'test-marketing' picked out 383 dishonest assistants.

Not all the new-style store detectives rely on a 'just shopping' cover. Some are drafted in behind the counter. Particularly successful in this undercover role are teenage girls. Frequently they will adopt an air of dreamy indolence, which invites damning confidences from dishonest colleagues and at the same time provides an excuse for the store manager to 'sack' them at the end of the week.

Adept though private detective and security firms are at plucking bad apples from the personnel barrel, their clients would obviously prefer to stop blemished fruit getting into the barrel in the first place. This partly explains why application forms for even the humblest jobs are becoming increasingly detailed and intrusive in their questioning. Predictably, the trend first showed up in British subsidiaries of American-owned companies. An application form drawn up by one British company shortly after its control passed to American hands, asked (among other things):

1. *Single? Engaged? Dates married and remarried? Date separated? Date divorced? Date widowed?*
2. *Do you own your own home? Do you rent? Live with parents? If so, do you pay for board or room?*
3. *Have you life insurance? Have you disability and hospital insurance?*
4. *Were you ever injured while working? Did you ever draw workmen's compensation?*
5. *Is your husband/wife employed?*
6. *Please note any clubs, lodges or other organisations of which you are now a member.*
7. *Wife, husband, father, mother and other immediate members of your family living in Great Britain? Relation? Name? Employed by?* (*Name of company and address.*) *Occupation?*

After strong representation from the trade unions whose members were involved, the above was finally boiled down to:

1. *Single?*
2. *Are you a member of any voluntary organisation which might require absence during working hours?*

As British-owned firms have begun to ape the current fashion for American personnel techniques, they too have started to pry deeply into the private lives of those who apply for jobs. Sections Two and Three of the 'Associate Record Form' sent out to job applicants by a well-known British insurance company look something like this:

2. Date and place of birth...... Passport No...............
   Marital status................. Country of issue........
   No. of Children.............. Any other Dependents?
3. How much assurance do you currently have?
   If you own your house state approximate value £......... Do you own a car?
   Nature and amount of current investments.......................
   Current monthly expenses...
   Your present financial situation will allow you to support yourself without any additional income for...........months.

To their annoyance, personnel managers have discovered that the deeper they dig, the less likely they are to get truthful answers. In America, a lie-detector is often used to resolve the difficulty. In England, a private investigator may be called in instead. While checking the replies to questions asked on the application form or during interview, he may be asked to uncover the answers to questions which even the thickest-skinned personnel manager would not dare to ask.

It would, for example, be interesting to know if the man still loved his wife; held extreme political views; lived within his means; was homosexual or accident-prone; what his health record was like. All these factors and many more could affect his efficiency, or make him susceptible to bribery or blackmail. But probably more than anything else, he would like to know if the man had a criminal record.

For some time, the security industry has been agitating for a 'National Register of Crime'—an official publication listing those who, with the exception of first offenders and juveniles, have ever acquired a criminal conviction. Alternatively, it has been proposed that, as in Sweden, an applicant for a position of trust should be entitled to a police certificate confirming that he is not listed in the criminal records. The proposal for a National Register of Crime has received support from no less a personage than Sir Ronald Howe, former Deputy Commissioner and head of the C.I.D.

'Crime is a *voluntary* act,' he has stated. 'It must be remembered that it is not necessary to commit crime. If people do, I do not see why employers and others should not know whom they are dealing with. On the whole criminals are nasty people who much prefer to commit crime than do an honest day's work.'

An earlier age arranged for an ex-criminal to be instantly recognised on sight—by cropping his ears. It thus became impossible for him to do an honest day's work even if he wanted to; no one would give him the chance. But for a long time now it has generally been felt that a man who has 'paid his debt to society', should be allowed a fresh start. In April 1968, the *Security Gazette* pointed out some inconsistencies in this attitude. We already have what amounts to a *partial* 'National Register of Crime'. The daily press covers any newsworthy court action, while debt judgements and bankruptcies are reported in full by official publications such as the *London Gazette*. What can be wrong with a more systematic approach? Moreover, recruits to certain branches of the Civil Service and the Armed Forces are always required to fill out a form which includes the question: 'Have you ever been convicted by the civil powers?' They may also be subjected to Positive Vetting—a system of snooping supported by government and opposition alike because it is for the safety of the state. Why then, the article implies, should similar safeguards not be made available to *private* employers?

The foremost champions of a National Register of Crime are to be found in the larger security firms. Many of these offer to screen their clients' key personnel on a fee basis; access to official records would plainly simplify this task. More importantly, it would help them enormously in checking their *own* recruits.

The guarding and cash-carrying sides of the security business offer unparalleled temptations to the weak and the reckless. This is why Security Express, Securicor and their competitors have been the first employers in this country to adopt national security standards of screening for commercial purposes.

In America, this attitude to recruitment has spread across the entire industrial spectrum. Firms making anything from rubber goods to biscuits often scrutinise the backgrounds, antecedents and opinions of prospective employees as though the fate of the nation hung in the balance. There, the trend was accelerated by the large numbers of policemen and government security staff drawn into industrial security work by retirement or better prospects. The same process is well under way here.

The first Chairman and Managing Director of Security Express was the late Sir Percy Sillitoe, former head of MI5. Detective Superintendent Butler, for two years head of the C.I.D. at West End Central, joined the same firm in 1968 as Head of Security, controlling its 1,000 guards and 400 armoured vehicles. In the same year, Deputy Commander Lewis, once one of Scotland Yard's 'Big Five', resigned his post as Director of Prison Security to join Chubb's. Securicor's staff includes eight ex-chief constables, four ex-assistant commissioners from Scotland Yard, and a former top-flight Interpol man.

The same pattern is visible at all levels of recruitment, not just in the higher echelons. Provincial police forces, in particular, have become seriously worried by the loss of some of their most promising men to industry long before retirement age. Higher pay forms the chief lure. Nottinghamshire police lost six C.I.D. men up to the rank of Sergeant in the last few months of 1968; the Metropolitan Police lose 30 to 40 men a year in the same way. Most join industry as security officers, but many use their skills as free-lancers: over 60% of the entire membership of the Association of British Detectives is made up of ex-policemen. All these men take with them the training and attitudes instilled by years in the Force: they leave behind a wealth of contacts. In America, this 'second police force' liaises closely with the first, exchanging information across a common background. For Britain, land of the 'old boy net', there is a clear moral here.

It is easy to see why the ex-policemen who form so substantial a proportion of the top management of security firms should champion not only a National Crime Register, but a universal fingerprinting system as well. Security is now very big business indeed, and is getting bigger all the time. Securicor, with just over 60% of the 'guarding' and cash transit market, has increased its business at well over 20% a year for the past six years. In 1968, a spokesman for the company said on television: 'We spend between £100-£200,000 on screening and positive vetting each year.' That was in a year when Securicor's turnover reached £11½ million. By 1975 it is expected to hit the £100 million mark. By then, the screening bill for just this one company, let alone the whole industry, will be astronomical. Access to official criminal records would cut it considerably, while a universal fingerprinting system would remove the security officer's greatest fear: that a new recruit's carefully checked identity and character may turn out to have been 'borrowed' from another.

Securicor's screening process closely follows official lines—which is hardly surprising considering the background of those in charge of the operation—and embodies a field investigation which delves as far back as the subject's schooldays. But security firms will never be satisfied until they can add official sources of information to their own. They will admit that the idea may seem distasteful, but plead special circumstances. After all, they point out, we make no secret of our methods. No one is *forced* to apply for a job with us.

By extension, the same argument could be carried over to scores of other jobs involving the handling of money or secrets. If access to official records is allowed in this case, then why not to employers of bank clerks, draughtsmen, or cashiers? No one is more acutely aware than the security firms of the rich opportunities for embezzlement, pilferage and the theft of secrets to be found in almost any business organisation. This uncomfortable fact forms the basis for much of their sales literature. Open the doors of official record depositories to just one outsider, and personnel managers all over the country would be clamouring for entrance.

Employers can already check the names of job applicants against such private stockpiles of information as the 'Records Research Unit', run by Management Investigations Ltd. This chiefly exists to provide the circumstances of any dismissal from previous employment, but can sometimes supply details of criminal convictions as well. For an additional check, they can consult Ian Withers, of Christopher Robert and Co.

Mr. Withers holds the key to the backdoors of more confidential records systems than it is comfortable to think about. He and his staff will tackle all the usual run of jobs which come the way of the private detective. But he offers a plus—his 'Confidential Information Service'.

For the modest fee of five guineas, he will pass on to an inquirer the size of your bank account. Details of withdrawals and deposits cost a little extra. For another five guineas, he will find out if you have a criminal record, and if so, the number of your file in the top-secret Criminal Records Office. In certain cases, he can discover just what that file contains; the fee for this will be the subject of negotiation.

Your driving licence record is most reasonably priced at a mere two guineas. Three guineas will buy your ex-directory telephone number; another three, the address to go with it. A forwarding address from the G.P.O. is slightly more expensive, at four guineas.

Mr. Withers also offers a number of bargain basement items: debt records priced at ten shillings and sixpence; cheque clearance for a guinea; vehicle index numbers, also a guinea. These snippets are cheaper than the rest because, with time and a knowledge of the ropes, Mr. Withers explains, you could probably discover them for yourself. Telephone a credit rating bureau, for instance, giving the name of a local store, and you can often discover what they have filed under your name (or that of your neighbour) by simply asking in a brisk voice: 'Have you anything on Mr. Blank at such-and-such an address?'

At the cost of nothing but a little ingenuity, you can sometimes discover for yourself at least one of the dearer items on the list as well—the state of someone's bank account. Ring his bank and explain that you wish to make a credit transfer in his favour, so could you have the account number, please? A few days later ring back again, quote his account number, and ask for a balance. Often the clerk at the other end of the line will assume you are the account holder, or that your knowledge of the account number entitles you to receive the figure on his behalf.

This approach is a favourite with professional investigators. Asked why it so often succeeds, one London bank manager said defensively: 'What do you expect, with the quality of staff we can afford to employ these days?'

Mr. Withers does not have to rely on uncertain gambits like these. He gets his information straight from the horse's mouth, by employing an extensive network of contacts.

Engagingly, he explains that his prices are governed by the size and number of retainers he is obliged to pay for each category of information. Where he needs to recruit only one contact, he is naturally able to charge less than where he must employ several.

Mr. Withers claims to have spies strategically placed inside all the major banks: at £10 a week apiece, this side of the network alone must cost a fortune. But the retainer stays the same no matter how many inquiries it may cover, and so he has been able to adopt the classic tactic of offsetting his overheads against increased turnover: his fellow-investigators have been circularised with details of his services, and are able to take advantage of them at trade rates. Now tradesmen, loan companies, personnel managers and other interested parties all over the country can take advantage of them too.

Sometimes the details available under the standard 'Confidential Information Service' may not be enough. In such cases, Mr. Withers will quote for a full-scale background investigation. The price for this can run as high as one hundred guineas, and will usually cover not only the subject's possible 'character defects', but a visit to his home and an interview with his wife.

'We'll say anything to get into a house,' admits Mr. Withers. 'We've no moral scruples in that regard. Our clients are paying us X-pounds and we have to get into that address . . . Our agent will call on the wife, neighbours or relatives as if he were conducting a market survey, complete with a convincing-looking form. I can get a letter of authority printed within a couple of hours.'

If a man drinks, beats his wife, enjoys a flutter at the races or maintains a mistress, a 'market researcher' calling next door will usually get to know about it. 'Neighbours can be very helpful,' Mr. Withers emphasises.

To the trained eye, a visit to a man's home can obviously provide all sorts of oblique clues to his character and manner of living. It can also provide evidence of a more direct sort. Investigators of many different categories have discovered to their joy that the moment the average housewife lets a 'market researcher' through her door, she throws discretion out of the window—particularly if she is first sweetened with a gift. Some investigators rely on the persuasive power of a crisp new ten-shilling note. Mr. Withers prefers the more subtle inducement of a large carton of the thickest cream. Once the housewife feels under an obligation she will freely pass on information which she would defend to the death from her neighbours.

The investigator will commonly borrow the name of a perfectly genuine market research firm for his purpose. One spurious survey form much used in the London suburbs—although not by Mr. Withers—is headed with the name of the largest polling organisation of them all. By the time an investigator using this form has completed an interview, he will know the financial affairs of the household concerned in the most minute detail: total income; how spent and by whom (down to bus fares and newspaper bills); consumer durables owned, and if bought on H.P., the monthly payment and name of the finance company concerned; and the exact amount left over as savings when the year's bills have been met.

'Market researcher' is not the only cover available to an agent compiling a 'status' or 'means' report.

'He might knock on the neighbours' doors on the pretext of selling some insurance and ask some questions about the family,' Mr. Withers explains. 'It's surprising what you can find out when you say you are an insurance salesman.'

Those who commission status and means reports turn a blind eye to the cheating, the lies and the bribery so often used to compile them.

'Employers don't ask us how we get our information,' says Mr. Withers. 'They have no scruples about that.'

Big Brother Incorporated

'. . . when a man sets himself up as a hired discoverer of delinquencies, when the amount of his pay depends upon the extent of his employment, and the extent of his employment depends upon the discoveries he is able to make, then that man becomes a most dangerous instrument.'

Comment from the Bench
in Sopwith v. Sopwith, 1859

Credit investigation—christened Big Brother Inc. in America, land of its most luxuriant growth—caters for department stores, insurance companies, finance houses and other enterprises with sound commercial reasons for curiosity about their customers' 'private' affairs. Several hundred million dollars a year go into satisfying that curiosity. Detailed dossiers are available on more than 110 million Americans—almost the entire adult population.

Because a dossier may be consulted by many different organisations, each with its own different conception of the ideal customer, those who compile them provide as complete and detailed a picture as they can, down to including relevant newspaper clippings.

In the U.S. as elsewhere, many credit rating companies have broadened their services to include the investigation of job applicants—one of the many instances of overlapping to be found between different branches of the snooping business—and for them a 'rounded picture' is especially important. Retail Credit Co., one of the largest companies in the field owes a substantial sum of its $135 million annual revenue to this source.

In any file the most important item will naturally be a complete 'credit history' with details of every credit transaction its subject has ever entered into, and of whether he has ever defaulted or been guilty of tardy payment. Hardly less important: the subject's racial origins. Insurance companies are particularly interested in these.

In June 1968, the president of the Hooper-Holmes Bureau (which numbers 10,000 insurance firms among its clients) asserted that his inspectors were no longer specifically instructed to note a subject's colour. This would now be against American law. However, his clients have not lost their interest in the subject, and so he continues to supply the information when requested to do so. 'We have to,' he told the interviewer. Asked why he and his competitors file a subject's sex life, drinking habits and other personal details, he explained that homosexuality, adultery and alcoholism all carry special risks which insurance companies need to take into account when writing a policy.

Credit histories are largely compiled from reports sent to the rating companies by their clients. For other information they rely upon networks of 'neighbourhood spies' who are paid on a per capita basis for their trouble. Some work full time, gathering gossip from neighbours and shopkeepers; others—such as delivery roundsmen—simply keep their eyes and ears open while going about their daily business. Naturally, much of the information reaching the files from these sources is grossly inaccurate. But no one who has been investigated will ever be allowed to see his own file, let alone challenge an entry in it. The F.B.I., the Inland Revenue and other federal agencies, however, can ask to see any file they choose.

Numerous lawsuits and a mounting wave of distress and anger have at last forced Washington to investigate the activities of the credit rating organisations, with an eye to regulating their growth.

The time is ripe for a similar investigation here, where the biggest credit-based spending spree ever has brought the stockpiling of personal information to a pitch not far short of American proportions.

Not that the blacklist business is new to Britain. In one form or another it has been established here for well over a hundred years. What is new is the efficiency of its modern practitioners; the scale of their operations; the completeness of the information they now offer.

Altogether there are about 34 different 'trade protection organisations' in the U.K. Taken together, their files cover more than 20 million people. The lion's share of the business goes to the longest-established firm of them all—the United Association for the Protection of Traders. Founded in 1842, it can supply credit information on over 14 million people from its 26 offices scattered throughout the country. Each year it conducts about two million enquiries on behalf of its 12,000 subscribers.

Second largest in the field is British Debt Services. Founded only ten years ago, it now has details of about five million people on file—much less than U.A.P.T. But since it collects only derogatory information, B.D.S. claims to have an even longer list of 'bad eggs' than its larger competitor which catalogues good payers as well as bad.

The demand for credit information is growing so fast that there is plenty of business left over from the larger organisations to support numerous small firms operating on a local basis. Well over fifty per cent of those defaulting on any credit transaction will be found to have previous records as bad debtors. There has always been a hard core of desperate, dishonest or feckless men and women accustomed to buying goods on credit, selling them for a fraction of their worth, and using the proceeds to begin the whole cycle over again. These people may have literally dozens of convictions behind them. But there is an increasing number of people—tens of thousands of them—who, without making a profession of baulking the credit trader, nevertheless make a habit of it; and tens of thousands more who have in the past entered into transactions in good faith but have been forced into default through circumstances beyond their control.

Credit rating companies are ready with dozens of case histories to prove how dramatically a trader can improve his profits by using their services to identify these people. B.D.S. quotes the instance of a firm of multiple tailors which was at one time losing a steady 6% of sales through bad debts. By introducing a strict system of credit control, and checking out each applicant through B.D.S., losses were halved within two years. Today, bad debts amount to only 1% of their credit sales—a figure which most credit managers would be happy to attain.

The rating companies garner much of their information from *Stubbs Weekly Gazette* which publishes details of all County Court Debt Judgements involving more than £30, and for which payment was not made within a month of the court award. But the vast majority of the nation's bad debts involve sums far smaller than this. For a search fee of one shilling, the credit investigators can look through the central register compiled by the Lord Chancellor's Department, which lists similar details on all judgements involving as little as £10. Each year 400,000 new cases are added to this register, but even so official sources are not adequate for the trader's needs. B.D.S. have estimated that in about 80% of cases, no official facts are published on County Court Judgements; even where publication has taken place, no trader can afford the time to look through endless back-numbers of *Stubbs Weekly Gazette* each time he acquires a new customer.

The rating companies, however, take the vast flood of official information in their stride, and add to it from their own sources. Lists of bad payers sent in by their own clients are especially valuable; some companies even exchange similar lists between themselves on a reciprocal basis.

Every time U.A.P.T. receives a request to check on a name against which it can find no derogatory information, it will assume —unless it later hears to the contrary—that credit was granted and no difficulties encountered. In this way it has built up massive records on sound credit risks as well as bad. To escape their files, honesty is no longer enough.

It is easy for the inveterate credit swindler to change his name; less easy for him to change his address. To spot him, most credit rating firms organise their files on a street-by-street basis. A newcomer to an address with a bad reputation may experience considerable difficulty in obtaining credit until further checks have been made. Street-by-street filing also helps to obviate the risk of one dishonest John Smith blighting the credit prospects of every other John Smith in the neighbourhood. Mistaken identity is a hazard to the trader at large; with the smaller less efficient rating companies it is endemic. More serious still is the possibility that derogatory information may be entered in someone's file quite unjustifiably. A court award may go unpaid for a month, and thus go down in the records, solely because of an illness or absence from home. The fact that it was later paid in full will not appear on the record, unless the person concerned takes the trouble to clear his name with the Lord Chancellor's Department—which will charge him two shillings for the privilege. Even then, the chance that the smaller credit rating companies will pick up the correction and amend *their* records is remote. Rather than run individual checks on request, they issue jumbo blacklists at intervals. Once a man gets onto such a blacklist, he tends to stay there.

And what of the man who buys goods which turn out to be shoddy or defective, and quite justifiably refuses to pay for them? Or who pays for them only after a long battle with the supplier? He too runs a risk of being blacklisted.

The most fertile of all fields for injustice lies in the activities of the paid informers retained by many credit rating companies here, as in the U.S. to provide detailed 'status reports' on people who have applied for substantial sums of credit—to buy an expensive suite of furniture perhaps, or a new car.

U.A.P.T. alone employs some 6,000 part-time agents for this purpose. No doubt they are chosen with care and are most of them doing a disagreeable job conscientiously and with skill. But they live by gossip—a notoriously unreliable source—and are always subject to the temptation of padding their reports with pure invention. Market research firms, which also employ networks of part-time agents to conduct their interviews, have long realised that there will always be some who, when faced with a long walk on a cold day, will prefer to stay at home and fill in forms out of their heads in front of a cosy fire. To combat this problem, they employ large numbers of supervisors who run double-checks on the standard of each interviewer's work. The credit-rating companies run no comparable checking system.

The less reputable rating companies must also answer for the activities of inquiry agents who are *over*-zealous, and by bribery and smooth talking gain access to the confidential information available in such abundance to employees of health, education and other local authority departments.

The growth of private intelligence networks throughout the country does not go unopposed even within the trade. B.D.S., for example, retains no local agents and has a low opinion of status reports. 'I doubt their accuracy,' says Mr. Alan Barker, a B.D.S. director, 'and I feel that frequently they are not worthwhile. Specialist credit reporting is a complicated business and, in my opinion, you just cannot get a national network of suitable agents.'[1]

The credit investigator spends much of his time checking the answers filled in by applicants on the forms which inevitably accompany any H.P. purchase. At the very least, these will require to know a man's occupation, his employer's address, the number of children he has, his existing H.P. commitments. In an effort to reduce the mounting toll of bad debts, traders are increasingly inclined to ask for even more detailed breakdowns of his finances: his wages; his wife's wages; what insurance he carries; whether he owns a car; even his health record.

The answers to these and other intimate questions will often find their way back to a credit rating company's files, and so be-

[1] Quoted in 'Are You a Bad Bet?' Consumer Council survey in *Focus*, 3.4.68.

come available to any client who asks for them. As the rating companies move towards computerisation, and their capacity to handle data becomes virtually limitless, such forms can be expected to become more intrusive still.

British credit managers are already talking of a scheme (first mooted in the *Harvard Business Review* by a Mr. Boggett, of Booz, Allen and Hamilton) which involves the use of a computer to compare a credit applicant's 'profile' against a statistically-determined scale of acceptability. That scale would be based upon a careful analysis of the factors leading to default. Naturally, the more information the computer is given to go on, the more accurate its 'judgements' will be.

But however carefully he may check, and by whatever new methods, the credit trader will always be saddled with a number of defaulters. The computer can help here, too. H.P. companies and others can now buy time (through organisations such as Management Computer Services) on machines which automatically print out individually-addressed default notices the moment an account falls into arrears. Untouched by human hand, these letters are carefully worded to meet the gravity of the case.

The writing of collection letters is a minor art, with its own literature of criticism and fiercely-opposed schools of technique. It owes its development to the fact that the legal collection process is long, slow and expensive. Rather than undertake it, a protracted bout of postal shadow-boxing is often worthwhile. Some creditors themselves practise it on defaulters; others call in the professionals early on in the game.

The professionals fall into two distinct groups. There are those who (like U.A.P.T. and B.D.S., who offer debt collection services as well as credit investigation), are scrupulously careful to avoid the use of 'doubtful' or intimidating phrases. There are also those whose letters consist of little else.

'TAKE NOTICE that failure by you to make a payment . . . may result in your name being registered as a defaulter both locally and nationally,' warns the Central Agency of Defaulters, a London firm. 'This registration will stop you obtaining any further credit in the future.'

'Our Bad Debt Collection Vans (will make) personal calls on you at your home, place of employment or any such other place as you may be found,' promises another firm.

The 'blacklist' gambit is a favourite with collection agencies;

the threat to approach a man's employer (which may be followed by a telephone call to his boss to 'ask permission to interview Mr. X. on the firm's time') runs it a close second. But before resorting to such extremes a collection agency will usually try a straightforward threat of legal action. To make this more effective, it may be cast in the form of a 'Blue Frightener'. Crammed with legal jargon, printed in gothic type on the coloured paper from which it takes it name, this official-looking document is designed to convince its recipient that court proceedings are already under way; that prompt payment alone can halt the legal juggernaut.

The prize for composing the most emotive appeal of all should go to the Premier Debt Recovery Agency of Beckenham, Kent. Theirs is a true virtuoso piece, weaving every known theme of the debt collector's repertoire into a dazzling counterpoint of intimidation.

'We intend to collect if it takes us a Life Time. None of the steps to be taken are very pleasant. Our collectors will call by Day and Night. You will be on the next BLACK LIST to go out to SHOPS, H.P. companies etc . . . we will make you BANKRUPT. BANKRUPT—Receiving Order—Public Examination—Name in *Gazette*—The Petition Etc . . . The only goods we cannot take are your Tools of Trade, wearing apparel and bedding to the value of £20. Really the amount involved is not worth the trouble . . .'

A billet doux on these lines will often make the debtor positively eager to kiss and make up with his creditor. But some are made of sterner stuff. 'There are the hardened debtors who consign your "No. 6 rozzer" to the trash can with a contemptuous sneer,' as one credit-manager put it[2] and others who simply pack their bags and move away to a different address.

Some debt collection agents will go to almost unbelievable lengths to track down an absconder. His relatives and friends will have been primed not to pass on his whereabouts; his employer will probably refuse to do so as a matter of policy. To break the barrier of silence and get that all-important address, the investigator will pose on the telephone as a 'man from the Ministry' ('just checking our records . . .'); G.P.O. official ('An urgent telegram . . .'); hospital almoner ('there has been an accident—we want him to identify the patient . . .') or even Medical Officer of Health ('. . . typhoid contact—possibility of an epidemic—must get in touch with him immediately . . .'). Banks have frequently

[2] *Business Credit and Hire Purchase Journal*, March 1968.

been fooled by the investigator who rings up and poses as the very customer whose address he is after. ('I haven't received my statement . . . You *have* sent it? But to what address? I've just moved, you see . . .')

Armed with an address, the debt collector has two courses open to him. He can proceed with court action in earnest—which can be more trouble than it is worth—or use 'direct action' methods to extract payment or repossess his goods. To the unscrupulous debt collector this latter course can be highly profitable, if hazardous. To collectors operating on a 'no success, no fee' basis, the temptation to use intimidation and actual violence on a debtor who is abusive, or always 'unavailable', or eternally promises payment 'tomorrow' is obviously severe. Many succumb to that temptation. 'Collection agents are uninsurable,' says one specialist. 'It depends on whether you fancy your chances when you go in on a case.' He estimated that when he was not off work nursing his bruises a 'good' collection agent could make around £160 a week. As living on credit becomes even more widespread, and more and more people fall into default, he forecast that 'Repo. men will come into their own, and the violence will grow, whether we have strong laws or weak laws.'[3]

Reputable debt collectors (of whom there are many) are worried about the aura of violence which is growing up around their trade. 'At present,' said one man, who in fifteen years as a private detective has undertaken innumerable debt collection assignments, 'you can have the biggest rogue under the sun chasing a man who is much less of a rogue.'[4] He sees the only alternative as a vast expansion of the present private intelligence systems, coupled with even more intrusive methods of credit checking. The trader regards this prospect with as much gloom as the rest of us. He would dearly love to dispense with the services of debt collectors and credit investigators. They cost money. With more effective legal collection methods, the neighbourhood spy and the hired bully-boy would become superfluous.

Just what *is* wrong with the present legal collection machinery? Before the Debtors Act of 1869, anyone who failed to pay his bills could be thrown into prison. As a method of collection it was not very effective, but it certainly made people pause before running up debts they could not be sure of repaying. After the

[3] 'World in Action', I.T.V., 17.2.69.

[4] Ibid.

1869 Act, no one could be imprisoned for debt *as such*—only for failing to meet a court order to pay a sum thought to be within his means. This made him guilty of contempt of court, for which he could be gaoled for up to six weeks.

From the creditor's point of view, this procedure is strewn with snags. A court order to pay is often fixed at such low levels that it can take years to regain the full amount owed; the debtor can apply at any time to have the amount reduced; and may have to be dragged into court again and again in order to extract even the reduced sum. If a creditor loses patience, he can send the bailiffs in—but they may not find very much when they arrive, and the little they do find will probably not fetch much at today's low second-hand prices.

The extent to which creditors use the law as a weapon with which to threaten rather than strike is shown by the figures: well over 1½ million court warrants to seize goods were issued in 1966—but only just over 3,000 actual sales were held. In the same year, almost a quarter of a million orders to commit debtors to prison were made—but only 3,344 actually *went* to prison. It is hardly surprising that credit traders, in an effort to redress the inadequacies of the law, should have developed their own methods of protecting their livelihood.

Recognising the problem, the government has now thrown our antiquated legal collection machinery into the melting pot. We are now, it seems, to adopt a system which was formerly considered too totalitarian in character to suit the British temper: the attachment of earnings.

At first sight, a scheme whereby a creditor could count on payment deducted from a debtor's wage packet at source would seem ideal from the trader's point of view. Closer inspection reveals a number of flaws.

In Germany, for example, the attachment system works very well—but only because it is backed by highly-organised official tracing machinery. Identity cards and the necessity to register changes of address with the police make it next to impossible for a man whose pay packet is being bled by an attachment order to 'lose' himself.

Here, too, we are moving towards a totally regimented society. The national insurance and tax systems will usually bring a man to the notice of the authorities in time. But if he is determined enough—and particularly if he is self-employed—he can drop out of sight for years. The 'right to disappear' still exists in Britain, although in vestigial form. A moment's thought will show why it is important that it should continue to exist.

Critics of the new attachment system predict two possible consequences both of them unpleasant. Either it will be inefficient, in which case private intelligence networks will continue to flourish and the Rachmans of the debt collector's world will come into their own; or subsequent legislation will make it truly workable at the cost of totally extinguishing the 'right to disappear'.

Tools of the Trade

Not so very long ago, anyone with a deerstalker hat and outsize magnifying glass could imagine himself fully kitted out for the investigator's trade. Today, the Sherlock Holmes image has given way to that of the gadget-bedecked technician. So much detection and surveillance equipment has been devised that a pantechnicon would be required to carry round even a representative selection of it, while its cost would strain the fattest of bank balances.

The state-employed investigator has little need to count the cost of the equipment he uses, but even the humblest private-enterprise snooper finds that money spent in this way can be a worthwhile investment. Not only can it make his job much easier: a lavish display of equipment around the office serves to impress the clientele.

Much of it is American-made, and freely available (at generous discounts of up to 40%) through his trade association. Some British P.D.s retail it to their customers and competitors on their own account, and keep in their filing cabinets enticing catalogues put out by such firms as Criminal Research Products Inc., of Conshohocken, Pennsylvania, and Scientific Detection Products Corporation, of Moorestown, New Jersey. These publications offer reading guaranteed to make any schoolboy's eyes pop with excitement. For self-defence on a dangerous assignment, they offer a choice of over twenty different kinds of club and blackjack, ranging from a miniature shot-filled model in two-tone plaited leather to the sixteen-inch 'Shok-Baton', which at the moment of impact delivers a 'charge of harmless, moderate voltage, low amperage electricity' from its built-in batteries. There is also the Damascus Sap Glove ('give weight to your authority . . . a fine unobvious defensive weapon . . . contains six ounces of powdered lead built into either the knuckle or palm . . .') and the Iron Claw ('a slight twist to the right increases the tension of the grip . . . by numbing the nerve centres . . .').

For identifying that dead body, you can buy a Post Mortem Kit ('special inking tool is supplied to enable you to ink stiff and motionless fingers') and the Tissue Builder Kit ('used to inflate collapsed fingers . . . will enlarge shrivelled fingers to their normal size'). Other chemical aids include a Semen Stain Reagent Kit and other reagents guaranteed to show up anything from narcotics, blood and obliterated numbers to document forgeries and the presence of powder stains on a gunman's hand. Naturally much of this equipment has only the most limited use outside a police department. But the private investigator eager to print on his letterhead—as some of them do—'full forensic laboratory services offered' will acquire all these chemical aids, and many more, with the purchase of the 'Professional Crime Investigator Kit'.

Its 238 different items in a handsome carrying case, complete with 'easy to use instructions', make this a definite bargain at just over £100.

For £1,540 (plus tax) Criminal Research Products Inc. will supply 'an outfit so complete it will not be necessary to purchase additional equipment . . . One purchase and you have a complete, modern, scientific police investigation laboratory. Complete, easy instruction booklets are provided with every item.'

This kit comes complete with a fully equipped darkroom; a library of the 'ten most popular criminology books'; a first-aid kit; filing cabinets and photostat machine; even a lie-detector.

For those with more modest budgets, smaller kits are available to meet specialised aspects of the investigator's role. Private detectives are frequently called in to situations where the presence of the police would be embarrassing or inappropriate, but which demand the use of standard police techniques. For undercover work in a factory plagued by pilfering employees, the P.D. can buy an Official Undercover Investigator Kit. At about £45 this outfit is camouflaged to look like an ordinary briefcase. It contains fingerprinting equipment; a variety of invisible pastes, powders and dyes with which 'bait' can be coated; and a black-light lamp which will cause tell-tale traces on a suspect's hands or clothing to fluoresce brightly.

There can be few investigators who at one time or another have not been robbed of success by a locked door or filing cabinet. Thanks to Criminal Research Products Inc. and Scientific Detection Products Corp., this infuriatingly familiar situation need never occur again. Besides lock-picking outfits with up to sixty picks, tension tools and key pullers in a neat leather case, they supply complete sets of window opening tools, and master keys guaranteed to unlock just about any car on the market. For those who scorn such artificial aids, there is a treatise entitled 'How to Open Locks without Keys or Picks', besides invaluable works such as 'The Safe and Vault Manual', 'Combinations for Master Padlocks', 'Secrets of Locksmithing', and 'How to Make Keys by Impression Method'. Criminal Research Products Inc. also catalogues a tool ('sold only to law enforcement bodies') which even James Bond might envy—a lock release gun. This tool, the brochure claims, will open every kind of pin tumbler lock, including supposedly 'pick-proof' locks. 'Shoot it like a gun—just pull a trigger to open any pin tumbler lock! Simple and easy to use . . . never damages or harms lock mechanisms!'

The strong whiff of Ian Fleming blown into the workaday world of the investigator by chemists and engineers has been intensified to an overwhelming reek by the electronics experts. Again, most of the running has been made by the Americans, whose space programme has produced so many new micro-miniaturisation techniques.

The space-age link has been useful to manufacturers of snooping equipment not only for the technical 'spin-off' it provides, but for publicity purposes as well. Dehart Electronics, for example—a Florida company based almost within earshot of the blast-offs at Cape Kennedy—makes much of the fact that its chief engineer has worked for a space communications company. From the problems of transmitting data across the vastness of space, this man has turned to designing—'with the same precision required in our satellite programme'—devices to relay passionate whispers through a bedroom wall.

Dehart make such old spy-story favourites as the pen bug ('You've read about it. And now we have it'), the shirt-pocket eavesdropper ('powerful enough to amplify whispers 30 feet away') and the instant phone bug ('take out the mouthpiece of the phone, drop in . . . replace the mouthpiece. That's all . . . will run indefinitely from a small amount of current it samples from the phone. . . .'

Also from Dehart—the Minibug, so sensitive it can 'reproduce footsteps on a carpeted floor and transmit them up to a quarter mile'. For surveillance at still longer range they make a repeater unit. 'How often have you wanted a little more range to get out of a residential area?' their catalogue inquires. 'Dehart has done something about it . . . double, triple or even quadruple your range.'

For eyeball-to-eyeball encounters, Dehart's customers can take along the smallest, easiest to use phone bug ever ('Merely borrow the use of the suspect's phone and while talking place the bug under the phone . . . held in place with strong magnets . . .') or the micro-bug ('small and light enough to go undetected, it can be planted as easily as patting someone on the back or it can be slipped into a pocket or purse without arousing suspicion'). The cheapest item on their books is the appropriately-named Super Spy, 'designed exclusively for listening through doors and windows. Ideal for hotel work . . . Turn on the built-in amplifier and plug in the earphone. Presto! You can hear all voices in an adjoining room!'

Another Florida firm to exploit techniques first developed for the space programme at nearby Cape Kennedy is Tracer Investigative Products, of Palm Beach. Their catalogue is small, but contains some really choice items: 'the world's smallest unit for transmitting both sides of a telephone conversation', for instance. 'The size of 12 postage stamps stuck together, this tiny transmitter can be INSTALLED IN SECONDS—inside a telephone—or to the line ANYWHERE—.' Tracer Products also manufacture what they claim to be 'The World's Smallest Wearable Transmitter—the size of a paper book of matches . . . ideal for those "Just you and I conversations",' plus 'the World Famous Sugar Lump Transmitter. The World's smallest, self-contained microphone Transmitter . . . There are innumerable places this unit can be concealed where a larger unit could not, hems of drapes, narrow ledges, behind furniture, behind the flattest of pictures.'

The sugar lump transmitter, at £53.6.0d, is far from cheap. Spotting a hole in the market, a third Florida firm has produced a much more modestly-priced unit, marketed under the engaging name of Tiny Tom. This is 'designed especially for use in a hazardous location where there is a poor chance to recover the unit . . . Every agency should keep at least two of these on hand for use where recovery hazards tend to discourage the use of more expensive units.' Other items sold by this organisation—R. B. Clifton—include the Tiny Tim transmitter ('can be stuck under desks, tables or chairs in seconds') and the Tiny Tattler ('designed for one purpose only—wireless wiretapping. Cannot be detected on line except by visual sighting.').

A 'visual sighting' by his quarry can rob the investigator not only of expensive equipment, but of the opportunity to gather the evidence he seeks. Yet though a man who suspects he is being bugged might track down a transmitter hastily taped to the back of a drawer or behind a picture, modern equipment lends itself so readily to concealment that a visual search alone is most unlikely to detect it. Given time and opportunity, an investigator can build his devices into upholstery, furniture, even into the walls. Transmitters can be added to the circuitry of intercoms, telephones, radios or television sets in such a way that even a qualified electrician would be hard pressed to tell which wires and transistors form part of the original design and which are later additions.

Disguised as a T.V. repair-man or G.P.O. official, the investigator can sometimes 'modify' equipment in this way right under the eyes of his unsuspecting victim. Alternatively, he can plant a bug so cunningly camouflaged as something else that it can safely be left out in full view.

Perhaps the most famous example of this approach is the bugged martini, with swizzle-stick antenna and tiny transmitter nestling inside a hollow 'olive'. Anyone with about £200 to spare can buy one. Just as ingenious, and much more versatile, is the so-called cube tap.

Disguised to look like an ordinary three-way electrical adapter, this device actually functions as a perfectly normal adapter should. Indeed, any electrical appliance plugged into it will increase its efficiency, since it utilises flex as an additional aerial, with consequently greater transmission range. Best of all, it draws all the current it needs direct from the mains, and so can operate indefinitely.

To plant such items as the cube tap is a simple matter. The lonely housewife who offers a cup of tea to the engaging 'salesman' or 'evangelist' who calls at her door with a convincing line of patter unwittingly provides the few seconds needed for the job.

A more subtle variation of this Trojan Horse approach is typified by the 'market researcher' who leaves behind, say, an expensive table lighter. 'A new model we're testing, madam. Yours to keep, of course. May I call back in a week or so for your reactions?'

He may even keep his promise, and on his second visit solemnly note down the housewife's comments before switching the doctored lighter for a more conventional model.

However ingenious the equipment or the methods used to plant it, however well it may be hidden from the eye, the man who knows or suspects that it is there can find it in the end—but only by using electronics to fight electronics.

Commercial organisations on both sides of the Atlantic now offer to sniff out electronically any bugs or microphones that may be hidden on their clients' premises. But a room declared 'clean' today can be all too easily wired for sound in time for tomorrow's board-meeting or lovers' assignation. To meet this threat, debugging equipment to enable even the novice to do a near-professional job is freely obtainable. Needless to say, almost all of it is marketed by the people who make the very same devices it is intended to counter.

Catalogues extolling the undetectability of the latest bug, phone tape or mini-mike also carry—sometimes on the same page—details of equipment guaranteed to sniff them out. One Connecticut firm actually produces a kit in which bugging and debugging devices glare at each other from opposing halves of a neat pigskin case, while Criminal Research Products Inc. (in their typically flamboyant way) offer the Grandaddy of all bugging-cum-counter-bugging kits for a cool £1,665.

This, the 'Master Electronic Intelligence Investigation Outfit', comprises not only the cream of their smaller 'Undercover', 'Secret Agent', 'Espionage', 'Police Stakeout' and 'Counter-Spy' kits, with over fifty different devices including Windowpane, Cufflink and Fingernail Microphones, Broom Transmitter (Without Broom) and Shoe Heel Transmitter (Without Shoes): it also comes complete with Ferret Transmitter Locator and Squealer Microphone Locator.

The manufacturers simply can't lose.

Any good all-band radio receiver will locate hidden transmitters with a high degree of success if its tuning dial is swept slowly through the available wavebands. When the transmitting frequency of a nearby bug is encountered, the speaker sets up a howl which will increase in volume as the signal source is approached. But to save the constant knob-twiddling this process involves, manufacturers have developed a great variety of specialised instruments which scan all the possible frequencies automatically.

'Permits you to determine whether anyone entering your office is wearing a transmitter or has one concealed in his briefcase . . . without the necessity of touching the instrument and without the visitor knowing he has been searched' claim Tracer Products, describing their £75 'Model 195' Locator. 'Determine the exact location of any hidden Room Transmitter or Phone Transmitter within 5 to 10 minutes . . . Can also be used to determine if anyone has placed a Transmitter inside or on your automobile.'

If the clients of professional de-bugging organisations were to guess that (to quote again from the Tracer Products brochure) 'half an hour's practice is all that is needed to make an expert of a novice', then this newest of service industries might suffer a nasty set-back. Realising this, one manufacturer has provided an amiable piece of witch-doctory designed to heighten the mystique of the operation. For double the price of the basic model, they offer a 'built-in beep-tone'.

This optional feature, they candidly admit, 'adds nothing to the detection of ordinary transmitters'. But 'it sounds very similar to the tones from a satellite', and 'makes quite an impression on the client who has engaged you. It also tends to divert him from watching the meter over your shoulder . . .'

The same manufacturer offers a device to detect the presence on any telephone line of the so-called 'tone activated line microphone'. This gadget was first developed in a crude form over thirty years ago. Its highly-refined descendant enables an eavesdropper to listen in to any conversation taking place in the room where the handset is located, by simply dialling the subscriber to whose line it has been fixed. The telephone does not ring, but the cradled receiver is immediately converted into a microphone. The connection can be made from any part of the world from which direct dialling is possible—and without cost, since automatic equipment cannot sense this unauthorised use of the line.

Men whose business frequently takes them away on extended trips sometimes fit these gadgets to their own telephone in home or office so that they can check up on the games the mice are playing while the cat is away. Others fear that competitors may be using this method to eavesdrop on confidential business conferences, and are willing to pay good money for the means to set their minds at rest.

Such means are now available; an ingenious instrument known as a line sweep will infallibly warn of the presence of a line microphone (besides other cruder forms of tap) on its built-in meter. The instrument is very simple to operate, and for professional de-bugging experts its real beauty lies in the fact that they can check their clients' telephones without even leaving their own offices. As one manufacturer points out: 'It takes no great imagination to contemplate the profits available to you, by sweeping the lines of your clients on a regular basis. Do it right from your own office, in less than two minutes.'

Evidently realising that he had written himself into something of a corner by stressing the simplicity of the process so heavily, the brochure's author hastily adds: 'Naturally, some of your clients will insist on buying the line sweep and you may optionally sell them at whatever price you deem adequate.'

However minute or well-hidden a transmitter may be (and now available is a model so small it can be concealed within the thickness of a sheet of wallpaper), the appropriate electronic counter-measures will sniff it out. But a microphone linked by wires to earphones or voice-activated tape recorder is a very different proposition; experienced electronic snoopers always prefer to use this method where they can, especially for long-term surveillance. Radio-bugs are considered more suitable for 'hit and run' assignments.

Microphones of match-head size and almost unbelievable sensitivity can be slipped under doors and windows, or hidden in minute holes bored in plaster or woodwork. Metal detectors and devices to make them resonate can be defeated by burying microphones several inches below the wall surface and leading sound to them through plastic tubes.

Of course, even the best-hidden microphone can be silenced once the wires leading to it are found. But now the undetectable microphone has been matched by the undetectable wire. Conductive paints have now been produced, in shades to match any colour scheme, which will transfer current from microphone to listener as readily as any wire. So the homely paint brush has joined the snooper's armoury.

Mr. Ben Jamil, President of the innocuously-named Continental Telephone Supply Co. ('Contel') of New York, stated only the sober truth when he wrote to an English enquirer: 'Not too many years ago, the only place you could find the type of device contained in this catalogue would be in the pages of a science fiction thriller.'

Up till 1966, Contel's marketing effort in Great Britain had been confined to the mailing of catalogues to interested enquirers. But early in that year Mr. Jamil—a man proud of his nick-name of 'Bugman'—decided that the fast-expanding British market would repay much closer attention. He announced that he would himself head a sales team on a high-pressure attack on the British market, and that 75 of the most sophisticated bugging devices American technology could produce would be put on exhibition at the U.S. Trade Centre in London.

Mr. Jamil's announcement caused a mild stir in the G.P.O. pigeon-coop. 'We are interested in this report,' said a G.P.O. spokesman cautiously. 'What steps we take will depend upon what we discover.'

Mr. Jamil announced his visit at a time of mounting public unease about bugging devices. Only five months before (in December 1965) the Postmaster General had responded to M.P.s' probings with a promise that no further licences for the operation of radio microphones would be granted without his personal authorisation. Investigations into the whole subject of bugging were still in progress, he announced; the ban was designed merely as an interim measure.

Like so many 'interim measures', the one announced by the P.M.G. was little more than an empty gesture. Informed sources doubt if licences to operate equipment of the kind M.P.s were worried about have *ever* been granted to private citizens in this country, although it is rumoured that one private detective did manage to obtain one some years ago, presumably as the result of some official oversight. (It is further rumoured that he was paid a substantial sum by the G.P.O. to surrender it.)

In any case, the problem could plainly not be tackled from the licensing end alone. The chances of anyone actually being caught operating a short-range radio bug were (and are) remote—so remote that not a single prosecution for bugging had at that time been made since the Wireless and Telegraphy Act (which laid down a maximum penalty for unlicensed transmissions of £100 and/or three months imprisonment) had been passed in 1949. Any serious attempt to curb the increasing tendency of P.D.s and others to use bugs would have to concentrate on sweeping them from the market place.

No such attempt had at that time been made. It was perfectly legal to import, make or sell as many bugs as demand would justify—and demand was rising all the time. Only one factor kept it from rocketing to American proportions—price. British-made equipment was mostly thrown together from government surplus components in back-street workshops; the few reliable firms in the field not only lacked American 'know-how', but produced such small batches that prices were well out of reach of the casual purchaser. First-class American equipment was available in unlimited quantities, but distributors had kept profit margins at almost ludicrous levels.

It was this wide-open situation that had so attracted the wily Mr. Jamil. From his New York office, he pointed to the benefits a properly-organised marketing programme could confer upon the British consumer. Mass production, new techniques and stiff competition had led to dramatic falls in the price of American equipment. One device, which only five years before had cost £1,428 was now available for a mere £8.18.0d.

No longer was sophisticated eavesdropping equipment out of reach of all but the professional user. The jealous wife, the husband with a taste for practical jokes, the enquiring child—now they could afford to buy it too.

Another Contel spokesman emphasised that what was good for Contel and its competitors could also be good for companies in other lines of business—British real estate firms, for instance. A microphone hidden in a model home or flat could give the builder a candid insight into the reactions of potential customers, while the sales or rental agent could check on the effectiveness of the sales approach used by his staff.

Contel's spirited championship of orthodox free-market, free enterprise principles caused consternation among the powers that be. Just as 'dirty' books have been accorded a fair degree of toleration in this country so long as they remain in expensive hard-cover form, but often met with prosecution when produced in paperback editions at prices the masses could afford, so the prospect of eavesdropping equipment at popular prices caused official dismay. Inefficiency and high prices had thus far made it possible to ignore the problem. A threat to introduce aggressive marketing techniques (including consumer advertising) on the American pattern made some form of official reaction inescapable.

The G.P.O. announced that Mr. Jamil was free to stage his exhibition as planned. But he would not be allowed to demonstrate any of his devices. Perhaps it was hoped that this move might persuade him to change his plans. If so, it failed. The London exhibition took place, and although no equipment was demonstrated on the premises, at least some of it was later put through its paces at a private house in Wimbledon.

The widespread interest aroused by the Jamil affair prompted numerous 'follow-up' stories in the press. Public interest in the whole subject of electronic eavesdropping came to the boil, and was kept simmering by a number of unsavoury divorce actions fought on the strength of bugged evidence. In July 1967 the authorities brought the first-ever bugging prosecution, against two amateurish P.D.s. In the same month the same firm was convicted a second time, for an almost exactly similar offence.

The authorities' new 'get tough' policy had its effect. Snooping equipment that had been on open display in shops in London's Edgware Road, Lisle Street, Shaftesbury Avenue and Tottenham Court Road vanished under the counter overnight. A number of retailers who had enjoyed a brisk trade in devices for 'phone tapping—the form of bugging involved in the double prosecution—now stopped handling it altogether. But a *Guardian* staffer was still able to find an excellent selection of mini-bugs for sale with no questions asked, and seemed surprised by her discovery.

Since it was not illegal to sell these devices (only to *operate* them—not the shopkeeper's concern) it was not really so astonishing that this traffic should continue. What was astonishing was the degree to which the prices quoted fell below those of less than a year before. One transmitter the size of a packet of ten cigarettes could now be bought for £12; a really first-rate unit—popular with suspicious marriage-partners—with a 400 yard range cost only £65.

Most of the best available equipment was still of foreign origin—American, Japanese, Dutch or German—but in January 1968 British manufacturers received an invaluable piece of Government assistance in the shape of an Order under the Wireless and Telegraphy Act.

Ironically, this was interpreted by the press as an absolute ban on the import, manufacture and sale of bugging devices, and was reported under such headlines as 'Bug Ban will Hit Britain's Private Eyes'. The official explanation for the change in regulations—that it would help to cut down radio and T.V. interference—was seen as a subtle piece of dissimulation. In fact, it was no more and no less than the truth. All the Order amounted to was a ban on transmitters capable of operating on certain overcrowded frequencies: between 26.1 and 29.8 megacycles, and between 88 and 108 megacycles. Transmitters operating on frequencies outside these limits could still be made and sold exactly as before.

British manufacturers seized their chance. With an expanding market right on their doorsteps, it was for them an economic proposition to build equipment incapable of transmitting on the forbidden frequencies; for foreign manufacturers, by and large, it was not.

Today, Britain can boast of snooping equipment as sophisticated as any. Decades ago, the Japanese and Russians skimmed the cream of Western technology by purchasing a single example of each item over the entire stock range offered by their foremost competitors, and then produced faithful copies with improvements of their own. Some British manufacturers have used the same tactics to great advantage.

The discreet enquirer will be shown with pride the American and—poetic justice, this—Japanese originals, and be invited to judge for himself how much smaller and more powerful the British-made equivalent is.

Foreign products are still available on the British market, despite the import ban, but British equipment is improving so fast that the incentive to 'buy foreign' is constantly diminishing. So brisk is the demand that one firm of investigators—Christopher Robert and Co.—not only use bugging devices, but now manufacture them too.

'In 1969 we sold £50,000-worth of our own transmitters and detectors,' said their spokesman. 'We can't manufacture fast enough to fill the demand. In fact, this is our major interest now. We build transmitters into clocks, standard lamps, record players . . .' The firm is also doing its bit towards helping solve the balance of payments problem. 'We sell to a number of overseas governments,' they claim. 'Most of our stuff has gone out on tour in the Middle East.'

This new British growth-industry not only turns out sophisticated mini-bugs, but everything the well-equipped snooper could desire: induction taps, to pluck conversations from a telephone line without even touching the wire; 'spike mikes' which, when hammered (or fired by gun from a distance) into the fabric of a building, turn it into a gigantic sounding board; parabolic and tubular microphones to eavesdrop on conversations at ranges of five hundred feet or more.

Those fascinated by Mr. Vance Packard's catalogue of snooping devices designed especially for the American child, should know that in Britain too the junior spy is no longer neglected. A *Which* report on home-produced eavesdropping toys would probably feature as Best Buy the ingenious 'Space Receiver'. For £2.17.0d, this will pick up distant conversations and relay them through headphones just as daddy's shotgun mike will do.

Not content with churning out variations on themes whose full potential had already been developed by others, British pioneers have now made the Great Leap Forward from imitation to innovation. They are now out there in front, pushing back the frontiers of knowledge with devices such as the Laser Spy Beam.

For situations where access to a building under surveillance is difficult or impossible, this tool is ideal. The eavesdropper need never set foot inside, since he requires no planted transmitters or microphones. Instead, he utilises the minute vibrations set up on a room's window-panes by conversations going on inside. A laser beam focused on the window from outside will be fractionally modified by these vibrations, and the sounds which originally caused them reproduced.

Spy story addicts have been familiar with this principle for quite some time. In practice, it presented severe difficulties. Yet Pilkington's, Britain's go-ahead glass people, managed to perfect this device simply as a publicity tool.

Demonstrating it in London in July 1968, the company's chairman admitted: 'We developed it as a gimmick and then realised its enormous espionage significance.'

A great many other people realised it too. Present at the demonstration were delegates from forty countries, including Russia, Hungary, Czechoslovakia and Poland.

The laser spy beam can be guarded against by the simple expedient of fitting double-glazing: a moral which Pilkington's no doubt hoped would not be lost on their audience.

Double-glazing is not the only use to which glass can be put in an anti-eavesdropper role. The Americans have developed a demountable glass cubicle, to be set up as a room-within-a-room in embassies where they suspect the fabric to be so riddled with hidden microphones that it would have to be taken apart brick by brick to find them all.

It is in fact frequently safer to assume the presence of bugs or taps—to learn to live with them—rather than to rely too much upon the infallibility of 'squealers' or 'sniffers'. The problem then becomes not one of tracking down and deactivating them, but of finding ways to render them useless even though they remain in operation.

British manufacturers have now turned their ingenuity to solving this problem also.

The scrambler telephone, once the prerogative of V.I.P.s, has now been brought within the reach of everyone by an Essex firm, Standard Telecommunications Ltd. To the unauthorised listener, conversations put through their CODEC (short for coder and decoder) will sound rather like the sound-track of a Mickey-Mouse cartoon run in reverse. It is cheap to buy and (here lies its main innovation) is completely portable. It will work happily with any standard telephone, and so the security-conscious businessman can carry one with him at all times to defeat not only the professional telephone tapper, but curious switchboard staff in hotels and elsewhere.

A well-tested means of stopping concealed electronic ears is to hold confidential tête-à-têtes in the bathroom with all the taps running, or to the accompaniment of a radio turned up at high volume. The human ear is sensitive enough to tune out the confused background noise; the microphone is not. That, at least, was the theory until recently. Sophisticated audio-filters and highly selective microphones can now render this precaution useless.

To restore the status-quo, Lustraphone Ltd. sell a 'noise machine' guaranteed to baffle even the most up-to-date snooping equipment. Users of their 'Transphone' can carry on top-level discussions equipped with throat-microphones which ignore the deafening rushing sound generated by the machine, and relay only their voices to the earphones of the man across the table. Cumbersome, but effective, at about £100 for a two-man kit.

How do you cope with the man you suspect of using a hidden tape-recorder to take down your words for later use as evidence against you? A B.B.C. reporter who smuggled a recorder into the Russian embassy some time ago was chagrined to discover when he emerged into the street after the interview that his tape was a complete blank. This most tactful of all methods for dealing with the problem is now available to all. You need simply arrange for your departing visitors to pass through a magnetic field strong enough to erase any tapes they may be carrying. While the electricians are installing the necessary equipment, they can also put in detectors to 'frisk' your visitors for concealed weapons and other hardware as they arrive.

Having made up for lost time in what is clumsily termed the 'electronic audio-surveillance field', British researchers are now hard at work on the more difficult challenge presented by 'electro-optical' surveillance methods.

Much of the groundwork has again been done by the Americans, as a direct result of their space programme. With the availability of fist-sized T.V. cameras capable of relaying pictures from the moon, it was inevitable that a use would be found for them nearer to home—perhaps *your* home.

The old proverb that 'one picture is worth a thousand words' takes on new point in a world where T.V. cameras only four inches thick can be concealed within the thickness of a wall or ceiling, their lenses hidden by screens which shield them from view without in any way interfering with their picture-taking ability. Even the much larger cameras mass-produced by such Japanese firms as Shibaden and Sony—and readily available in Britain—can be pressed into unobtrusive service by the spy: concealed in any convenient piece of furniture, they can scan events and objects outside their immediate line of vision by utilising the reflections in a mirror hung on the wall. Nothing is hidden from these silent witnesses, even after dusk. Many years ago Alexander Baird, the great pioneer of television, dreamed of what he called 'noctovision'—the T.V. eye that would see in the dark. In October 1968, Marconi of Chelmsford demonstrated that Baird's dream is well on its way to fulfilment. The company now has television cameras which will work effectively in light no stronger than is given out by an overcast moon.

With the aid of an infra-red light source, first-class pictures can be taken even in pitch darkness, not only of objects actually present at the instant the picture is taken, but of the ghostly images of objects no longer there; while an observer armed with a military 'snooperscope' can use infra-red to observe nocturnal events as closely as he would hope to do with a pair of excellent binoculars at high noon.

In America, electronic snooping is no longer the exclusive province of professionals. It has become a national craze. If we in Britain ever had any justification to feel superior, to feel 'it couldn't happen here,' that justification has now disappeared. Every snooping device the Americans pioneered is now available here, down to that almost touchingly archaic device, the two-way mirror. An employee of J. Pearson and Sons, a London firm who sell their 'Peer-glasse' two-way mirrors at £2 a square foot, revealed a few years ago that 'The man who invented them was an American who put them into bathing huts. He ended up in Alcatraz.'

A Glimpse at the Future

'If you want a picture of the future, imagine a boot stamping on a human face—forever.'
George Orwell: 1984

Confronted with the canvas of the future, the prophets of the past have made it almost a point of honour to load their brushes with only the most sombre colours. Today they mostly confine themselves to one—an unrelieved black. From the editorial offices of *Amazing Stories* to the think-tanks of M.I.T., the forecasts are filled with gloom and desolation. Those which do not envisage the total destruction of mankind in an atomic holocaust foresee instead a rigid totalitarianism: brutally repressive, as in Orwell's *1984,* or camouflaged with hedonistic licence, as in Huxley's 'Brave New World'.

With nuclear weapons already available in quantity enough to sterilise the planet ten times over, a pessimistic view of man's survival is easily shared. But why the assumption, on the part of so many non-Marxist writers, that in the long run totalitarianism is sure to triumph over the democratic idea?

A universal Big Brotherdom may be created by ideological passion, or the love of power for its own sake. But the consensus of prophetic opinion holds that it is more likely to arrive as a mere by-product of the search for efficiency.

In government and business alike, efficiency was formerly regarded largely as the product of intuition and experience. Today it is seen rather as the product of *technique*. Organisation and decision-making have become increasingly formalised, approached in accordance with sets of standardised analytical procedures. The more precise the technique, the fewer the variables it can tolerate. The planner demands more and more control: his scheme is like a fine watch, in which every part must operate precisely and predictably. One faulty component acting in an unforeseen way will ruin the accuracy of the whole.

To the new-style politician and administrator, 'the State is not the expression of the will of the people nor a divine creation nor a creature of the class struggle. It is an enterprise providing services that must be made to function *efficiently* . . . Political doctrine revolves around what is useful rather than what is good . . . (and) as the political form best suited to the massive and unprincipled use of technique, dictatorship gains in power.'[1]

In wartime, even the most ardent democrat recognises the need to subjugate the individual to the collective; that it is more efficient for some central authority to decide priorities and pursue them ruthlessly. Individual freedom inevitably suffers in the process, but this is regarded as part of the price of victory. Totalitarian states regard that price as well worth paying in peace as well as in war: the democracies may soon be forced to pay it too. 'Cold war,' writes Ellul, 'is as productive as hot war in forcing the democracies to imitate the dictatorships in the use of technique.'[2]

To the rulers of a small overcrowded island burdened with vast overseas debts, the temptations of technique are especially strong—of *any* technique, so long as it promises to help us out of the mess we are in. Government has become increasingly authoritarian, increasingly inclined to lay down priorities and decide the 'one best means' of achieving them. There is a National Plan for everything now. As yet, the checks and balances of democracy force the planner to follow a zig-zag course. Like ancient trees in the path of a super-highway, these have weathered the storms of the past only to become obstacles on the path to progress and efficiency. Many have already been pruned back, or uprooted to allow the planners room to pass, and their mutilation has hardly been noticed by the average citizen. The State already controls huge areas of our lives once thought sacrosanct to individual choice and action. In the future, and from the highest possible motives, individual choice in any but the most trivial matters may be extinguished altogether.

The danger lies in the fact that to the planner, the State must be treated as an organic whole. Everyone and everything in it must be quantified, evaluated and reduced to streams of electrons for his computers to handle. There is a limit to the number of individual characteristics and aspirations that even the most sophisticated computer can handle; they must be averaged out and categorised. The technique that eventually emerges from the machine's calculations can take into account only broader categories still.

[1] R. K. Merton, in intro. to 'The Technological Society', by Jacques Ellul, Jonathan Cape Ltd.

[2] Jacques Ellul, op. cit.

On America's computer-run campuses, students frustrated by their treatment as walking I.B.M. cards have paraded with placards reading 'I am a human being. Do not fold, spindle, or mutilate.' To the planners, such protests seem irresponsible or senseless. They know themselves to be well-intentioned. Mathematically, their techniques cannot be faulted. Therefore any attack upon them must be the product of either frivolity, ignorance or mental instability, to be countered not by a change in the technique, but a change in the critic's viewpoint.

Here lies the main threat for the future. Standardised techniques ideally require standardised factors, standardised people. As William Whyte showed in his book 'The Organisation Man', large industrial corporations can achieve something close to this ideal, successfully moulding their employees into the corporate image. Planners who regard the State as a gigantic holding company for the individual enterprises wholly or partly under its control, and the evolution of remedial techniques of government as simply another management problem, tend to skate over one vital difference between 'Great Britain Limited' and an ordinary business. Large industrial corporations can only produce smoothly-engineered cogwheels for the company machine because their personnel selection techniques screen out all but suitably malleable recruits. The State however cannot pick and choose its 'personnel'.

If it demands rigid conformity and blind obedience from its citizens, then those too staunchly individualistic to be moulded must be ground into shape; those more obdurate still must be 'rejected' altogether. Up till now totalitarian regimes have tended to rely upon systematic terrorism to accomplish the grinding process. Rejection has usually taken the form of exile or (more usually) murder. The elimination of 'anti-social elements' from the body politic is a standard technique of tyrannies of both the right and left. Hitler liquidated six to eight million Jews; Mao Tse-tung has admitted to the killing of 800,000 'revisionists' even after armed opposition to his rule had long ceased; Stalin's murder of the half million people of the Chechen-Ingush Autonomous Republic was just one incident in a campaign of genocide that (according to Kruschev's famous speech in 1956) included the Karachays, the Balkars, the Volga Germans, the Crimean Tartars and the Kalmuks.[3] Such 'Final Solutions' to the problem presented by

[3] These figures are taken from 'The New Radicalism', by Brian Magee, Secker & Warburg Ltd.

stubbornly-individualistic persons or ethnic groups cannot of course be discounted as a future possibility.

By the end of the present century, conformity in all things and at all times may be a matter of practical necessity rather than ideological orthodoxy. A child born today will (on present trends) see within his lifetime the emergence of an almost exclusively urban society, with cities of 1,000 million inhabitants and more. If such monstrous antheaps are to function at all, regimentation of an unprecedented thoroughness will have to be imposed. Permits will be needed for everything from a walk in the park to a glass of water. But conformity, although more necessary, will be more difficult to enforce. Automation will see to it that a substantial proportion of the populace will be unemployable, living a battery-hutch existence in which idleness and overcrowding will combine to produce a socially-explosive mixture of aggression and severe alienation. Governments may be forced to hammer home again and again the truth of Chairman Mao's axiom: 'Political authority grows from the barrel of a gun.' In fact, thanks to science, the political authority of the future is more likely to grow from the test-tube or the electronics laboratory.

Whereas to Big Brother power was an end in itself, maintained through pain and the threat of pain, to the technocrats who are now transforming our society power is simply a means to an end: that of greater efficiency. As a means of encouraging obedience, the carrot is more efficient than the stick—or so the behavioural psychologists tell us. Although the stick will have its place in the tyrannies of tomorrow, it will be needed less and less.

When Aldous Huxley wrote his 'Brave New World' in 1931, he envisaged for the sixth or seventh century A.F. ('After Ford') a totalitarianism in which punishment played almost no part. 'Socially undesirable' characteristics had been almost entirely eliminated from the race by selective breeding. The malleable human material provided by the geneticists was then thoroughly conditioned to passivity from birth, and kept that way with unlimited quantities of drugs, sex and other distractions. When 'Brave New World Revisited' came out in 1958, Huxley compared his vision of the future with Orwell's, and argued that his own had stood the test of time far better. Orwell conceived the idea for *1984* in 1943, and published it in 1949, and so it was quite natural, said Huxley, that he should have taken Hitler and Stalin as his models for Big Brother. But developments inside Russia, and the progress of science and technology had reinforced Huxley's belief that the future lay with dictators of a less violent stamp. But first, he believed, there would be a transitional period in which totalitarian regimes would experiment with the techniques of 'Brave New World' while relying upon the more traditional methods of Big Brother as a backstop.

Some day the social engineers may indeed succeed in making rigidly orthodox thought as natural and involuntary a function of the human mind as breathing is to the body. Until then it will still be necessary for any dictator to watch ceaselessly for signs of deviation. With the sort of gadgetry discussed in earlier chapters, near-universal surveillance is a technical possibility even now. What new techniques of surveillance and control are on their way?

It is conceivable that *all* telephone calls (and routinely bugged conversations in bars, hotels, offices and elsewhere) will soon be scanned by high-speed computers for underworld jargon, obscenities, the names of political organisations, key words such as 'subvert', 'kill', 'strike', 'protest', 'organise', 'infiltrate', 'oppose'—even for argumentative or threatening tones of voice. Conversations distinguished in these ways will be automatically recorded for later investigation. Identification of the speakers will be a simple matter: the voice-pattern of every citizen will naturally be recorded (together with his retinal and caligraphy patterns and his fingerprints) on his dossier at the computerised national data bank.[4]

It would take a whole library of books to explore all the advantages which computers offer for mass-surveillance work. In France, they have evolved a new kind of 'punch card' passport to speed immigration facilities at airports. Under the new system—originally planned to come into operation before 1970, when the first jumbo jets will start bringing in passengers in batches of 300 and more—French citizens will simply drop their new postcard-sized passports into slots at the control barriers. Each card will carry a colour photograph of the holder; his personal details will be printed in magnetic ink on the back. The photograph will be projected life-

[4] A universal fingerprinting programme for all British males was officially mooted in 1967, and met with surprisingly little opposition. Opinion polls showed a substantial percentage of the public to be actually *in favour* of the scheme. To be successful, it would require computers capable of a finer degree of accuracy in pattern identification than is yet possible. Glasgow police and Strathclyde University are now working to overcome this problem, which is linked with research on cervical smear and calligraphy identification. The Strathclyde Investigation is additional to the long-term study being conducted by the Home Office Research Unit.

size onto a screen for the immigration officer to see; the coded information will be read off by a computer, recorded, and then checked against the files. The process is almost instantaneous. Any 'wanted man' will find himself under arrest seconds after his passport hits the slot.

In some American states, police are already able to draw on computerised records for an instant radio check on persons stopped in the street, while in New York, they have experimented with a system whereby the licence plates of cars crossing a bridge into Manhattan were passed to a computer programmed with the details of all outstanding parking and traffic violations. Drivers with unpaid tickets were arrested before they even got to the other side of the bridge. Soon the whole process could be automatic—an electric eye to read the number plates, and an automatic barrier to immobilise a lawbreaker's car until he fed the appropriate fine into a slot or (in more serious cases) until the police arrived.

A refinement of this system would release for other work many of the policemen now tied up on traffic-watch. Exceed the speed-limit on a deserted road late at night, or fail to obey a halt sign or a red light, and a computer linked to a vehicle-identification device would immediately start printing out a demand for a fine—or simply deduct the amount from your bank account.

New proposals for the control of London's traffic show how computers could even be used to keep tabs on the exact whereabouts of any citizen at any time. To deal with congestion in city streets, Britain's Road Research Laboratory has come up with a 'pay as you drive' scheme. This would involve fitting to every vehicle a meter which could be activated by impulses sent out by electrical 'check-points' set in the road surface. In February 1969, contracts to develop four different kinds of meter were placed with a number of electronics firms. One of those firms—Plessey—has been asked to devise a unit capable of transmitting a coded signal giving the vehicle's identity to a computerised central control, which would then notch up charges just as telephone equipment does—and presumably allow the same facility for tracing a 'call'.

One of the many developments which Orwell could not have foreseen was that Big Brother would go into orbit. In April 1960, an optics expert[5] at the University of Rochester stated that it was practicable to develop lenses capable of resolving two objects three inches apart from an altitude of 125 miles. By 1961, America had

[5] Howard S. Stewart, writing in *International Science and Technology.*

her SAMOS satellites in orbit over Russia; a year later, the Russians had their COSMOS spy satellites orbiting over the U.S.A.

SAMOS was designed to take photographs with detail equivalent to what the human eye could distinguish at 100 feet; in some orbits it could resolve objects only 30 inches across. The MIDAS satellites put into operation at about the same time used infra-red detectors to defeat darkness and cloud-cover. MIDAS equipment was so sensitive that, according to one source,[6] it could detect a lighted cigarette at eight miles. At one test-firing its sensors reacted to the presence of a simmering coffee-pot near the launching pad.

In recent years, a security blanket has been lowered over advances in the spy satellite programme. For all any outsider knows, the Pentagon may now be able to study photographs with enough detail to make it possible to count the fleas on a Russian general's mistress's dog's back. It has however become plain that surveillance from space has its uses outside the military and meteorological fields. A faculty member[7] at Berkeley (who combines a specialist knowledge of forestry with expertise in aerial photography) has suggested that it should be used to prevent the violation of atmospheric pollution laws; to suppress illegal fishing, mining and logging; and to detect tax-evasion through the use of land for purposes undisclosed to the authorities. But why stop there? Ultra-long range surveillance is only necessary on foreign territory because—as Powers discovered too late—anti-aircraft missiles can knock out of the sky even such high-flying aircraft as the U2. For domestic law enforcement cameras could safely be brought much closer to the ground. Courting couples and the lonely hiker may soon be brought under observation from the sky—and within earshot too. In 1963, it was learned that American planes flying over Cuba had been equipped with listening devices so sensitive that the noise of machinery operating on the ground—even the smallest portable generator—could be pinpointed from above.

Thanks to Orwell, the concept of universal monitoring has become inextricably linked in the minds of many with a regime both capricious and cruel, violent and cynical. But unremitting surveillance could just as easily become the hallmark of a mild and well-meaning paternalism. As electronic eyes and ears become cheaper, and familiarity with their use breeds public apathy, both government and business can confidently be expected to rely upon

[6] 'The Invisible Government' by Wise and Ross, Jonathan Cape Ltd.
[7] Robert Colwell.

them more and more. In America, and to a lesser extent in Britain, audio-visual monitoring is now commonly used in public transport systems, places of entertainment, banks, stores and the lifts and passageways of apartment buildings. In their study *The Year 2,000,*[8] Kahn and Wiener forecast that, perhaps as early as 1980, an escalating crime rate may lead to T.V. cameras and microphones being hidden as a matter of course in hotel rooms, offices and college dormitories. At first, monitering will be carried out solely for the protection of the public. But the increasing stress laid upon mental health, and the social engineers' burning desire to understand the 'whole man', may lead to psychiatrists and social scientists being given access to the tapes and films produced, and eventually to the monitoring devices themselves. To them, crime springs from maladjustment; it is something to be cured, not punished. Given diagnostic tools of sufficient accuracy—today's personality tests writ large—it then becomes perfectly logical to pull a man in for treatment *before* he breaks the law.

To some extent society does this already. But we distinguish sharply between the man who is 'responsible for his actions' and the man who is not. In the future that distinction may disappear entirely. Then there will be no crime—only maladjustment of varying degrees; no prisons—only hospitals; no policemen—only medical orderlies. And instead of a judge, a jury and an indictment, there will be a committee of men in white coats, a sheaf of graphs and a videotape machine.

To the technocrats who will run tomorrow's hive-state, what greater evidence of maladjustment could there be than a desire to thwart the beautiful logic of their planning? What worthier cause for treatment than the desire to make each citizen happy and contented in his appointed place in the computerised scheme of things?

Leaving aside for the moment the question of how hard-core dissidents would be dealt with—how could the rulers of a totalitarian Britain soothe the discontents of the overcrowded, under-employed masses?

For his 'Brave New World' Aldous Huxley dreamed up the wonder-drug 'soma'. It damped down aggression; increased receptivity to state propaganda and conditioning; and (according to dosage) produced happiness states ranging from lazy contentment to euphoric hallucinations. A dictator armed with such a tool would have no need of baton-charges or machine guns: his subjects

[8] Published by Macmillan (New York) 1967.

would find obedience and conformity not merely easy but agreeable.

Behaviour-influencing drugs already account for a substantial slice of Britain's medical prescriptions. The hypnotic/sedative barbiturates figured on 15 million prescriptions in 1961. By 1965, the total had risen to 17 million. Drugs to deal with the same basic problem while leaving the user reasonably alert are also gaining a wide popularity. Since the first tranquillisers—reserpine, chlorpromazine and meprobomate—appeared in the mid-fifties, dozens of variants have been hatched in the laboratories. In 1967, one or another of them appeared on 14,700,000 prescriptions in England and Wales. In the same year, doctors wrote 4,900,000 prescriptions for anti-depressants and 4,800,000 for stimulants and 'appetite suppressants'. In America, *one in every three* prescriptions is for pep-pills, sleeping tablets, tranquillisers or anti-depressants.

Every time a doctor makes out a prescription for any of these, he has a difficult question to ask himself: just what is a 'normal' or 'socially desirable' state of mind? We all of us experience tension and depression to some degree. At what point can we legitimately expect psychochemical help? The states induced even by such soma-substitutes as we already have are so attractive that one addiction expert has estimated that black-market usage alone may run as high as one in five of the population. If they were as freely available as alcohol or cigarettes, how high would usage run then?

Faced with a vast population of overcrowded, workless citizens, even such an ancient and unsophisticated drug as cannabis might seem the answer to a dictator's prayer. '. . . the effect of the drug is to create a proneness to inertia and lethargy, it is not likely to lead to aggressive behaviour, (but) is more likely to lead to a general passivity . . . it can also decrease sexual performance.'[9]

As yet there is no one drug combining all the characteristics of soma. But the crop of behaviour-influencing drugs is increasing yearly. The development of the right psychochemical package would seem to be only a matter of time. In 'Brave New World', it took six years' work by 2,000 pharmacologists and bio-chemists, and the work was done. We have not yet given 'Manhattan Project' status to the search; but Gardner Quarton, of Michigan's Mental Health Research Institute, believes that within the next 25 years the present systematic research into basic brain mechanisms will bear fruit in the shape of a whole new range of psychochemicals which will allow us to create and control any mood we choose—or

[9] 'Drugs and Civil Liberties'. NCCL, 1967.

which may be chosen for us.

Among them may well be a drug to enhance suggestibility. In sodium amytal, pentothal and scopolamine we already have three drugs for this purpose—although their side-effects rule them out for long-term use. More sophisticated versions could be added, like fluoride, to the water supply; or form a constituent of a state-supplied ration of happy pills. With backing like this, even the clumsiest propaganda would strike home with the power of divine revelation.

Too elaborate for mass use perhaps, but invaluable for the treatment of citizens so seriously 'maladjusted' that they actively oppose the regime, are new techniques for the direct stimulation of the brain. Experiments with the use of electrodes for this purpose have been in progress for almost a century. Now they have reached breakthrough point. At Yale, Dr. Jose Delgado has for several years been experimenting with hair-fine electrodes implanted in the brains of a colony of monkeys. The electrodes are connected to a socket cemented to the skull. A micro-miniature radio receiver is strapped to each monkey's back, and is then plugged into the socket. Using a transmitter, Dr. Delgado is thus able to stimulate chosen areas of the brain by remote control. A variation involves the implantation of very fine tubing instead of electrodes; in this technique, each monkey is provided with a minute pump, and carries a supply of drugs in a capsule slung around its neck. A radio signal is used to activate the pump, which injects a precisely-metered quantity of chemical through the tubing deep into the animal's brain. With electrodes and 'chemitrodes', Dr. Delgado has been able to produce responses which include: complete inhibition of appetite; aggression; terror; pleasure; sexual excitement; panic; disorientation; and agonising pain.

Dr. Fisher, a psychologist on the staff of the University of Pittsburgh, has conducted similar experiments on rats. An injection of acetylcholine at a certain 'interchange point' in a rat's brain will stimulate him to drink; testosterone will cause him to build nests; noradrenaline will produce hunger. At the University of Michigan, Dr. Bernard Agaroff has blanked out the memories of goldfish with injections of the antibiotic puromycin. Dr. Murray Jarvik, working at the Albert Einstein Medical School in New York, has developed a specialised electro-shock treatment that does the same thing to rats.

From monkeys, goldfish and rats the researchers have now turned to human experimental material. At Tulane University and elsewhere, patients suffering from mental and other diseases have been wired up just like Dr. Delgado's monkeys, with the difference that they are themselves given control over the excitation buttons. There are normally three of these, attached to a small device worn at the belt. Feelings experienced have ranged from euphoria of varying degrees to sexual excitement just short of the orgasmic, with occasional instances of nausea, frustration, fear and anger. Patients in the grip of violent seizures have been calmed in an instant by attendants who managed to get to the right button in time.

As the brain is charted in greater detail, the range of responses to be called forth by the excitation of the proper area will certainly increase. Theoretically, it should eventually be possible to manipulate a man like a puppet—to take him over completely by remote control. In fact, it would probably be enough to scramble the thought-processes of a hard-core dissident just enough to render him incapable of sustained or complicated thought, or to make him permanently timorous; and to fit an emergency 'pain circuit' which, when activated, would bring him to the hospital begging for relief.

Eventually it should be possible to conceal the signal receiver and power source inside his body in such a way as to leave no physical trace—and then to wipe from his memory all *mental* traces of the operation as well.

Candidates for this drastic form of therapy could easily be singled out long before they had the chance to threaten the status quo. Personality testing (already a standard feature of the American educational system) could single out potential deviants while still at school. Further investigation would of course be needed to establish the precise degree of their maladjustment. For this purpose, a more sophisticated version of the present-day electroencephalograph could well be used.

Some modern EEG machines have 34 channels; most have only eight—that is, they monitor the electrical activity of the brain through eight electrodes taped to the skull, and reproduce traces of that activity on a graph. Each channel will record information at the rate of approximately 3,600 amplitudes a minute. So in the course of an average recording period of about twenty minutes, the pens of even an eight channel machine will trace well over half a million peaks and troughs, all of them potentially meaningful. Until recently, only about one hundredth of one per cent of that information could be interpreted. The rest was unintelligible—mere 'background noise'. Gross brain damage or abnormality was fairly easily recognised, but in the normal brain little could be distinguished from the pattern except the onset of dreams in a sleeping subject, and marked mood changes in a waking one. Now however computer analysis has made much of the 'background noise' intelligible. Experimental subjects have been exposed to a wide range of stimuli, and the resulting pattern changes analysed by computer. (Each subject is exposed to the same stimulus several times, since on any one recording the background noise tends to blanket the meaningful signals.) The responses are then averaged out, and the computer 'learns' to recognise that reaction in the future. This technique has now made it possible to isolate the response to stimuli as trivial as a flicker of light or a light tap on the arm. At M.I.T. there is a specially-designed machine whose very name is a warning. It is called ARC—Average Response Computer.

ARC is still a long way from being able to unravel the complexities of human thought, but could already be used as a highly efficient lie-detector. Traditional lie-detectors rely upon measurement of changes in heart-beat, blood-pressure, breathing and the electrical resistance of the skin—techniques first applied to interrogation work late in the nineteenth century, and combined in the first really practical machine (the Keeler Polygraph) as long ago as 1926. Only minor refinements have been made since, yet under the most favourable conditions and in the hands of an expert, these comparatively crude machines have an established reliability rate of 80-95%. Not good enough for a court of law, perhaps, but quite accurate enough for Big Brother. The C.I.A. is currently developing a lie-detector so camouflaged that a subject can be examined without even knowing it. Christened the 'wiggle seat', the machine looks like an ordinary office chair—but isn't.

With a really sophisticated EEG lie-detector at his disposal, Big Brother would not need to watch all of the citizens all of the time. He would merely run periodic checks on everybody, as some American employers already do. As one of them explained to a reporter some years ago, regular checks are of great value in 'assisting employees to give greater attention to matters of integrity, honesty and loyalty'. Yes indeed.

The most satisfactory way to produce standardised people for a standardised world would of course be to breed them that way. In 1931 Huxley imagined a Brave New World inhabited by three specially-bred classes of sharply differing intellect; random reproduction was a thing of the past. In 1958 (in 'Brave New World Revisited') he wrote that although the centralised control of reproduction could not be completely discounted for the future, it could 'for practical purposes' be ruled out. Today it is difficult to be so sure.

There are three main ways in which a society of Alphas, Betas and Gammas could be produced. These are: 'selectionist' eugenics; 'transformationist' eugenics; and bio-engineering.

Selectionist eugenics would involve breeding for required characteristics while preventing all 'genetically undesirable' births. This could be accomplished by adding a birth-control agent to the water-supply, and will almost certainly be a technical possibility within the near future (the Vatican is particularly worried by this thought). An antidote, or supplies of pure water, would only be made available to selected breeding stock.

There are numerous practical drawbacks to this scheme. To eliminate all undesirable characteristics from the genetic stock of an entire nation would be either painfully slow, or would involve cutting back the population to a quite impracticable extent. John Maynard Smith, Professor of Biology at London University, has pointed to a more satisfactory solution—clonal copying. Soon, he says, it may be possible to remove the nucleus from a human egg (fertilised or unfertilised, it makes no difference) and to replace it with the nucleus from a germ-line cell from an individual whose genotype Big Brother may wish to reproduce. The result? An exact genetic duplicate of the donor, as like him as an identical twin. Even with artificial insemination, only half the donor's genes can be transmitted; clonal copying will pass them on in their entirety, making it possible to produce a dozen carbon-copy Einsteins, or ten million near-moronic machine-minders. This process, says Professor Smith, is 'likely to be feasible in the fairly near future'.[10] If no entirely suitable genotype for clonal copying is available, 'transformationist eugenics' may make it feasible to create one. Molecular biologists have recently made rapid strides in the identification of many of the genes leading to the formulation of sex, physical characteristics and even mental defects. Further research may allow the removal of any imperfections which mar the gene

[10] 'Eugenics and Utopia'. Essay in Vol. 5 of the Daedalus Library: 'Utopias and Utopian Thought' Ed. by F. E. Manuel, Houghton Mifflin, Boston, Mass.

string of an otherwise ideal donor. The bio-engineers could then go to work, refining the development of the offspring still further with surgical and chemical techniques. The educators and propagandists would complete the job. What Huxley called 'the nightmare of total organisation' would then truly be with us.

No one can say when that nightmare will begin. Indeed, its very nature will ensure that by the time it is in full swing, the populace will be too well-conditioned to see it as a nightmare anyway. Like the kindly parents of idiot children, our rulers will do their best to satisfy every popular whim. They will chastise only when forced to it, and will rarely need to chastise at all. Occasionally there may be throwbacks who, dimly remembering something of what is lost, struggle to regain it. Winston Smith, rebel hero of *1984*, was driven back along the road to orthodoxy by torture and overwhelming humiliation. For the errant citizens of a computer technocracy the return to acceptance and conformity is likely to be wholly painless, but although the means of reformation may differ, the end in view is the same. The rebel would be taught not merely to accept the status quo, but to cherish it. He would be brought to realise that 'it was all right, everything was all right, the struggle was finished. He had won the victory over himself. He loved Big Brother.'

Some Suggestions For Further Reading

'The Power of the Prime Minister', by Humphry Berkeley. Published by George Allen & Unwin Ltd., 1968.

'Will Parliament Survive?', by C. Hollis. Published by Hollis and Carter Ltd.

'What's Wrong With Parliament', by Hill and Whichelow. Published by Penguin, 1968.

'More Power to the People', edited by Lapping and Radice. Published by Longmans, Green & Co. Ltd.

'A Radical Future', edited by B. Whitaker. Published by Jonathan Cape Ltd., 1967.

'The New Radicalism', by B. Magee. Published by Secker & Warburg Ltd., 1962.

'The Growth of Central Government Manpower', by F. Knox. *Pamphlet* published by Aims of Industry, 1968.

'Memorandum to the 1965 Speaker's Conference on Electoral Reform'. *Pamphlet* published by the Electoral Reform Society.

'Government by Deceit', by B. Reading. *Pamphlet* published by the Conservative Political Centre, 1968.

'The Ombudsman', edited by D. C. Rowat. Published by George Allen & Unwin Ltd., 1965.

'British Government Observed', by B. Chapman. Published by George Allen & Unwin Ltd., 1963.

'Law and Orders', by C. Kemp Allen. Published by Stevens & Sons Ltd., 1965.

'The British Election of 1964', by Butler and King. Macmillan & Co. Ltd., 1965.

'Anatomy of Britain Today', by A. Sampson. Hodder & Stoughton Ltd., 1965.

'No Vision Here', by D. G. Stewart-Smith. Foreign Affairs Publishing Co., 1966.

'Masters of Indecision', by G. K. Young. Methuen & Co. Ltd., 1962.

'The System: The Misgovernment of Modern Britain', by M. Nicholson. Hodder & Stoughton Ltd., 1967.

'Civil Services of the U.K.—1853-1970', by E. N. Gladden. Cassell & Co. Ltd., 1967.

'Crisis in the Civil Service', edited by H. Thomas. Anthony Blond Ltd., 1968.

'The Fulton Report' on the Civil Service. H.M.S.O., 1968.

'Patronage in British Government', by P. G. Richards. George Allen & Unwin Ltd.

'Ramshackledom', by L. G. Pine. Secker & Warburg Ltd., 1962.

'The D-Notice Affair', by Hedley and Aynsley. Michael Joseph Ltd., 1967.

'Not in the Public Interest', by D. Williams. Hutchinson Publishing Group Ltd., 1965.

'The Future of the Press', by C. King. Second Series of Granada Northern Lectures, reprinted by McGibbon & Kee Ltd., 1967.

'Essays in Constitutional Law', by R. F. V. Heuston. Stevens & Sons, 1964.

'Constitutional Law', by Wade and Phillips. Longmans, Green & Co. Ltd.

'The Public Records', by V. H. Galbraith. Oxford University Press Ltd., 1934.

'Studies in the Public Records', by V. H. Galbraith. Oxford University Press Ltd., 1948.

'Report of the Committee on Departmental Records' (The Grigg Report). H.M.S.O., Cmd. 9163 of 1954.

'A Guide for Departmental Record Officers' (Revised Edition). Published by Public Record Office. Restricted circulation.

'Keeping the Peace', by D. Williams. Published by the Hutchinson Publishing Group Ltd., 1967.

'The Invisible Government', by Wise and Ross. Jonathan Cape Ltd., 1964.

'The Espionage Establishment', by Wise and Ross. Jonathan Cape Ltd., 1967.

'Intelligence at the Top', by K. Strong. Cassell & Co. Ltd., 1968.

'The Codebreakers', by D. Kahn. George Weidenfeld & Nicolson Ltd., 1966.

'The Police and Civil Liberties', by S. Bowes. Lawrence & Wishart Ltd., 1966.

'Scotland Yard', by H. Scott. André Deutsch Ltd., 1954.

'Freedom, the Individual and the Law', by H. Street. Pelican, 1967.

'The Intruders', by E. Long. Praeger, New York, 1967 and distributed in U.K. by Pall Mall Press Ltd.

'Privacy and Freedom', by A. Westin. Atheneum, New York, 1967.

'The Erosion of Freedom', by R. Blackburn. The Times Press, 1964.

'The Right of Privacy in England and the United States.' *Reprint* published by the Tulane Law Review. First published Feb. 1963.

'The Protection of Privacy', by B. Neill. *Reprint* published by The Modern Law Review. First published July 1962.

'Privacy—The Right to be Let Alone', by Ernst and Schwarz. Macmillan, New York, 1962.

'Privacy Under Attack', *Pamphlet* published by the National Council for Civil Liberties, 1968.

'Industrial Personnel Security', edited by L. H. Weaver and published by Charles C. Thomas, Springfield, Illinois, U.S.A.

'Scope and Limitation of Industrial Security', by Knight and Richardson. Published by Charles C. Thomas, Springfield, Illinois, U.S.A.

'The Booster and the Snitch: Department Store Shoplifting', by M. O. Cameron. Free Press of Glencoe, Collier-Macmillan Ltd., 1964.

'Private Enquiries—A Handbook for Detectives', by V. Meek. Gerald Duckworth Ltd., 1967.

'Industrial Counter-Espionage', by P. Hickson. Institute of Directors, 1968.

'The Protectors,' by T. Clayton. Oldbourne Press, 1967.

'Report of the Committee Appointed to Inquire Into Security Procedures in the Civil Service.' H.M.S.O., Cmnd. 1681.

'Lord Denning's Report', H.M.S.O., Cmnd. 2152 of 1963.

'Report of the Committee of Privy Councillors Appointed to Inquire Into the Interception of Communications.' H.M.S.O., Cmnd. 283 of 1957.

'Report of the Tribunal Appointed to Inquire Into the Vassall Case and Related Matters.' H.M.S.O., Cmnd. 2009 of 1963.

'The Back Duty Manual', by A. J. Roper. Butterworth & Co. (Publishers) Ltd., 1953.

'Render Unto Caesar', by A. G. Davies. Elek Books Ltd., 1966.

'The Inland Revenue', by A. Johnson. George Allen & Unwin Ltd., 1965.

'The Tax Gatherers', by J. Coffield. The Hutchinson Publishing Group Ltd., 1960.

'The Gnomes of Zurich', by T. R. Fehrenbach. Published by Leslie Frewin Publishers Ltd., 1966.

'An Expenditure Tax', by N. Kaldor. Unwin University Books, 1955.

'The Organisation Man', by W. H. Whyte. Jonathan Cape Ltd., 1957.

'Cannabis: Report by the Advisory Committee on Drug Dependence.' H.M.S.O., 1968.

'Drugs and Civil Liberties' (Revised Edition). The National Council for Civil Liberties, 1969.

'The Technological Society', by J. Ellul. Jonathan Cape Ltd., 1965.

'Utopias and Utopian Thought', edited by F. E. Manuel. Daedalus Library, Vol. 5. Houghton Mifflin, U.S.A.

'The Mind.' Time Life Science Library, 1968.

'The Year 2,000', by Kahn and Wiener. Macmillan, New York,, 1967.

'The Naked Society', by Vance Packard. Longmans, Green & Co., 1964.

'Brave New World Revisited', by Aldous Huxley. Harper & Row Ltd., 1958.

'Profiles of the Future', by A. C. Clarke.

'Control of the Mind', by Farber and Wilson. McGraw Hill, New York, 1961.

'The World in 1984', edited by N. Calder. First Published by *New Scientist*, 1964. Published by Penguin, 1965.

The titles of numerous more specialised books and pamphlets (and of those with only a partial relevance to the subject) have been omitted from this list. Reference to some of them will be found in footnotes to the text, as will details of many useful magazine and newspaper articles. The 'British Humanities Index' provides a constantly updated source of others.

Appendix

1. In 1969, the chief accountant of one engineering firm with 770 employees calculated that, without counting P.A.Y.E. work, it took 801 man-days of work each year to provide the government with all the information demanded by way of surveys, questionnaires and records. With 260 working days a year, this task is equivalent to one clerk concentrating on government form-filling for *three whole years.*

2. The armed forces had adopted such a re-checking system several years before.

3. This does not include officials of the G.P.O., the Treasury or the Ministry of Defence.

4. The dead cannot be libelled, unless some piece of scurrilous invention were held likely to cause a breach of the peace, by inciting the deceased's relatives to revenge. In practice, even this roundabout remedy would nowadays be extremely difficult to obtain.

Index